The Industrial Revolution in America

PROBLEMS IN AMERICAN CIVILIZATION

The Industrial Revolution in America

Edited and with an introduction by

Gary J. Kornblith
Oberlin College

Houghton Mifflin Company   Boston   New York

Editor-in-Chief: Jean Woy
Associate Editor: Frances Gay
Project Editor: Magdalena Hernandez/Gabrielle Stone
Associate Production Coordinator: Deborah Frydman
Manufacturing Coordinator: Andrea Wagner
Marketing Manager: Sandra McGuire

Cover Image: The Mason Machine Works, at Taunton, Mass., founded in
1829 by William Mason. Collection of the Boston Athenaeum.
Cover Design: Sarah Melhado

Printed in the U.S.A.

Library of Congress Catalog Card Number: 97-72506

ISBN: 0-669-39472-6

23456789-DH-01 00 99 98

For Carol

The Editor

Gary J. Kornblith received his B.A. from Amherst College and his M.A. and Ph.D. from Princeton University. Since 1981 he has taught at Oberlin College, where he is currently Associate Professor of History and Director of the Oberlin Center for Technologically Enhanced Teaching (OCTET). He has published articles in *Business History Review, Journal of the Early Republic,* and other scholarly journals. His most recent publications include "Artisan Federalism: New England Mechanics and the Political Economy of the 1790s," in *Launching the "Extended Republic": The Federalist Era,* ed. Ronald Hoffman and Peter J. Albert (Charlottesville, Va., 1996); "Becoming Joseph T. Buckingham: The Struggle for Artisanal Independence in Early Nineteenth-Century Boston," in *American Artisans: Crafting Social Identity, 1750–1850,* ed. Howard B. Rock, Paul A. Gilje and Robert Asher (Baltimore, 1995); and "The Making and Unmaking of an American Ruling Class," co-authored with John M. Murrin, in *Beyond the American Revolution: Explorations in the History of American Radicalism,* ed. Alfred F. Young (DeKalb, Ill., 1993).

Preface

This new addition to the Problems in American Civilization series reflects the maturation of scholarship on American industrialization over the past generation. Although setting precise dates for the beginning and end of the Industrial Revolution in America is problematic, the selections in this anthology pertain mainly to the nineteenth century. These selections purposely bridge the Civil War era, which often serves to divide the undergraduate study of American history into two parts. I have sought to bring together and juxtapose work by scholars who approach the historical analysis of industrialization from different perspectives and who employ a wide range of methodologies and modes of interpretation. Thus I have included selections by business historians and labor historians, intellectual historians and social historians, urban historians and environmental historians, historians of technology, and historians of gender and race in American culture. Although I have omitted examples of the highly statistical work done by "new" economic historians, their analyses have influenced the themes and design of this volume. At a time when historical scholarship is becoming more sophisticated, specialized, and hence more fragmented, this anthology aims to provide readers with a diverse yet well integrated set of views on the causes, dynamics, consequences, and meaning of the Industrial Revolution in America.

The volume is organized along both topical and chronological lines. Section I focuses on the origins of American industrialization in the late eighteenth and early nineteenth centuries. Sections II and III examine, respectively, the rise of the factory system and the transformation of handicraft production before 1850. Section IV examines the dynamics of class, gender, and race that shaped social experience in the mid-nineteenth century metropolis. Section V explores the development of a truly continental market and the concomitant rise of big business during the second half of the nineteenth century. Section VI analyzes the diverse responses of intellectuals, working people, business people, and other Americans to the immense changes wrought by the Industrial Revolution by the century's end. Each section, indeed each selection, can stand independently of the others, but the editor hopes that the anthology, taken as a whole, will have an impact on the reader greater than the sum of its separate parts.

This book grows out of a course by the same title that I have taught at Oberlin College since 1982. I am greatly indebted to the many students who have taken the course over the years for repeatedly raising unexpected questions, for engaging in intellectually stimulating classroom debates, and for constantly pushing me to expand and deepen my own understanding of the subject. Oberlin students take pride in challenging authority and hold their professors to high standards. I have rarely found teaching at Oberlin easy, but I have always found it rewarding.

A funny thing happened on the way to the completion of this project. In the summer of 1995, I was named Acting Director of Computing at Oberlin College. My year-long sojourn in that job slowed my progress on this book, but also gave me added insight into the complex relationship between technological change, market dynamics, social organization, and cultural transformation. I thank the staff of the Irvin E. Houck Computing Center for making my experience on the front lines of the Information Revolution so enjoyable and enlightening.

A number of professional colleagues have helped me with the organization and content of this volume. They include Jeff Blodgett, Bruce Laurie, Walter Licht, Roy Rosenzweig, and Steve Ross. I would also like to thank the following reviewers who provided helpful comments and suggestions on the content of this volume:

Hamilton Cravens, Iowa State University
Thomas Dublin, State University of New York, Binghamton
Susan E. Hirsch, Loyola University
Edward F. Keuchel, Florida State University
Naomi R. Lamoreaux, Brown University
Larry Owens, University of Massachusetts, Amherst
Carroll Pursell, Case Western Reserve University
John K. Smith, Lehigh University

I am especially grateful to Tom Dublin and my wife, Carol Lasser, each of whom has offered constructive criticism and emotional as well as intellectual support at every stage in this project's development. I sincerely appreciate the cooperation of all the authors and publishers who granted permission for the republication of material that first appeared elsewhere.

I thank Sylvia Mallory, formerly at D.C. Heath, for embracing my original proposal to compile an anthology on American industrialization and for encouraging me to proceed. I also thank Laurie Johnson and Frances Gay for their expert editorial guidance and Magdalena Hernandez and Gabrielle Stone for their efforts in coordinating final production.

Finally, I would like to acknowledge the personal and scholarly debt I owe to the late John William Ward, my mentor at Amherst College. Bill inspired me to become a historian, and I trust he would find it fitting that this volume appears in a series long associated with Amherst's creative approach to the teaching of American studies and American history.

G. J. K.

Contents

IV. The Emergence of the Metropolis

V. Expansion, Concentration, and Invention in the Age of Capital

VI. Progress and Its Discontents

Introduction

The Industrial Revolution in America was unexpected. When George Washington took office as president in 1789, the United States was an overwhelmingly rural and profoundly agrarian society. Only one in twenty Americans lived in a community of 2,500 people or more, and three out of four adult men made their living in agriculture. By contrast, less than one-tenth of American men worked primarily in manufacturing, and most of those were artisans using hand tools and relying on their own strength for power. The largest economic enterprises were slave plantations that specialized in raising staple crops for export, such as rice and tobacco. Although women and children produced substantial amounts of yarn and cloth in private households, Americans depended heavily on foreign, especially British, imports for finished manufactures. In global terms, the United States stood on the periphery of a maturing capitalist system centered in Europe. In the contemporary context the American standard of living was relatively high, but by modern standards the new republic's economy was essentially undeveloped, even backward.

Yet a century later the United States had become an economic superpower, one of the most highly developed nations in the world. To be sure, two-thirds of Americans still resided in communities of fewer than 2,500 inhabitants, and two-fifths continued to work mainly in agriculture. But there had been a major shift away from farming toward manufacturing, which by 1890 employed one-fifth of the nation's total work force and accounted for over half of its total economic output. Manufacturing establishments routinely used water- and steam-powered machinery, and in major cities the typical worker labored for wages in a factory with over 100 employees. Slavery had been abolished, and the nation's largest private enterprises were now railroad corporations and huge industrial companies such as Carnegie Steel and Standard Oil. From a global perspective, the United States had moved from the periphery to the core of the international capitalist system. According to recent scholarly estimates, in 1890 the United States generated one-third of the world's entire industrial production, surpassing Great Britain and every other country.

The essays in this book explore how and why the American Industrial Revolution took place and evaluate its multifarious consequences for American society and culture. Some readers may find the term "Industrial Revolution" overly dramatic and hence inappropriate. Indeed, historians have debated the term's meaning and utility ever since Arnold Toynbee applied it to British developments in a series of lectures he delivered at Oxford in 1881–1882. According to Toynbee, "The essence of the Industrial Revolution is the substitution of competition for the medieval regulations which previously controlled the production and distribution of wealth." Because such regulations never took firm root in Britain's North American colonies, the relevance of Toynbee's conception to American history is clearly open to question. Yet if, following the lead of Raymond Williams, we compare the meaning of the adjectives *industrial* and *industrious,* the usefulness of the term "Industrial Revolution" in the American context may become more evident. Both adjectives are derived from the noun *industry,* but whereas *industrious* refers to personal motivation and effort, *industrial* suggests an institutionally organized form of production. To a large extent, this basic difference in connotation encapsulates the social, economic, and technological transformation examined in this book. Whether a historical process that spanned a hundred years can be properly called a "revolution" is a separate, albeit related, matter. The real test may be the extent of the transformation and the turbulence the process entailed, not how long it took. Given the deep contrast between how most Americans lived in 1790 and in 1890, the term *revolution* seems to the editor more appropriate than the alternative *evolution.* But readers are encouraged to draw their own conclusions on the basis of the diverse essays collected in this volume.

The book is divided into six sections, which proceed in chronological and topical order. Section I focuses on the origins of American industrialization. Compared to the enormous literature on the preconditions and causes of British industrialization, the scholarship on the American case is relatively sparse. Over the past thirty years, however, historians have debated in depth how best to characterize preindustrial American society. One issue of dispute is whether Americans were or were not "capitalistic" long before they began to industrialize. To a considerable extent, this question turns on one's definition of capitalism. If any sort of acquisitive behavior qualifies as capitalistic, then Carl Degler was surely right when he argued that "capitalism came [to America] in the first [European] ships." Nor is there reason to doubt that early colonizers brought with them notions of private property and a penchant for trade. But many scholars prefer a narrower definition of capitalism, applying the term only to market economies where wage labor serves as the main productive basis for capital accumulation. By this more restrictive definition, the United States was commercially oriented but not truly capitalistic at the time of the American Revolution. From this perspective, the question "Why industrialization?" becomes tied to the larger question "Why capitalism?"

Related to this controversy is a debate over the role of republican ideology in shaping the political economy of revolutionary America. Bernard Bailyn, Gordon Wood, and many others have traced the worldview of leading patriots to the "real Whig" or Country tradition of English thought—an intellectual tradition marked by nearly obsessive fear of power, tyranny, and corruption. By this interpretation, the patriots rejected not only British claims to sovereignty over North America but also the whole British model of political and economic development. They hoped to establish an agricultural republic comprising landed citizens who would possess both the material independence and the moral virtue necessary to promote the public good, even at the expense of their own private interests. J. G. A. Pocock has gone so far as to characterize the patriots' vision as a "quarrel with modernity." Yet out of the American Revolution emerged both a federal republic and a dynamic market economy. If the patriots really were looking backward when they declared independence, then what explains the new nation's rapid economic development? Some historians argue that the demands of nationhood forced a basic reconsideration of republican priorities after independence was won. Other scholars contend that the mass of Americans embraced the liberal principle of self-interest long before the patriot gentry did. Whatever the explanation, much of American discourse on political economy continued to be framed in the terms of Country and republican rhetoric well into the nineteenth century.

Section II examines the coming of the cotton mill to the United States. According to the eminent British historian Eric Hobsbawm, "Whoever says Industrial Revolution says cotton." The classic image of British industrialization is William Blake's description of "dark, satanic mills." Were American cotton mills similarly depressing and exploitative institutions? Contemporary proponents of American industrialization argued that working conditions in the United States differed fundamentally from those of Great Britain. In America workers enjoyed more economic opportunities and political rights than downtrodden English factory operatives. Moreover, as virtuous republicans and wise businessmen, American mill owners took a paternalistic interest in the welfare of their employees. Not all contemporaries agreed with this optimistic assessment, however, and historians remain divided. Some scholars contend that early mill villages in the United States were carefully designed to ease the transition from agricultural to industrial ways of life and that generally harmonious labor relations prevailed in these settings. Other scholars take a more pessimistic view, arguing that early mill operatives found industrial discipline oppressive and resisted exploitation by means ranging from stealing to quitting to striking.

Although hardly representative, the most famous showplace of American industrialization during the 1830s and 1840s was Lowell, Massachusetts. Developed by a group of wealthy investors known as the Boston Associates, Lowell boasted a series of large, incorporated textile factories that employed mainly young women recruited from the New England countryside to run the machinery. Foreign observers such as Charles Dickens reacted to Lowell with astonished admiration, lauding in particular the cultural accomplishments of the Lowell "mill girls," who for several years produced their own literary magazine with corporate support. Lowell's success seemed to prove that, unlike Europeans, Americans could make an Industrial Revolution without social conflict or mass suffering. Yet even in Lowell's "golden age," the projected image of social harmony was belied by brief work stoppages and a concerted campaign for a shorter workday. After 1850, managers encountered increasing trouble attracting Yankee women to the mills and turned to Irish immigrants instead.

Compared to the scale and sophistication of the Lowell textile mills, enterprises in most other fields of manufacture remained quite rudimentary through the mid-nineteenth century. Nonetheless, many artisanal trades underwent important structural changes during this period, especially in the Northeast. Section III examines the transformation of craft production and its implications for producers and consumers alike. In certain trades, most notably shoemaking, merchant capitalists reorganized the division of labor and established a system of "putting-out" materials to men and women operating in their own households or backyard workshops. In other trades, especially in urban centers, traditionally trained master craftsmen initiated the enlargement of shops, specialization of tasks, and application of new technologies. Whoever took the initiative, the results were often dramatic. Efficiency and output increased, while opportunity for advancement within the trades declined. Whereas in the late eighteenth century, apprentices and journeymen could realistically expect to become self-employed masters later in their careers, by the middle of the nineteenth century, most young artisans looked forward to a lifetime of earning wages and working for someone else.

For consumers, the transformation of craft production proved a mixed blessing. As more manufactured goods became available at lower cost, many people preferred to buy what in the past they might have made themselves or simply done without. Some historians argue that nineteenth-century Americans were significantly more eager than Europeans to purchase relatively standardized, unstylish yet functional articles because American culture was fundamentally more democratic and more utilitarian. Other historians note, however, that not all Americans could afford the same level of quality. The distinction between custom-tailored suits and slop-shop clothing, for example, was obvious for everyone to see. The increase in supply of manufactures did not translate automatically into egalitarian patterns of consumption or display.

From a technological perspective, the Crystal Palace Exhibition held in London in 1851 marked American industry's coming of age. During the early nineteenth century, the United States had borrowed (or stolen) most of its advanced manufacturing technology from Great Britain. The Crystal Palace Exhibition demonstrated that Americans were now initiating impressive technological improvements on their own, especially in the production of firearms with interchangeable parts. In the wake of the Exhibition, the British Parliament appointed a committee to investigate the so-called American System of manufacture. The committee reported that American arms makers employed a combination of special-purpose machines and highly precise gauges to attain true interchangeability. By making it easier to fix malfunctioning weapons under battlefield conditions, American know-how promised to alter the nature of war.

Section IV shifts attention from the transformation of production to the rise of the metropolis. Thomas Jefferson and various other Founding Fathers feared the growth of big cities because they believed (on the basis of European examples) that urban masses lacked civic virtue and would make bad citizens. One purpose of the Louisiana Purchase and the later addition of Texas and the Mexican Cession was to preserve the agrarian character of American society as long as possible. Yet at the same time that some Americans went west, many others moved into cities. Indeed, the processes of westward expansion and urbanization were interrelated: the gains in agricultural productivity afforded by access to better soil, more efficient transportation and communication networks, and improved farming technology enlarged the supply of foodstuffs, which quite literally fed the increase in urban population.

Existing cities expanded dramatically while new cities sprang up virtually out of nowhere. Philadelphia, the nation's largest city at the time of independence, grew from 42,000 people in 1790 to 340,000 in 1850 and over 565,000 in 1860. New York City developed even faster, rising from a population of 33,000 in 1790 to 515,000 in 1850 and more than 1,080,000 in 1860. Farther west, Cincinnati increased from 500 residents in 1795 to 161,000 in 1860; Chicago skyrocketed from under 5,000 in 1840 to 109,000 in 1860 and nearly 300,000 in 1870. By 1890, more Americans lived in metropolises of at least a half-million people than had inhabited the entire country a century before.

Scholars in recent years have approached nineteenth-century cities as social laboratories for the study of class, gender, race, and ethnicity. At issue are patterns of group behavior and bases for group identity. In a famous passage of his magisterial work *The Making of the English Working Class,* published in 1963, Edward Thompson defined *class* not "as a 'structure,' or even as a 'category,' but as something which in fact happens (and can be shown to have happened) in human relationships." "Class happens," he explained, "when some men, as a result of common experience (inherited or shared), feel and articulate the identity of their interests as between themselves, and as against other men whose interests are different from (and usually opposed to) theirs." In the years since Thompson offered these propositions, historians have debated their validity. They have also raised the related question of whether other social concepts, too, are better understood as mutable constructions rooted in historical experience than as fixed categories based in "objective" reality. Against the backdrop of these scholarly controversies, the essays in Section IV explore how and why city dwellers came to think of themselves as members of separate classes, complementary genders, distinct ethnic groups, and antagonistic races during the middle decades of the nineteenth century.

One important topic not addressed at length in this collection is the relationship between industrialization and the American Civil War. Seventy years ago, in their classic synthesis *The Rise of American Civilization*, Charles and Mary Beard characterized the Civil War as an "irrepressible conflict" between the forces of industrial capitalism and agrarianism. While minimizing the significance of slavery as a causal factor, the Beards deemed the war "the Second American Revolution" because it enabled Northern capitalists to wrest control of the national government away from Southern planters. Most historians writing today regard slavery as the most important cause of the Civil War, and some question whether the war greatly affected the course of American industrialization. Contrary to the Beards' assumption, antebellum Northern and Southern economies complemented each other rather well, as evidenced by the rapid pace at which both sectional economies grew before 1860. Instead of unleashing the forces of industrial capitalism, as the Beards maintained, the Civil War may have slowed American economic development by wreaking massive destruction on the South. Yet several prominent scholars, including Eric Foner, Eugene Genovese, James McPherson, and Barrington Moore, have revived the Beards' thesis by recasting it in new, less narrowly economic terms. They portray the Civil War as a contest between essentially irreconcilable social and cultural systems, one based on chattel slavery and the other on free labor. By this account, although Northerners and Southerners shared a common republican heritage and a mutual desire for material prosperity, they came to interpret the principles of liberty, property, and equality in ideologically incompatible ways. By implication, without the Civil War and Northern victory, slavery would have survived in the South, the United States might well have dissolved, and American political and economic development would have taken a sharply different turn in the late nineteenth century.

As events actually unfolded, the Civil War ushered in an era of corporate expansion and concentration of capital. Section V examines the rise of big business. As Alfred Chandler and his students have documented, American railroads pioneered modern forms of bureaucratic management during the 1850s and 1860s. Confronted with an unprecedented need for close coordination of complex operations over large geographical areas, railroad corporations introduced layers of middle managers both to formulate and to implement standards for efficiency and safety. To finance this organizational transformation and the huge cost of basic equipment and labor, the corporations sold stocks and bonds in amounts unprecedented for private enterprises. As a result, the New York Stock Exchange flourished, and the railroads spread across the continent. These developments in turn led to the creation of a truly national market and a number of truly national companies. From the 1870s forward, entrepreneurs in other industries adapted the railroads' business strategies to the production and distribution of commodities ranging from oil and steel to sewing machines, cigarettes, and dressed beef. Small businesses did not suddenly disappear; indeed, they remained the norm at the local level, even in metropolises. But for the first time, big business became a central institution in American life.

The book's sixth and concluding section evaluates the outcome of the Industrial Revolution in America. Conflicting evidence makes any cost-benefit analysis of industrialization's impact on American society a daunting task. Take, for example, the often debated issue of workers' standard of living. By one estimate between 1860 and 1890 the average earnings of manufacturing workers rose by 50 percent in real terms (that is, actual buying power). Yet this figure obscures the social price attached to working for somebody else rather than oneself, and it may also underestimate the impact of periodic unemployment. If the tendency to go out on strike or to join a union can be taken as a basic measure of workers' discontent, then ever-growing numbers of American wage earners felt their situation was deteriorating in the late nineteenth century. The Knights of Labor, at its peak the era's largest organization of working people, warned in its constitution against "the recent alarming development and aggression of aggregated wealth, which, unless checked, will invariably lead to the pauperization and hopeless degradation of the toiling masses."

Not everybody shared the Knights' foreboding. Steel magnate Andrew Carnegie, for one, proudly celebrated the material and cultural abundance wrought by industrial capitalism. In an essay first published in 1889 and later reprinted as "The Gospel of Wealth," Carnegie acknowledged the existence of dramatic inequalities in American society but argued that they were the necessary and morally acceptable result of progress. "Much better this great irregularity, than universal squalor," he declared. ". . . The 'good old times' were not good old times. Neither master nor servant was as well situated then as today. A relapse to old conditions would be disastrous to both—not the least so to him who serves—and would sweep away civilization with it."

A series of grand exhibitions and well-orchestrated public events commemorated the achievements of American industrialization in the late nineteenth century. Among the most notable were the Centennial Exposition in Philadelphia in 1876, the opening of the Brooklyn Bridge in 1883, the inauguration of the Statue of Liberty in 1886, and the World's Columbian Exposition in Chicago in 1893. But juxtaposed to these celebratory occasions were major outbreaks of social turmoil and labor strife: the Great Railway Strike of 1877, the May Day strikes and the Haymarket Riot of 1886, the Homestead conflict of 1892, and the Pullman Strike of 1894. From all appearances, late-nineteenth-century Americans were deeply at odds in their assessment of the Industrial Revolution and the quality of life it produced. Not surprisingly, historians writing a century later seem little more united. Yet as we embark on an Information Revolution of similarly huge proportions, we may find that reflecting on the past helps us to make better sense of our own predicament. That, at least, has been a guiding hope in compiling this volume.

1776   The United States of America declare their independence from Great Britain.

1781–
1782   The Bank of North America, the first commercial bank in the United States, is founded.

1780s   Artisans and others establish associations to promote American manufacturing.

1785   Oliver Evans develops a fully mechanized flour mill in Delaware.

1787–
1788   The Federal Constitution is drafted and ratified, establishing a national political and economic framework.

1790   British immigrant Samuel Slater constructs America's first successful system of mechanized cotton spinning in Pawtucket, Rhode Island. Congress passes the first Patent Act.

1791   Alexander Hamilton issues his *Report on Manufactures* calling for federal encouragement of industrial development.

1794   Eli Whitney patents his cotton gin.

1790s   Philadelphia and New York journeymen in selected trades organize societies to advocate their interests separately from master craftsmen.

1806   Conviction of journeymen cordwainers in Philadelphia on a charge of conspiracy to raise wages (*Commonwealth* v. *Pullis*).

1807   Robert Fulton demonstrates the economic viability of the steamboat on the Hudson River.

1814   Francis Cabot Lowell and the Boston Associates establish a large-scale cotton textile factory in Waltham, Massachusetts, with a work force composed mainly of young women.

1817–
1825   New York State constructs the Erie Canal.

1819   Financial panic.

1823   Boston Associates opens textile mills in East Chelmsford, Massachusetts, which is renamed Lowell in 1826.

1824   Rifles with fully interchangeable parts are manufactured at Harpers Ferry armory under the direction of John H. Hall.

1827	The Mechanics Union of Trade Associations, a citywide confederation of journeymen societies, is founded in Philadelphia.
1829–1832	Rise and decline of Working Men's parties in Philadelphia, New York, and elsewhere.
1831	The Baltimore and Ohio Railroad begins operation, inaugurating the era of steam-powered locomotives in the United States.
1832–1833	Nullification Crisis: South Carolina challenges the federal government's authority to levy a protective tariff.
1833–1837	Upsurge of labor organizing and strikes in northern cities. Patents are issued to Obed Hussey, Cyrus McCormick, John Deere, and others for improvements in farm technology.
1833	Seamstresses and other women workers in Philadelphia form the Female Improvement Society.
1834, 1836	Lowell mill women go out on strike.
1837	Financial panic; collapse of labor organizing efforts.
1842	The Massachusetts Supreme Judicial Court affirms legality of labor unions in *Commonwealth* v. *Hunt*.
1840s–early 1850s	Workers and reformers press for legislation establishing a ten-hour day.
1844	Samuel F. B. Morse demonstrates long-distance telegraphy between Baltimore and Washington, D.C. Nativist riots in Philadelphia.
1845–1855	Upsurge in immigration of Irish, Germans, and Chinese to the United States.
1851	Crystal Palace Exhibition in London provides an international showcase for American technological achievements.
1850s	Leading railroads emerge as the nation's first big businesses with modern managerial hierarchies. The New York Stock Exchange achieves national and international prominence. Resurgence of labor activism; founding of national trade unions.

1856 A patent agreement among sewing machine producers paves the way for I. M. Singer's mass-marketing strategy.

1857 Financial panic.

1860 Massive strike by shoemakers of Lynn, Massachusetts, and vicinity.

1861–

1865 The Civil War leads to the abolition of slavery. To finance the Union war effort, Congress establishes paper currency ("greenbacks") and a national banking system. Investment banking develops in the North. Labor agitation increases in the North.

1865 Alexander Holley and partners introduce Bessemer steel-making process to the United States.

1866–

1872 The rise and decline of the National Labor Union. Grangers organize cooperatives and oppose railroads' pricing policies in the Midwest.

1867 Transatlantic telegraph cable begins transmission.

1869 Transcontinental railroad is completed. Oil is discovered in Titusville, Pennsylvania. Holy Order of the Knights of Labor is founded.

1869–

1870 The rise and decline of the Colored National Labor Congress.

1870 John D. Rockefeller and partners establish Standard Oil Company of Ohio.

1873 Financial panic.

1875–

1877 Long Strike, coal-field violence, Molly Maguire trials and executions in eastern Pennsylvania.

1875 Andrew Carnegie and partners open the Edgar Thomson Works to produce steel rails on an unprecedented scale.

1876 The Centennial Exposition is held in Philadelphia. Alexander Graham Bell patents the telephone.

1877 The Great Railway Strike sweeps across nation, prompting a state and federal military response. The Supreme Court upholds state regulation of railroads in *Munn* v. *Illinois*.

1878–

1884 The rise and decline of the Greenback Labor party.

1879   Henry George publishes *Progress and Poverty*. Thomas A. Edison develops a practical incandescent lamp.

1880s   An upsurge in immigration from eastern and southern Europe. The Farmers Alliance develops. Value added by the manufacturing sector surpasses that added by the agricultural sector.

1882   Congress passes the Chinese Exclusion Act. The Standard Oil Trust formalized.

1883   The Brooklyn Bridge opens.

1885   The U.S. Senate holds hearings on "relations between labor and capital."

1885–
1886   An upsurge in membership of the Knights of Labor headed by Terence V. Powderly.

1886   The Great Upheaval: May Day strikes for an eight-hour day and Haymarket Riot. American Federation of Labor organized by Samuel Gompers and others.

1887   Congress passes the Interstate Commerce Act.

1888   Edward Bellamy publishes *Looking Backward*. New Jersey revises its general incorporation law to permit holding companies.

1889   Andrew Carnegie propounds "The Gospel of Wealth."

1890   James Duke and others form the American Tobacco Company. Congress passes the Sherman Antitrust Act. A modern, steel-framed skyscraper opens in Chicago.

1892–
1897   The rise and decline of the People's party (Populists).

1892   Confrontation at Homestead, Pennsylvania.

1893   Financial panic. World's Columbian Exposition is held in Chicago.

1894   "Coxey's Army" of the unemployed marches on Washington, D.C. The Pullman Strike and boycott end in failure. Henry Demarest Lloyd publishes *Wealth Against Commonwealth*.

1895   The Supreme Court restricts federal authority under the Sherman Antitrust Act (*United States* v. *E. C. Knight Co.*).

1895–
1904   A great merger movement leads to consolidation among manufacturing firms.

The Industrial Revolution in America

I

The Origins of American

Industrialization

John F. Kasson

REPUBLICAN VALUES AS A DYNAMIC FACTOR

At the time of the American Revolution, most patriot leaders believed that agriculture would provide the best moral as well as economic basis for a republic. Manufacturing, they feared, bred social degradation and political corruption. Yet as the United States struggled to achieve stability after the Revolution, an increasing number of Americans began to advocate economic diversification and governmental encouragement of manufacturing. In the following selection, cultural historian John F. Kasson traces the transformation of republican ideology in the late eighteenth century and analyzes the emerging belief that manufacturing technology would serve the public good in a modern republic. Kasson is Bowman Gray Professor of History at the University of North Carolina, Chapel Hill. This selection is excerpted from his book *Civilizing the Machine*.

In the late eighteenth century America began not one revolution but two. The War of American Independence coincided with the advent of American industrialization, and these dual transformations ultimately conjoined in a way that has shaped the character of much of our history. The ideological links between technology and republicanism, however, were only gradually forged. For the new nation, the meaning of both the Revolution and modern machinery was uncertain and the relationship between the two problematic. Dispute over the implications of technology for the new nation involved critical issues of American destiny. Influential citizens argued whether introduction of domestic manufactures would ensure America's political independence, economic and social stability, and moral purity or subvert them; whether technology would help to integrate the country into a cohesive nationality or prove a divisive agent. These and related questions were anxiously discussed throughout the entire Revolutionary period, from the Stamp Act crisis through the

From "Emergence of Republican Technology," from *Civilizing the Machine: Technology and Republican Values in America, 1776–1900,* by John F. Kasson. Copyright © 1976 by John Kasson. Used by permission of the Stephen Greene Press, an imprint of Penguin Books USA, Inc.

ratification of the Constitution, by men highly conscious of the precariousness of the republican venture. Yet within a half century such questioning was pursued only by a relative few. For the dominant voices in public discussion, doubt was unthinkable; they hailed the union of technology and republicanism and celebrated their fulfillment in an ever more prosperous and progressive nation. The transition between these two positions, whereby technology came to be regarded as essential to American democratic civilization, was of fundamental importance to the nation's history.

Examination of this dual revolution of politics and technology must begin with the ideological background of the American Revolution. Ideology alone, of course, did not cause either of these great transformations, but it shaped the understanding that formed the basis for action. It constituted the configuration of assumptions, values, and beliefs by which Americans sought to interpret and transform their political and social relationships. The center of American Revolutionary ideology was the concept of republicanism. For the Revolutionary generation, republicanism was not an intellectual superstructure, not an external, artfully contrived weapon of propaganda, despite the manner in which later historians would perceive it. Nor was it simply an invention of the moment. The roots of republican ideology extended deep into English politics and the English libertarian tradition, Puritanism, Enlightenment rationalism, ancient history and philosophy, and common law, and these roots were strengthened rather than severed by being transplanted into the fertile soil of America. The notion of republicanism began with a conception of the relationships among power, liberty, and virtue. The balance among these elements, Americans' reading and experience taught them, remained delicate and uneasy at best. Power, as they conceived it, whether wielded by an executive or by the people, was essentially aggressive, forever in danger of menacing its natural prey, liberty, or right. To safeguard the boundaries between the two stood the fundamental principles and protections, the "constitution," of government. Yet this entire equilibrium depended upon the strictest rectitude both within government and among the people at large. To the eighteenth-century mind republicanism denoted a political and moral condition of rare purity, one that had never been successfully sustained by any major nation. It demanded extraordinary social restraint, what the age called "public virtue," by which each individual would repress his personal desires for the greater good of the whole. Public virtue, in turn, flowed from men's private virtues, so that each individual vice represented a potential threat to the republican order. Republicanism, like Puritanism before it, preached the importance of social service, industry, frugality, and restraint. Their opposing vices—selfishness, idleness, luxury, and licentiousness—were inimical to the public good, and if left unchecked, would lead to disorder, corruption, and ultimately, tyranny. The foundation of a just republic consisted of a virtuous and harmonious society, whose members were bound together by mutual responsibility. . . .

The history of the emergence of republican technology cannot be fully grasped unless one first understands the extent to which Americans on the eve of the Revolution conceived of their identity in terms of agriculture. The country stretched before them, an apparently inexhaustible wilderness to be subdued and cultivated. One could begin to smell pine trees as far as 180 nautical miles from land, and the forests extended far beyond the Appalachian frontier until they trailed off in legend. Such a fertile and spacious setting spurred extraordinary growth. From a population of approximately 250,000 in 1700, the colonies had swelled to 1,170,000 by 1750, 2,148,000 by 1770, and by the end of the century the United States would boast of more than five million people. Roughly 80 percent of the population worked on farms, and many others depended directly upon the farming economy for their living. Colonial Americans, of course, shared quite unequally in the prosperity of the New World. Yet despite the great extremes of conditions separating aristocrats, indentured servants, and slaves, the colonies had achieved to an unprecedented degree a middle-class society based on their rural economy. . . .

Under the pressure of ideas and events in the years after 1765 this image of agrarian America was intensified and transformed into a revolutionary symbol of republican virtue. Revolutionary spokesmen placed special emphasis upon what might be called the ecology of liberty. Americans, they maintained, stood in a particularly strategic position as the defenders of freedom against corruption and tyranny because they were uniquely favored by nature and history in the abundance of land and tradition of independence essential for a free people. The independent yeoman was elevated as the symbolic hero of the American struggle and the farmer became a favorite persona of revolutionary literature. In such a role J. Hector St. John de Crèvecoeur described the way in which a European immigrant was transformed by his new environment: A man comes to America, hires himself out to a farmer, works well, and is treated with respect. After he has established himself, he buys land and begins a farm of his own. "What an epocha in this man's life! He has become a freeholder, from perhaps a German boor. . . . From nothing to start into being; from a servant to the rank of a master; from being the slave of some despotic prince, to become a free man, invested with lands to which every municipal blessing is annexed! What a change indeed! It is in consequence of that change that he becomes an American." It was a normative as well as a descriptive definition of an American that Crèvecoeur proposed. A republican society was a society of free-holders, and praise of husbandry amounted to a national faith.

But if agriculture assumed a position of special importance in the republican enterprise, so did technology. The word "technology," of course, did not acquire its current meaning until the nineteenth century. In eighteenth-century usage "technology" denoted a treatise on an art or the scientific study of the practical or industrial arts, but not the practical arts collectively. Indeed, men made little or no distinction in this period between theoretical science and mechanical ingenuity, contentedly grouping both under the rubric of "useful knowledge." When, for example, in 1743, Benjamin Franklin called for the establishment of the colonies' first learned society, he titled his paper *A Proposal for Promoting Useful Knowledge among the British Plantations in America.* Intended to pursue "all philosophical Experiments that let light into the Nature of Things, tend to increase the Power of Man over matter, and multiply the Conveniencies or Pleasures of Life," the proposed society would range from botany and mathematics to labor-saving inventions and manufactures. For all knowledge was deemed related and advantageous, and even those whose investigations did not aim at specific, practical ends remained confident that whatever truths they uncovered would ultimately prove useful. Observing the first balloon ascent in Paris, Franklin heard a scoffer ask, "What good is it?" He spoke for a generation of scientists in his retort, "What good is a newly born infant?" He and his American contemporaries shared the Enlightenment assumption that as knowledge increased, so inevitably would its practical applications and rewards, and thus they took steps to promote the two together. . . .

With the achievement of independence, the issue of the place of domestic manufactures and the promotion of technology reached [a] critical juncture. Though English tyranny had at last been repulsed, questions of political power, economic policy, and moral virtue—the issues which had swept Americans into Revolution in the first place—continued to consume the nation. The possibility that the republic, at last freed from external oppression, might fail from internal excesses, haunted their minds. There exists an emotional as well as an intellectual continuity between the War of Independence and the period of Confederation: a sense of expectancy, of energy, but also a deep, even anxious concern to hold true to course, a determination not to relax the effort. The powerful lens of republican ideology by which Americans had earlier examined England they now trained on themselves, and many were dismayed at what they saw. The simplicity, self-sacrifice, and virtue which they had so esteemed in 1775 appeared in danger of degenerating into what one critic call "political pathology."

Particularly alarming in this context was the character of America's foreign commerce. Once hostilities had ceased, British goods poured afresh into the United States, their way smoothed by generous extensions of credit. After years of homespun and austerity, Americans bought the wares of their erstwhile oppressors quickly and eagerly. They found, however, an important outlet for their own materials in the British West Indies closed to their ships. Unable to repay their debts, they soon plunged deep into economic depression, and attempts to climb out of debt through the issuing of paper money only increased the confusion. . . . Once again, then, Americans faced a crisis of economic independence which threatened the entire republican venture. Encouragement of domestic manufactures as a vital defense of republicanism had earlier been a rallying cry in the colonial boycott movements and the Revolutionary War itself. The question now arose whether these efforts should be fostered as the springboard for a permanent system of manufactures.

On this subject certainly the most familiar contribution is Thomas Jefferson's celebrated argument that America remain a nation of farmers, contained in *Notes on the State of Virginia* (1785). The notion of European political economists that every nation should manufacture for herself, Jefferson contended, was mistakenly applied to America, where the abundance of land might support the industry of all the people. The root of Jefferson's objections were not economic, however, but moral:

> Those who labour in the earth are the chosen people of God, if ever he had a chosen people, whose breasts he has made his peculiar deposit for substantial and genuine virtue. It is the focus in which he keeps alive that sacred fire, which otherwise might escape from the face of the earth. Corruption of morals in the mass of cultivators is a phænomenon of which no age nor nation has furnished an example. It is the mark set on those, who not looking up to heaven, to their own soil and industry, as does the husbandman, for their subsistance, depend for it on the casualties and caprice of customers. Dependance begets subservience and venality, suffocates the germ of virtue and prepares fit tools for the designs of ambition.

What, then, did it matter if foreign manufactures might sometimes be dear? If that was the price of liberty, who could dissent from Jefferson's injunction, "for the general operations of manufacture, let our work-shops remain in Europe"?

> It is better to carry provisions and materials to workmen there, than bring them to the provisions and materials, and with them their manners and principles. The loss by the transportation of commodities across the Atlantic will be made up in happiness and permanence of government. The mobs of great cities add just so much to the support of pure government, as sores do to the strength of the human body. It is the manners and spirit of a people which preserve a republic in vigor. A degeneracy in these is a canker which soon eats to the heart of its laws and constitution.

Jefferson's moral stance, his insistence upon the interrelationship of freedom, industriousness, and virtue, was unimpeachable. No one would argue that America should sell her republican birthright for a mess of pottage; nor would anyone deny that agriculture would properly remain the basis of America's economy and the overwhelming occupation of her people for the indefinite future. . . .

But if all willingly acknowledged the preeminence of agriculture, an increasing number of Americans in the 1780s demanded that the nation stop the rapid sapping of her economic, political, and moral strength through European trade and restore her vigor by promoting domestic manufactures. Against the background of economic and social crisis, these men launched upon a reassessment of America's potentialities and a renewed consideration of the possibilities of republicanism. Building on the arguments and experience of the 1760s and '70s, advocates of manufactures contended with increasing boldness that public virtue and the public good might best be achieved and defended through the establishment of an independent and balanced economy. Their arguments helped pave the way for the establishment of a stronger national government empowered to control trade under the Constitution and to solidify the developing alliance between technology and republicanism. . . .

An anonymous "plain, but real friend to America" challenged agrarians' objections to manufactures in the *American Museum* [magazine]. In insisting upon farming as the sole natural occupation, he suggested, they construed the possibilities of nature in the New World too narrowly. Precisely because nature had been so "profusely liberal" to America, it became her to use her gifts to the utmost. This meant engaging not solely in agriculture but in manufactures as well. Essentially, the author justified promotion of domestic manufactures by arguing for a divine utilitarianism:

> Nature does nothing in vain. Her operations are regulated by the nicest and best rules. What she gives us in our own country, we may rest assured, if rightly used, will be found to be the best for us. Conduct not yourselves, therefore, my countrymen, as if you believed that nature bestowed on one country what ought to be given to another, which absurd idea would be chargeable on you, for your spurning at her gifts, by either wholly neglecting them, or sending them abroad to be manufactured. How contrary this to the dictates of common reason! Be wise for the future. Learn to prize the numerous blessings which God and nature have favoured you with.

For Americans to import finished goods instead of making their own was thus a violation of the economy of nature, a rejection of her beneficence, and a flouting of America's destiny. True frugality and industry meant the pursuit of both agriculture *and* manufactures. Nature, technology, and republicanism wonderfully cohered. Only sentimental pastoralism, the writer suggested, blinded critics from perceiving that nature's purposes were not fulfilled until her powers were fully utilized. "It is not hills, mountains, woods, and rivers, that constitute the true riches of a country. It is the number of industrious mechanic and manufacturing as well as agriculturing inhabitants." America, in fact, was not immune to the laws of natural and political economy which governed the rest of the world, and therefore to gaze dreamily at the scenery while the fortune and morals of the nation declined was to court disaster. . . .

The clearest and most sustained statement at this time of modern technology's special significance for the republican enterprise came on August 9, 1787, when the Philadelphia merchant Tench Coxe delivered the inaugural address before the Pennsylvania Society for the Encouragement of Manufactures and the Useful Arts. . . . In his opening remarks to the Society, Coxe gestured grandly to "the AUGUST BODY," the Constitutional Convention, then laboring through the summer heat; yet for Coxe the assurance of American republicanism depended not alone upon the revision of political institutions but also upon the cultivation of domestic manufactures. Such sentiments had become widespread by 1787, even though resistance to manufactures still remained. The importance of Coxe's speech, however, was that he revealed the special implications of contemporary technology for America; he showed how the machine might be harnessed to a republican civilization. New machines and sources of power, Coxe contended, made objections to American manufacturing on grounds of the scarcity and dearness of labor and raw materials and the work's harmful effects upon laborers no longer tenable. The vision he heralded was the American ideal of a workshop without workers: an automated factory in which employees would perform light preparatory and supervisory tasks while the bulk of the work went forward by machines. As Coxe described the prospect to his audience: "Factories, which can be carried on by water-mills, wind-mills, fire, horses, and machines ingeniously contrived, are not burdened with any heavy expence of boarding, lodging, clothing, and paying workmen; and they multiply the force of hands to a great extent, without taking our people from agriculture." Recent labor-saving inventions, such as those developed by the English textile industry, Coxe foresaw, promised to benefit America far more than Europe. The nation's scarcity of labor, no longer a liability to manufactures, on the contrary became an asset, an incentive toward mechanization, whereas in England, where labor was more plentiful and hence cheaper, the advantages were not as great. Coxe cited the example of a European factory which, with "a few hundreds of women and children . . . performs the work of twelve thousand carders, spinners, and winders," and enthused over the possibilities of power-driven machinery for America: "Perhaps I may be too sanguine, but they appear to me fraught with immense advantages to us, and full of danger to the manufacturing nations of Europe: for should they continue to use and improve them, as they have hitherto done, their people must be driven to us for want of employment: and if, on the other hand, they should return to manual labour, we shall underwork them by those invaluable engines." Savoring the irony, Coxe was telling his audience that England had, by her own artful devices, surrendered her competitive advantage in manufactures to America.

The effect of the new technology, as Coxe described it, was to reverse not only economic objections to manufactures, but moral ones as well. The overwhelming character of American life would continue to be agricultural; as for manufactures, "Horses, and the potent elements of fire and water, aided by the faculties of the human mind (except in a few healthful instances), are to be our daily labourers." Machine-powered factories would serve in effect as republican institutions and provide a strong moral antidote to elements of dissipation and corruption. By employing those poor unsuited for other work, factories would relieve discontent and potential disorder. As Coxe observed, "A man oppressed by extreme want, is prepared for all evil: and the idler is ever prone to wickedness: while the habits of industry, filling the mind with honest thoughts, and requiring the time for better purposes, do not leave leisure for meditating or executing mischief." Similarly, native manufactures would combat luxury. Coxe pointed to America's "untimely passion for European luxuries as a malignant and alarming symptom, threatening convulsions and dissolution to the political body." This debauched taste could also be cured by manufacturing simple domestic goods. American manufactures thus emerged at the conclusion of Coxe's address as the beacon of republicanism: "It will lead us, once more, into the paths of virtue, by restoring frugality and industry, those potent antidotes to the vices of mankind, and will give us real independence by rescuing us from the tyranny of foreign fashions, and the destructive torrent of luxury." . . .

Thus the seeds of the great era of American industrial and technological growth in the second half of the nineteenth century were planted much earlier and cultivated meticulously through the

Revolutionary period to the ratification of the Constitution. That document which many historians have taken to mark the beginning of American industrial consciousness and have regarded as uniquely prophetic, Hamilton's *Report on Manufactures* of 1791, was in fact the culmination, gathering together and summarizing arguments that had been developing for a generation. An apologia for manufactures and a justification for expanding America's protectionist policy, the *Report* was distinguished more in the boldness of its specific recommendations for protective tariffs and bounties than in the originality of its thesis of the importance of a balanced economy. The popular image of Hamilton, encouraged by some scholars, as a Machiavellian figure who smuggled in the blueprints for American industrialization behind the backs of an idyllic and unwary nation of farmers wildly exaggerates not only Hamilton's personal character but the thought and character of the rest of the nation as well. The promotion of American manufactures and modern technology generally was not a conspiracy hatched in private but a campaign relentlessly urged in public, under the banner of American republicanism, for twenty-five years before Hamilton's *Report*. By 1791 their position in the nation's ideology and culture was established. . . .

Thomas C. Cochran

AN INNOVATIVE BUSINESS SYSTEM

Scholars and policymakers have long sought an explanation of why some societies modernize much more readily and rapidly than others. In the selection that follows, business historian Thomas C. Cochran identifies several shared cultural traits that predisposed Great Britain and the United States to launch the world's first industrial revolutions in the late eighteenth century. Yet Cochran also draws important distinctions between the American and British experiences, and he portrays the emergence of a uniquely innovative business system within the northeastern United States. Cochran is Professor of History Emeritus at the

From *Frontiers of Change: Early Industrialism in America*, pp. 5–15 by Thomas C. Cochran. Copyright © 1981 by Thomas C. Cochran. Used by permission of Oxford University Press.

University of Pennsylvania and the author or editor of more than twenty books. This selection is from *Frontiers of Change.*

The rulers of Saudi Arabia and numerous other men currently responsible for the development of nations must crave to know the critical factors in the rapid British and American industrialization of the late eighteenth century. Can history tell them the absolute essentials, or were there any? So far, scholarly study has failed to provide simple answers. . . . Economists place varying weight on such factors as a demand that could be readily increased by lowering prices, new technology producing cheaper supplies, better mobilization of capital through financial institutions, and changes in economic organization and business attitudes. But why, at that particular time, did social forces, relatively stable and well adjusted to each other for hundreds of years, move in new directions that disrupted the traditional order? History has offered broad answers, such as a previous "commercial revolution" that had opened up worldwide trade, or the pursuit of the national aspirations of aggressive monarchies, or the rise of scientific thought and experimentation. But all of these must seem too general or remote to satisfy either historians wanting to know more exactly how change occurred or current planners having to allot specific resources.

I

In addition, no one of these primary causes nor all of them together explain the fact that among the many countries of the North Atlantic and Mediterranean communities the industrial revolution occurred most rapidly in two English-speaking nations. At the beginning of the eighteenth century Britain had no marked superiority over France, Switzerland, the Low Countries, the Hanseatic cities, or the Mediterranean region in basic or accessible knowledge of commercial or technological matters. Americans, who had only recently knit together commercially remote ports on the fringes of the continental wilderness, seemed even less likely to be leaders. Yet in the ensuing century and a half Britain and the United States became rapidly growing industrial nations while the others were hardly getting a start.

Historians have given a number of reasons for this remarkable lead, although most of these writers have not been sufficiently familiar with the advance of American technological development. One line of reasoning is that the feudal system and its comprehensive net of cultural values had a stronger hold on continental Europe than on the English-speaking world. Another calls attention to geographical conditions more favorable to transportation in Britain and the northeastern United States. Obviously these two nations were not troubled as much as continental Europe by the devastation of wars. Or the most simple answer of all sees the continuance of an initial eighteenth-century speedup as the result of natural resources: of abundant wood for the charcoal smelting of widespread iron ore in America or of good coking coal near to such ore in Britain. This last argument has been elaborated to show that British coal metallurgy early gained a lead that France could not overcome. All of these answers contain partial truths and can be fitted into a more generalized model of favorable conditions. But in themselves they produce no agreement on first causes or prime movers; from them it is impossible to make even a tentative list of "necessities" for the continued change from a relatively static, traditional society to a dynamic society built on innovations in agriculture, commerce, and industry.

Furthermore, the muse of history seems to have playfully scattered false clues about what happened in Great Britain. On the surface it appears that mechanization of textile manufacture was the leading edge of a general industrialization. But subsequent history belies any generalization, for in the following two centuries many agricultural nations mechanized textile manufacture and then went no further toward an industrial revolution. Obviously the jennies in spinning mills in eighteenth-century America and Britain were not basic causes, but only manifestations of deeper social forces. Similarly, the example of Britain suggests that steampower is a prerequisite for industrialization, yet textile and other mills on the Northeast Coast of America were usually located out in the countryside, along rivers, to take advantage of much-cheaper waterpower.

II

In recent years scholars on both sides of the Atlantic have seen the false character of some of the old material clues and have moved in the general direction of cultural explanations for industrialization.

The meaning of culture has not changed in essence since its initial formulation by Edward B. Tylor over a century ago, but the implications of his definition of a "complex whole which includes knowledge, belief, art, morals, law, custom and any other capabilities and habits acquired by man as a member of society" have been elaborated on as applied to social problems. From the standpoint of the present study, Anthony F. C. Wallace's formulation is useful. He sees culture, in part, as "those ways of behavior or techniques of solving problems which, being more frequently and more closely approximated than other ways, can be said to have a high probability of use by individual members of society." Ward B. Goodenough illustrates another facet of the same general point of view by defining culture as the concepts and models that people have in their minds for organizing and interpreting their experience. By applying these formulations to the American colonies and states, one might observe that the Northeast coast had a majority or modal culture, based on its traditions and environment, that recognized innovations in craftsmanship and business policy as essential "techniques of solving problems." In addition, the necessities of the developing colonies and states enforced a continued emphasis on utilitarian ways of "organizing and interpreting . . . experience," one generation after another.

While Wallace and others see culture as capable of change, they recognize the strength of traditional elements and hence the origins of some American traits in the European background. Both economists such as John U. Nef and noneconomic social scientists recognize that cultural commitment to material improvement arose in Europe, at least, as early as the period of colonization. Max Weber argued that a suitable religion was important. As the American experience shows, applying the artisan knowledge of mature European culture to overcoming the problems of a wilderness was highly educational; and as Britain demonstrated, the favorable social influences of skilled artisans, commercial entrepreneurs, interested aristocrats, and tolerably friendly government were important stimulants. But the generally propitious culture must also have had some special characteristics if the great advances around 1800 are to be explained.

In America and Britain of the eighteenth century there were already widespread wood and metal working industries, which, in these cultures at least, seem to have been crucial. The technological innovations that started the upsurge of industrialization, that is, were congenial to the existing culture and not, as in the case of less-developed nations, exotic imports. While the later Japanese experience might argue that "high technology" industries can be introduced by experienced artisans who have studied foreign machinery, this observation merely adds the corollary that, even if rapidly enlarged, a traditional, indigenous metalworking industry, like Japan's, was essential to bringing in the age of iron and steel. Since later industrial machines continued to be made of metal, history assures us by hindsight that the metalworking industry was the essential of advanced technology in 1800. . . . Furthermore, the early industrial nations progressed chiefly in response to consumer demands, not by government acquisition of exotic equipment belonging to more developed societies.

In any period, a favorable general culture that has produced the right type of indigenously advancing technology seems essential in the environment upon which new economic conditions of supply, demand, and capital come to operate. Anglo-American culture in general serves to explain eighteenth-century inventors such as James Watt or Oliver Evans, while the governmental institutions common to the two nations helped by giving entrepreneurs legal security and freedom to act. Also, by providing relatively high protection against the ravages of war, politics, or other nonmarket forces, both governments encouraged rapid private investment.

There is nothing novel, per se, in listing as essentials to rapid development a favorable culture, a well-developed artisan background in the proper industries, freedom for entrepreneurial action, and a high degree of governmental security against interference although continuous wars on the European continent after 1793 gave unusual importance to this last factor. The view put forward here, however, is that the long-run force of these factors is not dependent on market conditions at any given time. The long-run forces are qualitative aspects of the society and its culture, and, for meanings useful for other periods, history should be pursued on this institutional level. Innovators had to succeed in the market, but their successes are a measure of results rather than causes. The statistics, unreliable as they are, can only suggest what happened, not why it happened. As the philosopher William Barrett has cautioned, "Thinking must learn again to descend into the poverty of its materials."

III

In tracing the social patterns that led to rapid industrial growth, it is necessary to examine particular cultural characteristics in more detail and, because this is a study of America, how these operated in its particular culture. At the very core of cultural difference between America and other nations, including Britain, was a greater interest by the urban upper class and most of the well educated in improving material devices. For example, the American Philosophical Society in Philadelphia, the largest city, honored men who worked on practical problems, while the great hereditary landed aristocrat Robert Livingston of New York financed experimental steamboats.

This basic regard for the practical or useful is reflected in many characteristics of American culture, including, among others, the relationship of the business community to the law courts and to new legislation. Under the pressure of lawyers the courts became distinctly favorable to entrepreneurial action. Starting initially from the colonists' desire to buy and sell land freely, the common law in America grew to favor the operator, or internal developer, sometimes at the expense of absentee investors or the traditional rights of land owners. European, including English, land law had grown up around the concept of security both for inheritance and against harmful changes in the environment. American land law grew around facility of improvement and transfer. But the effects stretched far beyond the land; business transactions were freed from a mass of archaic legal ceremony. Guilds, for example, were never powerful in America, and cities readily granted artisan's licenses, where necessary, to all applicants. Associations of master craftsmen were never able to exercise exclusive controls over journeymen. After 1750 business lawyers came to be the shapers of new judicial interpretations. Ease of incorporation and protection of contracts against state interference were post-Revolutionary stimulants to investment. While successful industrialization without leadership from the business community and its lawyers seems almost unthinkable, the importance of their contribution has been too often overlooked.

Since it is men from the existing mercantile system who commission or invest in internal improvements, a well-coordinated and flexible business system seems a basic cultural prerequisite for rapid economic development. In America up to 1820, at least, efficient communication, transportation, finance, marketing, and law, all products of the business system, were collectively more important in reducing costs than were contemporary improvements in the fabrication of goods. It pleased early nineteenth-century Americans to have the price of cottons reduced, but the "new world" they lived in was more the product of faster and cheaper finance, trade, and transportation than the result of steam engines, power saws, and other new machines. Speeding the movement of goods from maker to receiver was the chief economizer of scarce working capital.

Inseparably associated with the dynamic American business system of the late eighteenth century were exceptionally flexible workbench artisans—men who knew how to use tools and could improve on old processes. Outside of American or British cultures, the relative lack of such all-purpose artisans was a major block to development. The United States in particular benefited from the generalized abilities of this group. In Europe artisans tended to become highly skilled at a particular craft, whereas in America migration and the ever-present need for new construction tended to make the artisan omnicompetent, on at least a moderate level. Consequently, many artisans moved readily from making furniture or hoes to erecting textile machinery and ultimately to fashioning parts for steam engines; or from building houses to constructing paper mills; or from working for wages to becoming independent entrepreneurs. Americans were short on book learning or artistic craftsmanship but long on know-how for building crude but effective machines. These traits were the result of the total culture acting on its members over generations. They were probably transmitted from generation to generation more by observation and practice than by formal apprenticeship or schooling, making for a flexible labor supply of relatively high competence.

After 1790 the interdependence of business and technical skills rapidly increased where concentrations of population made for easy communication. Regions favored by this concentration can industrialize independently of the nation as a whole. In a large urban area the man who wants credit can apply to a nearby bank; the shop supervisor who needs a new part can walk a few blocks down the street to get it. The innovator with a fresh inspiration can study existing practices, talk with informed friends, and consult useful books at hand. Historians of technology have come to think that it is from this working with new machines in locally competitive production—from this stage of trial and error in and around urban centers—that the large gains in efficiency arose. Seen another way, a concentration of workshops produces an informal all-purpose machine tool industry, and such an industry seems essential to autonomous growth or successful borrowing. The inescapable element in progressive industrialization appears to be machines for making machines. Furthermore, history indicates that once this stage of development has been reached, regression will come only from powerful external factors such as exhaustion of resources, war, or other major social disturbances.

IV

A conscious decision to innovate is governed by an artisan's or businessman's perception of the possibilities open to him. Philosophers and social scientists alike agree that what is perceived depends on what is already known; one sees what is behind the eyes rather than in front of them. Therefore, perception that leads to development is a matter of culture. The vision of the innovator is guided by generally held knowledge and social conditioning; the businessman manipulating the elements of his trade may instinctively see the possibility of new uses or combinations because the culture has encouraged artistic creativity. The tendency to innovation and ready acceptance of the new in American culture had unique qualities stemming from the total historic environment.

To begin with, the colonists came from the European frontiers of change in respect to business and technology. By their decision to migrate, to risk the formidable dangers of a trans-Atlantic voyage from which perhaps a quarter to a third would die, they must have represented a segment of European populations with an unusual willingness to take new risks. Upon arriving, many went to partially settled areas where learning different ways of doing things was necessary to survival. The ways of life arising from continual migration into new areas, which at one time or another affected a large percentage of eighteenth-century Americans, also led to new ways of doing business and making things. One writer has gone so far as to say Americans developed a "habit of habit change."

As in the rest of the Western world, public education was minimal and apprenticeship was relied on for training in crafts, including housework and cooking, but in America no social stigma was attached to the status of apprentice. Wealthy planters apprenticed their sons to merchants, and the latter often preferred to have their sons trained by experience in another office. It was this type of education that was by 1780 partly responsible for a group of American businessmen and artisans who appear to have been as able as any in the world.

Continual migration produced a large group of consumers who were satisfied with crude articles. The migrant to a new settlement made what was needed. He often shifted readily from one occupation to another. Americans, in general, became jacks-of-all-trades, and perhaps true masters of none. The results of this experience were to show in the adoption of machinery. American craftsmen had great confidence that they could make machinery work. Often they failed to do so profitably, but occasionally in trying they made important innovations, like those of John Fitch and James Rumsey in steamboats, for example.

In addition, continual migration accentuated the open class structure of society. The new arrival in a community was judged by what he could do rather than who his parents were. There were, of course, exceptions at both top and bottom of this largely horizontal society. At the top were large merchants and landowners who in the Northeast were usually also investors in a number of commercial activities. At the bottom were men lacking in either ability or character, who worked as laborers, and also able young men who started in this status but soon became landowners, skilled artisans, or traders. None of these generalizations apply to enslaved black men who were not numerous in the areas of early industrialization. But the potential for upward mobility no doubt inspired most young men in America in a way not possible in more stratified societies.

High mobility, both geographic and social, also weakened family ties; men expected to leave home early, and in many cases the farm of their childhood memories was soon sold. The same was true of family business firms. Few sons felt the obligation, common in continental Europe, to perpetuate the farm or firm as a family enterprise. Money, or "economic rationality," rather than land or family ties, was the common measuring rod of the society. New opportunities drew away from ablest young men, and partnerships continually changed. Seen from another angle, this constant shifting meant that many new firms started up, and since Americans were inclined to overoptimistic and superficial assessment of risks, there were likewise many failures.

Nathaniel Griswold said that, of a hundred New York City merchants he had known in the first half of the nineteenth century, only seven had completely avoided failure. But since "failure" was largely a matter of shifting accounts, continuous new starts set a trend of innovation in the economy that more than compensated for any stalling due to the temporary misallocation of money that resulted from insolvency.

The combination of two rapidly advancing cultures with a common language was a stimulant to technical progress in both Britain and America. Except during periods of war, immigrants (often illegal) from the British Isles were an important source for America of both labor and technical information. The linguistic compatibility between the cultures led to continuous movement of businessmen between the two nations, with many of the British coming to America to stay.

V

Culture is necessarily based on, although not always dominated by, geography. Industrialization might have first developed under relatively adverse geographical circumstances, but historically it did not. Furthermore, differing cultures, as illustrated by adjacent parts of France and Germany, may exist in areas quite similar geographically. Britain and the northeastern United States shared geographic environments highly favorable to industrialization. Both had fertile agricultural land, penetrated by many bays and rivers, and both had the types of natural resources needed for early mechanization. That a geographic interpretation cannot supersede a cultural interpretation, however, is illustrated by Japan, where an excellent geographic endowment did not lead to industrialization until cultural forces, specifically nationalism, demanded such development.

The general fertility of land and the trading advantages of coastal Britain and much of northeastern America had produced an agricultural and commercial society that by the late eighteenth century had a relatively high standard of living. Geography, that is, permitted a culture with a good margin of economic surplus that could be used for experiments in new methods and forms of production. It would be hard, by contrast, to imagine industrialization occurring in the minimal subsistence culture of Tierra del Fuego.

Geographic resources such as raw materials needed for expanded or new types of production obviously constitute another factor in development, but one that is not, as illustrated in phases of Japanese growth, a *sine qua non* on the same basic level as some of those already discussed. Coking coal close to iron was a major factor in Britain only after 1785 and was of no great importance before 1850 in the United States. If, however, the generalization is rephrased to say that abundant material for smelting and refining near to iron ore is a factor in development, it has a place in a generalized explanation. Until the mid-nineteenth century, the forests of the northeastern American seaboard produced plenty of fuel for processing iron ore and running steam engines, while scores of mill streams could produce power more cheaply than in Britain.

VI

Geography and culture, by helping to determine the types of local production and demand, affect business decisions and hence the directions of industrial progress. In general, the technical writings and workbench skills of the late eighteenth century were common throughout the Western world. English craftsmen, however, were taught high degrees of specialization, while those in America were prepared by necessity to do whatever they had to do. Fortunately, a civilization in which wood was superabundant allowed American bunglers to write off mistakes and push ahead. Meanwhile, traditional British skills frequently hindered attempts at new methods. Hence there is often little meaning in close comparisons of the journeys by the two cultures to mature industrialization. Given the state of Western world knowledge, either would have made rapid progress without the other, and, in spite of traditional writing to the contrary, their paths often diverged rather widely and fruitfully.

Among many diverse responses to different local demand, three examples will suffice. When an Arkwright water frame for spinning thread, often viewed as the most important early invention (1769) of the industrial revolution, was brought to Philadelphia in the 1780s it failed to attract local capital because its advantages in reducing costs in the local market seemed questionable. At the same time Oliver Evans's completely mechanized flour mills in Delaware did not seem worth the investment to British millers who, like the

Philadelphia spinners, produced on a small scale for local demand rather than for export. Similarly, incorporated joint-stock banks gave a lift to development in land-rich but capital-hungry America from 1782 on, while in geographically stable and financially wealthy Britain private bank influence prevented such charters until 1825. Therefore, in cases of rapid development such as in Britain and America, differences in production based on local circumstances make it useless to speculate on who is ahead at any given time. With a relatively rapid interchange of knowledge and what came by the early nineteenth century to be near equality in practical skills, each nation led the way in meeting its own special needs and exploiting its own opportunities. . . .

Anthony F. C. Wallace

THE FRATERNITY OF MECHANICIANS

Inventors are often pictured as extraordinary individuals who single-handedly altered the course of history. In the following selection, Anthony F. C. Wallace highlights instead the collective dimension of technological innovation. Focusing on the early development of industrial machinery, he portrays a small, transatlantic fraternity of mutually supportive "mechanicians" who traded information and ideas in a common pursuit of progress. This core group of innovators, Wallace suggests, supplied the practical knowledge necessary for successful industrialization. Wallace is a cultural anthropologist and University Professor Emeritus at the University of Pennsylvania. This selection is from *Rockdale,* his highly acclaimed case study of a nineteenth-century Pennsylvania mill village.

The production machines—the machines that transformed raw materials into consumer products, that generated power, that propelled bullets—were made by a small group of highly skilled men . . .

termed "mechanicians" [in the early nineteenth century]. They designed these machines and often themselves worked with forge and lathe, and hammer, cold chisel, and file, to make the mules and looms, the steam engines, the firearms parts, and all the other machinery that made up the Industrial Revolution. These men were also the inventors and users of machine tools—the machines that made machines.

The presence of a substantial cadre of mechanicians in England, France, and the United States was probably a main reason for the rapidity of the spread of manufacturing in those countries. The production machines themselves did not move easily across oceans until the latter part of the nineteenth century. Thus, although Great Britain was the source of most of the basic *ideas* for textile machinery, few if any of her machines were actually being imported into America. Whether English or American in concept, American machines were made in America in American machine shops, largely by American-born machinists. . . .

The machinist's practice in the early nineteenth century merged imperceptibly into that of the blacksmith, the iron master, the machine maker, the engineer, the draftsman, the artist, the inventor, and the natural scientist. Established and successful manufacturers and merchants—men of good family—were quite willing to commit their sons as apprentices in machine shops. The trade was an old one and had a sense of community, which encouraged the transmission of technological information by methods of demonstration and practice, as well as by the immigration of experienced operatives and the travel of American machinists abroad.

Although some successful mechanicians were manufacturers, the culture of the machinist was fundamentally different from that of the manufacturer: the machinist thought with his hands and eyes, and when he wished to learn or communicate he made a drawing or a model; the manufacturer and manager thought with his larynx, as it were, and when he wished to learn or communicate, did so with words, in conversation or in writing. The machinist had dirty hands from working with tools; the manager had cramped hands from writing.

In contrast to the British machine shops, where the workers, "according to the English plan of division of labor, were only perfect on a single branch," the American shops emphasized the acquisition of general technical skills and the perfection of machinery. George Escol Sellers, in his visit to England in 1832, was constantly amazed at the technological backwardness of the British machinist trades (even in their most advanced forms, as in the famous Maudslay Works). In England there was a strict specialization of labor, some "men working a lifetime with hammer and cold chisel," others devoting themselves to the lathe, and all (with the exception of planers) working with relatively clumsy tools. . . .

Another notable feature of the American shops was the heterogeneity of workers. In the Sellers' shops one might meet, work side by side with, and learn from, a veritable social potpourri: German princes traveling incognito to learn the mechanician's art, gentlemen's sons, college professors, professional artists, English artisans with literary tastes, third-generation American mechanics. American workmen tended to be respectable, literate, independent, jealous of seniority and privilege, and ready to fight foreigners: John Morton Poole at Matteawan recounted how an English master mechanic was beaten up by the man he replaced, and the youthful George Escol Sellers learned with dismay of the plot to abuse his friend Henri Mogeme, the wandering German mechanic of noble blood. . . .

It would be interesting to develop a census of the fraternity [of mechanicians] in order to measure its size and other social characteristics. Although this task would go far beyond the needs of the present study, some notion of an order-of-magnitude kind is worth having. The materials provided by the mechanicians of the Sellers family, who were among the leaders in the group, give an intimation of the number of mechanicians—the creative, innovative master mechanics working in metal—in the English-speaking world. In the period 1820 to 1840, something like three to four hundred such men were working. The whole group, including journeymen and apprentices, totaled probably no more than six thousand persons, if one estimates (generously) an average of twenty journeymen and apprentices for every master.

The memoirs and recollections of George Escol Sellers even provide a minimal list of names for the members of the network whom the Sellers family of this period counted as kin, as teachers, as business associates, or as friendly acquaintances. Although the Sellers network included some people from the worlds of politics and commerce, its male members were primarily people who worked with their hands as mechanicians, artists, scientists, and naturalists. Taken all together they made up a substantial portion of the leadership of the technological community of the lower Delaware in the early nineteenth century; as the century wore on, many of them contributed largely to America's industrial and scientific development. Many names in the fraternity are missing, but their absence does not necessarily imply lack of acquaintance, for George Escol Sellers was writing in his eighties and being deliberately selective. His roll call is impressive, nonetheless, numbering perhaps one hundred men in America and England whose names are well enough known even 150 years later to justify inclusion in the national biographical dictionaries, and another fifty who were at least significant figures in their own communities during their lifetimes. Sellers' description makes it plain that nearly all the several hundred master mechanicians of the English-speaking world knew each other by name and reputation, and that each man probably had met and talked with most of his peers on one occasion or another or had corresponded in writing. The mechanicians' fraternity of England and America was a tightly woven network of men, who shared a common awareness of the state of the art, the problems to be solved, and the progress each man was making. The fraternity can only be compared to the practitioners of a discipline like physics or mathematics, or of a school of art or a theological tradition. It was, in Thomas Kuhn's sense, a paradigmatic community. . . .

The work of the mechanician was, in large part, intellectual work. This was true in spite of the fact that he dealt with tangible objects and physical processes, not with symbols, and that some of what he did was done with dirty hands. The thinking of the mechanician in designing, building, and repairing tools and machinery had to be primarily visual and tactile, however, and this set it apart from those intellectual traditions that depended upon language, whether spoken or written. The product of the mechanician's thinking was a physical object, which virtually had to be seen to be understood; descriptions of machines, even in technical language, are notoriously ambiguous and extremely difficult to write, even with the aid of drawings and models.

As with the work of those who think in words, schools of thought or traditions flourished among the mechanicians too, embracing a preference for a particular kind of solution to a type of mechanical problem, or a devotion to a particular expertise. Some of these traditions could be subsumed under the relics of the ancient craft guild system. There were turners, tinsmiths, masons, millwrights, brass founders, and so forth. The master in each of these crafts was the custodian of highly specialized skills, which he passed on to the coming generation of apprentices, teaching largely by demonstration and example. But the other kind of tradition depended upon the collaborative working out, by generations of mechanics, of the potentialities hidden yet implicit in a certain principle of mechanism, and the solving of the problems each successive improvement called forth. Their situation was not unlike that of scientists in the normal development of what has been called a paradigm. When a basic innovation was introduced, it was embodied in an actual machine; the machine, and copies of it, rather than verbal descriptions, communicated the paradigm. But with each machine came problems to eliminate and improvements to add, all within the ambit of the original conception. Thus the mule of Crompton—a synthesis of the jenny and the water frame—constituted a paradigm for mechanicians to work on for the next 150 years. Machines were not "invented" in complete and finished form; rather, they were the product of generations of collective effort. The paradigms themselves often were never patented, and if they were, the patent was rarely left valid and uninfringed for long; what was patentable was not the paradigm but an improvement.

The kind of thinking involved in designing machine systems was unlike that of linguistic or mathematical thinking in its emphasis on sequence as opposed to classification. To the linguistic and mathematical thinker (for mathematics is merely very formal language), the grammar that embodies the rules of sequence is a given; what is crucial is the choice of the correct word or phrase, denoting a class of concepts, and the collection of attributes appropriate to describe the thing in mind. To the mechanical thinker, the grammar of the machine or mechanical system is the successive transformations of power—in quantity, kind, and direction—as it is transmitted from the power source (such as falling water or expanding steam), through the revolutions of the wheel, along shafts, through gears and belts, into the intricate little moving parts, the rollers and spindles and whirling threads, of the machine itself. The shapes and movements of all these hundreds of parts, sequentially understood, are a long yet elegantly simple moving image in three-dimensional space. In this mode of cognition, language is auxiliary—often so lagging an auxiliary that the parts and positions of a machine have no specific name, only a generic one, and if referred to in words, have to be described by such circumlocutions as "the 137th spindle from the left," "the lowest step of the cam," or "the upper right hand bolt on the governor housing."

The complexity of thought required to understand mechanical systems would seem in no way inferior to what is required for the trains of reasoning in mathematics or the common language. Thinking visually and tactilely has an inherent disadvantage, however, in comparison with thinking in language. Those who think in words— on subjects which are thought about effectively in words—can think a sentence and then utter it for others to hear. If one visualizes a piece of machinery, however, and wishes to communicate that vision to others, there is an immediate problem. Speech (and writing) will provide only a garbled and incomplete translation of the visual image. One must make the thing—or a model, or at the least a drawing—in order to ensure that one's companion has approximately the same visual experience as oneself.

In the Western world, an effect of this special problem in communicating technological information has tended to be the growing isolation of those who think in mental pictures. Theologians, humanists, even scientists can converse freely because the thinking is done with the same system of symbols as those used in communication. Indeed, it has become conventional to assume that thought itself is merely a kind of internal speech and to disregard almost completely those kinds of cognitive processes that are conducted without language, as though they were somehow more primitive, and less worthy of intellectual attention. Those who think about machinery have tended to undervalue their own accomplishments, or to deny that the process is intellectual at all, and to belittle "intellectuals" in turn. . . .

The problem of the relationship between science and technology has remained. In the 1830s, the inventive mechanician needed to have some knowledge of basic physical principles and, increasingly, an awareness of the rigorous requirements of the experimental method of proof. Yet, although he thus profited from some scientific training, his improvements in machines and industrial process

seem to have been suggested less by new scientific discoveries calling for application than by interesting old technological problems
calling more urgently for solution because of economic pressures.
And as often as not—perhaps more often than not—the solution
was suggested by other innovations within the mechanicians' tradition rather than by advances in science. The problem is still being
argued 150 years later.

II

The Coming of the

Cotton Mill

Gary Kulik

A FACTORY SYSTEM OF WOOD

In the United States, as in Great Britain, the master symbol of early industrialization was the cotton mill. The mechanization first of cotton yarn production and then of cotton cloth production transformed how people worked as well as what they wore. In appearance and structure, however, the initial cotton mills hardly signaled a radical break with the past. Located on rivers in rural settings, they looked more like traditional gristmills than massive modern factories. In the following essay, Gary Kulik explores the extent of change versus continuity in the early Industrial Revolution by examining closely the materials used in building and equipping the "Old Slater Mill" in Pawtucket, Rhode Island, America's first enduring cotton mill. Kulik is Deputy Director of Library and Academic Programs at the Henry Francis du Pont Winterthur Museum and Library.

In 1792, the wealthy Rhode Island manufacturer Moses Brown, two of his kinsmen, and a young English immigrant named Samuel Slater resolved to build a "factory house" for the spinning of cotton yarn. It would be located on the west bank of the Blackstone River in Pawtucket, Rhode Island, just a few hundred yards upstream of the clothier's shop which had served as the company's first waterpowered production site. In that shop in December 1790, Samuel Slater had set in motion the first mechanized system of cotton yarn production in the United States. Slater had learned his technical skills as an apprentice to Jedidiah Strutt, a prominent Derbyshire cotton manufacturer, once a partner of Richard Arkwright. It was Arkwright who had assembled the pieces of the new carding and spinning technology, the ideas for which many of his contemporaries believed he pirated, into an interconnected system of factory production. And so the factory system, which Andrew Ure defined as "the combined operations of many orders of work people . . . in tending with assiduous skill a series of productive machines continuously impelled by a central power," was born.

From Gary Kulik, "A Factory System of Wood: Cultural and Technological Change in the Building of the First Cotton Mills," from Brooke Hindle, ed., *Material Culture of the Wooden Age* (Tarrytown, N.Y.: Sleepy Hollow Press, 1981). Excerpted by permission of Gary Kulik.

It was this system which Slater transported to the United States. He did not do so through that enormous feat of memory usually credited to him, nor without the critical assistance of local artisans whose skills gave effect to his ideas, nor without the financial backing of Moses Brown. But it was still Slater who, like Arkwright before him, envisioned the entire system and its possibilities. As modest as were Slater's technical accomplishments on that December day, nothing like this had existed before in America. There had been textile workshops, "manufactory houses," as they were known, equipped with the latest improvements in hand technology, and some even with power-driven carding machines. But nowhere had there been a system of production which converted hand-cleaned cotton into yarn by means of specialized machines, linked together through gears, shafts, and ropes and driven by a single source of power—in this instance, by a waterwheel. Slater had introduced the factory system to America. And now, in 1792, he and his partners were about to build the first American factory.

Yet if we interpret the building of that first factory simply as a fundamental novelty, we would obscure much that is central to historical understanding. For the "Old Slater Mill," as it would be known, and all of its constituent elements—machines, gears, shafts, waterwheel, dam, and raceway—evoked the past as much as the future. The mill and its component parts were the product of an essentially continuous artisan tradition, a tradition which expressed itself through the intricate skill of carpenters, joiners, turners, millwrights, and pattern makers—the workers in wood. . . . The use of wood in the early years of the Industrial revolution expressed both the continuity of history and the enduring connectedness between nature and humanity. For despite the transformative changes of these years, the Industrial Revolution emancipated humanity neither from its own history nor from the limits of nature. . . .

Two and one-half stories high, 43 by 29 feet in plan, the wood-frame mill had twenty-eight windows, a single outer door, and separate rooms for carding, spinning, and storage—rooms which likely corresponded with each of the mill's floors. The builders employed post and beam construction and wood joists to support the single layer of planks which comprised the floors. Vertical siding covered the exterior. The small "factory house," with its gable roof, did not look noticeably different from the houses, barns, and artisan shops which surrounded it. A method of production with revolutionary implications had been enclosed in an essentially traditional architectural form.

There were, of course, English precedents—some of which Slater himself knew. Large masonry mills of commanding presence overlooked the Derbyshire dales. These were the initial British expressions of what William H. Pierson, Jr. has called "the first new building type of the modern world." . . . Compared to buildings such as these, the spinning mill of Almy, Brown, and Slater was a modest, simple, and unassuming affair. . . . In its initial appearance, the mill presented itself in forthright American terms. It was not just that it was built of wood, at a time when its British counterparts were built of stone and brick. That was important, but so too was the way the wood was used. The carpenters framed the mill with wooden posts and beams, morticed and tenoned together. They then nailed sections of vertical siding directly to the mill's framework, dispensing with the use of studs. This was a practice with long antecedents in American colonial history, but one rare in Britain. Houses in certain areas of New England, and American barns, gristmills, and sawmills frequently employed vertical siding in place of studs. Such a practice, in a society where wood was plentiful and labor was scarce, made sense. Reciprocating sawmills, themselves characteristic American responses to labor scarcity, could easily produce the boards and planking necessary to the technique. Further, any apprentice carpenter could nail boards to a house frame, while studs had to be carefully morticed, a task requiring skill and experience. The most distinctively American feature of Almy, Brown, and Slater's mill then—the use of vertical siding—was one which had evolved as a technological response to the particular patterns of eighteenth-century American life. The very form of the mill evoked the problem of labor scarcity. There was no small irony in that, for the textile industry in its early years would be forced to wrestle with the identical problem.

The use of wood as the building material for America's first factory had additional, and perhaps deeper, cultural meaning. The first British cotton mills had been stone or brick, and with good reason. Masonry was more resistant to fire than wood. But masonry forms also had a monumental quality, which wood could only strain to achieve. The early British cotton mills were structures of utilitarian stateliness and arrogant grandeur. Whether they were seen as palaces of industry or as prison-like workhouses, whether described as "luminously beautiful" when operating at night or as "dark" and "Satanic," the effect was the same. They inspired awe. These were structures which forcefully expressed the Promethean pride of their owners, a pride which derived both from a sense of superb technical mastery—evoked by the clean, elegant lines of a bridge or by the mechanical achievements of a well-run factory—and from a growing cultural self-confidence. . . .

Almy, Brown, and Slater's simple wooden factory [by contrast] expressed the still tentative and insecure nature of industrial capitalism in early national America. An imposing brick or stone spinning mill, in a small village which had no structures built entirely of masonry, would have called attention to itself in a way which might well have intensified social tensions. . . . What took place inside that factory was different than anything that had ever taken place in Pawtucket; but visually, the factory blended easily into the village landscape. There was nothing jarring about its visual presence, nothing in the image it projected likely to provoke further animosity. Indeed, given its style and proportions, it resembled nothing so much as an unadorned, eighteenth-century New England meeting house—an image of sober rectitude.

Some New England spinning mills did, in fact, look like ecclesiastical structures. The most notable example was the Lippitt Mill, built in 1809 on the Pawtuxet River in south-central Rhode Island, and still standing. With its stately end-belfry and octagonal cupola, it bore a distinct resemblance to the new-style New England churches of the early nineteenth century. Bales of cotton and not dutiful parishioners, however, passed through its main gable-end entrance. There is little reason to claim, though, that the first American cotton mills derived their form and style from the New England meeting house; but some mills clearly expressed a close affinity with one or other of the principal variants of that religious form—and the symbolism of that was extraordinary. As British mills increasingly invited comparison with prisons and workhouses, some American mill owners were building structures which invested their thoroughly secular designs with an aura of religious purpose. What better way to try to dispel opposition than to appropriate the deep and pervasive religious symbolism of New England.

If the use of wood in early American spinning mills could assume symbolic meaning, it had other important—although more mundane—uses as well. Wood, for example, was the principal element in the power-generation systems of the first cotton mills. At Almy, Brown, and Slater's Pawtucket mill, wooden gates controlled the flow of water through the flume, and pine boards covered the floor of the flume immediately under the water wheel. Wooden flooring generally decreased hydraulic turbulence in the flume, and thus increased the efficiency of the waterpower system. The centerpiece of that system was, of course, the wheel. No contemporary descriptions of the mill's wheel survive, though it was certainly built of wood. . . . Pawtucket's first historian, David Benedict, remembered it as an "old clumsy wheel." It was, in fact, largely traditional in form. First, it was likely an undershot wheel. The height of the dam was insufficient to support an overshot wheel, and breast wheels, the type most commonly used in textile mills during the first half of the nineteenth century, were rare in Pawtucket until the second decade of the century. Second, it was an exterior wheel, located at the side of the mill rather than under it. There is positive evidence of the latter. . . .

The Arkwright [spinning] machines themselves, however, represented the most important and innovative breakthrough—though they did so at the same time as they expressed the essential continuity of the western European technological tradition. The chief difficulty in the mechanization of spinning lay in efforts to replace the delicate action of the spinner's hand in gently attenuating the cotton, wool, or flax fiber as it was being spun. Arkwright's use of three drafting rollers arranged in series, the latter two rotating slightly faster than their predecessors, affected the substitution of mechanical for human motion. . . . The drafting rollers were the critical innovation, although they were not an idea original to Arkwright. In other respects as well, Arkwright's spinning frame embraced a number of previously conceived solutions to recurring technical problems. The brass gears which drove the four-spindle spinning heads were no different in kind than the gears long used in clocks. In fact, the early textile-machine builders referred to the spindle gearing as "clockwork," and Arkwright himself initially advertised for clockmakers to fabricate such gears. Moses Brown did the same when he commissioned clockmaker John Bailey in the spring of 1788 to construct two spinning heads based on the Arkwright machines then owned by the Commonwealth of Massachusetts. And the spinning mechanism itself operated on the same principle as the hand-spinning wheel. Arkwright's U-shaped flyers, which revolved around each spindle and affected the winding of yarn onto the bobbins, closely resembled the flyers of household flax wheels. Arkwright's improved flyers, and those which Slater used, were different from their traditional counterparts in only two respects. They had no eyelets to regulate the winding of yarn onto the bobbins—that would be done instead through cams—and they were made of iron rather than wood.

Wood, however, was the principal material used in the construction of Arkwright spinning frames, just as it had been in the building of household spinning wheels. Pawtucket's Sylvanus Brown, a carpenter and millwright, supplied the wood for Slater's "little Frame" (the machine of twenty-four spindles which Slater first built), and the "Oak for Spindle Rails." But Brown did far more than simply supply wood. He also built the wooden frames, using traditional mortice and tenon joints, wooden pegs, and an occasional screw. . . . Brown, in similar fashion, built . . . the carding machines, with their wooden cylinders, feed rollers, frames, top flats, and pulleys. With its use of wooden pulleys and rope drive to connect the motion of the main cylinder to that of the doffer, or final cylinder, and to the feed rollers, Slater's surviving carding machine made greater use of wood than its British counterparts, which employed metal gearing to perform the same linkages. In most other cases, the moving parts of Slater's machinery were brass or iron, but the major structural elements were wood. The critical fact of Arkwright's and Slater's success, however, could not be found in this or that machine, but in the way in which all the machines fit together. Arkwright's major innovation was the system he conceived—a system of interconnected machines linked together by gears, shafts, and a central power source, and designed to produce a single product. And the actual form of that system rested centrally on a traditional technology of wood.

The successful American implementation of that system, wholly British in origin, was not based on Slater's skill alone. It required native intelligence and the craft skill of others. It required the work of men such as Sylvanus Brown, and Oziel and David Wilkinson.

Moreover, the general form in which that system was embodied was strikingly American. American millwrights employed wood to a greater extent, and for a longer time, than their British analogues. Plentiful wood and scarce labor shaped the appearance of the American factory, its machinery, and its system of power transmission. And the outward form of the first American factory, a humble structure of wood, was deeply affected by the popular antagonism which its presence evoked. The factory which Almy, Brown, and Slater built in Pawtucket in 1793, although enlarged in subsequent years, would remain the model for almost a generation of cotton mill owners.

The influence of that first cotton-spinning mill was pervasive. In the first place, Slater and his partners, by 1807, controlled approximately one-fifth of the total cotton spindlage in the United States. The company's new mills in Rehoboth, Massachusetts, built directly across the river from the first mill, and in Smithfield and Warwick, Rhode Island, all followed the pattern initially elaborated in 1793. Secondly, former associates or employees of Slater began at least nine spinning mills of their own, spanning an area from New Ipswich, New Hampshire, to Whitestown, New York. These and other spinning mills built from 1790 to the years of embargo drew their lessons from Pawtucket, and almost exclusively they were constructed of wood. . . .

When American millwrights built the machinery and buildings which comprised the constituent elements of the first factory systems, they did so with resources near to hand. Those resources may have been virtually unlimited in extent, but they were sharply limited in variety. Eighteenth-century artisans did not have the alloys nor the chemical compounds common to the twentieth century. Given that, their work bore closer resemblance to that of medieval artisans than it did to that of contemporary builders. And like their medieval predecessors, they relied centrally on wood, shaping it with skills developed and transmitted over centuries.

Wood was the principal material in America's first factory systems. The abundance of wood in America had profound influence on the shape and structure of the American factory. The distinctive features of American technology did not lie simply in the development of labor-saving machinery, as important as that was. . . . But as Nathan Rosenberg has argued, American technology was resource-intensive as well as labor-saving—and the resource that was most intensively used was America's abundant supply of wood. The prodigal use of wood influenced a wide range of American technologies and business practices, from the reciprocating sawmill to the development of balloon-frame construction, from high-pressure steam boilers to the Blanchard lathe, from vertical siding to the persisting importance of charcoal iron production. The abundance of wood directly influenced the first American textile factories, their exteriors, their machines, their systems of power generation—and wood remained a critical element of the factory system longer in America than in Britain. With the increasing use of stone, brick, and iron in the years from 1815 and 1840 American factories entered a new phase of their development, but it was a phase grounded on the skills and knowledge first expressed in America's wooden age. . . .

Jonathan Prude

SOCIAL CONFLICT IN THE EARLY MILLS

One barometer of the social impact of early industrialization was the reaction of those who worked in the new cotton factories. Mill owners often portrayed their relationship with factory operatives in benevolent and paternalistic terms. Whether workers shared this perspective is open to debate. Many scholars have interpreted the scarcity of strikes as prima facie evidence that harmony reigned in the early mills. In the essay that follows, Jonathan Prude questions this interpretation and identifies various means other than strikes by which workers expressed their dissatisfaction both individually and collectively. Prude's works include *The Coming of Industrial Order: Town and Factory Life in Rural Massachusetts, 1810–1860* (Cambridge, Eng. 1983). He teaches American history at Emory University.

From *Working-Class America: Essays on Labor, Community, and American Society.* Copyright 1983 by the Board of Trustees of the University of Illinois Press. Used with permission of the author and the University of Illinois Press.

In 1812, in the rural Massachusetts township of Dudley, fifty miles southwest of Boston, five local entrepreneurs built a woolen mill, several tenements, and a store. Initially titled Merino Village, this manufacturing compound suffered reversals and in time even passed on to other proprietors. But in one form or another it remained a presence in Dudley's history throughout the next two generations. In 1813, Samuel Slater—the celebrated English immigrant to Rhode Island who in 1793 had helped construct America's first successful water-powered spinning mill—arrived in Oxford, abutting Dudley to the east, and opened a cotton factory. Along with its workshops, store, cottages, and boardinghouse, this establishment was styled the East Village. By 1828, Slater had added the South Village woolen mill and the North Village thread factory, both in Dudley— his three enclaves lying north of the Merino Village in a triangle roughly four miles around and all of them, like the Merino Village, surviving downturns and setbacks to endure through the succeeding decades. . . .

While the Slater and Merino villages were not the first American textile manufactories, employers and employees working in these enclaves still ranked among the earliest new-world participants in factory labor. As a result, their complex choreography of friction and accommodation should actually be viewed as an early installment in a critically important educational process: a kind of learning which is unavoidable in industrializing societies; which initial generations of every American occupation affected by industrialization had to undergo; and which—in different ways and degrees—in fact often provided the prelude and backdrop to whatever overt militancy some American industrial workers achieved. Put briefly, what early textile employers and employees taught themselves was how to respond to one another. They deciphered—or, more accurately, they created—the rules of the game for being industrial employers and employees. And by doing so they implemented a pivotal lesson in the social meaning of industrial capitalism.

The size and structure of society in the Slater and Merino villages can be set out fairly easily. Available data suggest that between the early 1820s and the early 1830s the Merino labor force grew from around 60 to 108, of whom 40 percent were men, 50 percent were "women and girls," and 33 percent were attached to families. The aggregate roster of the three Slater compounds increased from 54 operatives in 1813 to around 260 in 1840, and in the East Village—requiring fewer skilled adult employees than a woolen factory—men accounted for 25 percent of the employees, women and children hovered around one-fifth and one-half, respectively, and two-thirds were attached to families living inside the compound. To these statistics we should add the ten to fifteen managerial officials—all adult, all male—resident in each village. And we should also add the various mill-village inhabitants—of both sexes, all ages, and totaling perhaps 20 percent of each compound's labor force—who coresided with working parents, siblings, or children but did not themselves hold berths.

But how did this social structure function? What were its dynamics and lines of force? We may begin unraveling these issues by exploring management and the regimen it sought to impose. And the point of departure here is the highly personal character of the Slater and Merino administrative structure. For a striking fact disclosed by the records is that several Merino owners served supervisory stints at their mills, and that even in the early 1830s—after Boston investors had purchased stock—the entire proprietary retinue met regularly at the Dudley factory. It is striking too that Samuel Slater, despite business interests scattered throughout New England, frequently visited his southern Massachusetts mills. Along with his sons, who began shouldering administrative duties around 1825 and who took control of the villages after their father's death in 1835, Slater intervened frequently: establishing wage guidelines, evaluating work turned out, setting requirements for "steady," punctual, "industrious and temperate" workers, providing favorite employees with cash gifts, scolding others for "unfaithfulness"—all enough to communicate a continuing personal involvement with the "hands."

Below the proprietors were the agents, charged with overall daily supervision of the villages, and the room overseers, responsible for the "business" of each factory room. Hired mainly from mercantile positions or administrative posts in other mills, and working for the most part in secluded offices, the former officials were not intimate with the rank and file under their authority. But agents were sufficiently involved in the ongoing operations of these mills to develop ties with some operatives and to be at least known to all of them. Overseers were even more familiar to the labor force. Typically recruited from experienced male operatives (one-third of Slater's East

Village overseers were drawn from the payroll of this compound) these front-line supervisors were every day brought into direct, continuous contact with the hands under their charge.

Coupled with this administrative inclination to personal contact—providing an important animus for this tendency and legitimizing its capacity to embrace both strictness and generosity—was management's claim of "interest" in employees. Antebellum mill masters (or commentators writing on their behalf) commonly declared that efforts by managers to prevent tardiness and drinking, for example, were merely "prudent and effectual" attacks "against disorderly and immoral behaviour"; and along with more obvious expressions of altruism—such as Slater's cash presents—these efforts disclosed the industrialists' "kindly and paternal" concern in the workers' "welfare." . . .

The relationship that gradually developed between employers and employees in these . . . compounds took various forms, some of which were devoid of any trace of friction. This was because one strategy Slater and Merino operatives adopted for coping with the industrial order was simply obedience. And this in turn, of course, was in large measure a consequence of the personal and "kindly" dimensions of management's authority and the resulting loyalty and sense of indebtedness some workers came to feel toward their employers.

But workers also acceded to the formal, bureaucratic structures of the regimen: time discipline, for example. During Slater's first years in Rhode Island, operatives had sometimes drifted away for a few hours or days to pick berries or to protest delayed wage payments. Others, accustomed to the pre-industrial convention of quitting work at sundown, had bridled when mill masters demanded they labor past dusk on winter evenings: "The first night I lit candles," Slater acknowledged in 1795, "[Benchley] sent for his children to come home" and it took "considerable and warm debate" to retrieve them. By 1812, however, a cultural accommodation had taken place. Attendance continued to dip slightly in autumn as operatives took off occasional hours to help harvest nearby fields. But working long days the year round no longer sparked debates, and, by 1830, the average Merino operative—even counting the 10 percent staying only a half a month—registered 77.9 percent perfect attendance. The comparable figure for the East Village was 91.3 percent, which included a steady 20–21 percent with no absenteeism at all.

Such pliability and loyalty obviously raise the possibility that at least some operatives accepted the legitimacy of industrial rhythms and structures. And the notion becomes all the more compelling when we remember that churchgoing residents of these villages inclined to worship among the discipline-minded Methodists and Baptists. In the end, however, docility is only a small part of the story. Throughout these years, in widely varying ways, Slater and Merino operatives blended obedience and deference with efforts to push back against the men and rules governing them. Prompted by the novel and increasingly intrusive pressures of factory life, prompted also by the unwillingness of post-Revolutionary Americans to submit entirely to a regimen so frequently labeled "tyranny," perhaps inspired by the hostility Yankees occasionally vented at milldams, or by the cocky independence of first-time wage earners— evoked and encouraged in all these ways, resistance emerged as a fundamental motive of the industrial social system.

Often the opposition was individualistic: the fact that even in the 1830s ties among workers remained limited tended to channel opposition into gestures essayed alone or in small groups. Often too it involved operatives' directly challenging fundamental managerial policies or threatening the mills' existence: the broadening accommodation of Yankees to elements of the industrial regimen did not prevent some employees from being thoroughly repulsed by factory life. And often these two themes intersected. Thus, we find parents protesting the daily separation from their children. Peter Mayo— acting alone, refusing to compromise, almost certainly knowing his resistance precluded continuing employment—was dismissed from the East Village in 1827 for trying to "controul his family whilst [it was] under charge of the Overseers."

And thus we find hints of arson. Rumors abounded in antebellum New England that fires suffered by textile factories were often of "incendiary origin." As a result, while the Merino mill never burned, Slater was never certain the several conflagrations striking his properties were all accidental. His suspicions were never proved, nor were the precise issues that might have prompted such attacks ever explained. But if it did occur, this expression of opposition would have closely resembled the uncompromising attacks on milldams Yankees living around factory villages occasionally mounted. And it would clearly disclose the presence of operatives on Slater's payroll committed only marginally to industrialization and deeply offended by its implications.

From the outset, however, many Slater and Merino employees also resisted in ways that accepted the continuing existence of the mills and their own continuing involvement as operatives. This was accommodation that avoided docility. Here workers—not just men, as was the case with the more aggressive opposition, but women and children too—pushed back, but in measured ways: to bolster their earnings or to assert the precious antebellum republican value of independence, and sometimes both at once. Absenteeism should be cited here, for even as punctuality increased, staying away from the mills remained a satisfying, relatively nondisruptive means of expressing autonomy from factory pressures. After all, the attendance rates quoted earlier suggest that Slater and Merino operatives in 1830 were still absenting themselves about 15 percent of working hours. Equally important, many millworkers—again acting alone—supplemented their incomes and demonstrated their independence by stealing raw materials and finished goods from their employers. The practice was evidently common among Slater's earliest Rhode Island employees and may well have looked back to the "almost traditional" thievery in the eighteenth-century English textile trade. In southern Massachusetts in the early nineteenth century stealing did not threaten the solvency of Slater and Merino mills, but officials had "to rise sometime before the sun" if they hoped to prevent operatives from making off with management's property.

This inventory of certain and probable resistance—seeking "controul" over their children, arson, absenteeism, stealing—persisted through the 1830s. As conditions changed, however, such continuity was bracketed by important shifts in the complexion of resistance. With the growing realization that textile mills would not soon fade away, and with the growing number of veterans dependent on these manufactories, tactics aimed at rejecting or destroying manufacturing establishments received less emphasis than efforts to achieve a *modus vivendi* with the industrial order. But at the same time, management's mounting stringency prompted new and more varied opposition. Thus by the 1820s there is reason to suppose Slater and Merino employees had begun sabotaging their machines—not to destroy the mills but simply to give themselves temporary respite from engines running "perpetually" at ever faster speeds. And by 1830, East Village residents had implemented another response to technology: women power-loom weavers were routinely pacing themselves so that, despite the looms' steady speed, they could pursue a psychologically more palatable slow-to-fast weekly work rhythm.

While rooted (like all resistance) in attitudes shared by operatives, these emerging responses to machine discipline were still essentially individualistic gestures. The drift toward at least more fellowship among workers, however, produced a further evolution: by the 1820s we find hints of collaborative resistance. Admittedly, the clues are elusive: collective opposition only once involved confrontation, and (like the workers' extrafamilial activities generally) never found institutional expression. Yet there are traces of whispering campaigns and slowdowns aimed at excessively demanding overseers. There are hints too of a strange choreography of funeral attendance, by which operatives took half-days off to bury their friends and relatives but declined to attend services for managers. And we can detect—if only after the fact, from shifts in factory routine they induced—the goals and efficacy of these tactics.

In effect, operatives collaborated to fill a vacuum. Lacking estab-lished traditions specifying normal demands in factory work, opera-tives sought to create norms. Time discipline was once more a focus, for if workers balanced punctuality with persisting absenteeism, they also collectively appropriated management's seventy-two-hour week and turned it to their own purposes. Thus, whereas in 1814 Slater's Smithfield employees were "willing to work as long as they do to [i.e., in] Pawtucket," even if that meant a few minutes longer, by the 1830s in the Merino Village and as early as 1817 in the East Village, demands for work beyond seventy-two hours, even five minutes worth, was "extra," to be purchased with "extra" pay. The stringency with which the mills calculated punctuality was thus paralleled by the workers' invention of overtime.

Comparable boundaries appeared around production. In the years before machine-made cloth undercut their position, handloom woolen weavers in the Merino Village set output ceilings and de-manded bonuses for added work. Similarly Slater's mule spinners and power-loom weavers did not reject assignments of more and faster machines during the 1820s, but they insisted the added out-put be accompanied by higher gross earnings. And women throstle spinners, who operated twice as many machines in 1835 as in 1817, received both more pay and pay at higher rates for "tending extra sides."

Thus developed a kind of balance. The increased stress on opposition which countenanced continued employment in the mills, and especially the emergence of collaborative efforts to distinguish normal from extra demands, suggests that many operatives were coming to accept the industrial order but simultaneously modifying the regimen with their own requirements. Accepting factory life on these terms—giving and taking in ways which both employers and employees could more or less accept but which also underscored the differences between them—this was an established pattern in the Slater and Merino villages by 1820, and significantly colored life and work in the compounds over the next two decades. But once, in 1827, the balance collapsed, precipitating the single expression of overt militancy these villages experienced before 1840.

The incident arose out of Slater's handling of handloom weavers—not the part-time outworkers, for they were too scattered and for the most part insufficiently committed to weaving to protest when they were laid off. Rather, it was the skilled cassimere weavers inside the South Village who rose into action. Responding to competitive pressures, Slater had cut the piece rates of these men in the spring of 1827. While the size of the reduction is unknown, it was evidently too large to be offset with compromises, and the affected weavers quickly voiced a "determination not to weave unless at the old prices . . .": in other words, to strike.

The 1827 turnout should be viewed in two ways. First: as the consequence of pressures playing across life and work in Slater's woolen village. The strike did not arise *ex nihilo*, or even simply as a reaction to a wage cut. The weavers' "determination" arose largely because they were skilled workers and hence particularly inclined to protest economic demotions. Doubtless, too, the weavers drew inspiration from the overall rise of labor militancy in this period; indeed, the operatives' transiency makes it possible that South Village employees had learned from events in other mills—the 1824 strike in Pawtucket, for example, which introduced turnouts to American manufactories. But most of all, the 1827 confrontation arose from the long-building momentum of resistance—the tradition of individual gestures, the collaborative insistence on extra pay for extra work—brewing in the Slater and Merino villages. Here, in fact, is where the

South Village incident illuminates a pattern common in overt labor confrontations. For throughout American industrialization, but perhaps particularly during its antebellum phase, strikes typically emerged from a background of employees and employers struggling to establish the lines and limits of their relationship. As in the South Village, so in other workplaces, strikes were usually conservative efforts to forestall changes—whether wage cuts or (sometimes seemingly trivial) amendments in work rules—that workers felt went too far too fast, as though a threshold had been reached that workers were unwilling to cross without a struggle. But as in the South Village also, such eruptions of militancy were usually shaped by—indeed, are often comprehensible only in light of—prior, more subtle histories of fencing between labor and management.

But it is also true that the South Village turnout must be viewed in a second way—as a failure. Despite advancing bonds of common experience among Slater and Merino employees, countervailing factors—the acceptance of discipline, the personal loyalty to managers among some workers, and the various obstacles to unity we have recounted—all remained too strong. The weavers stood alone, and management won simply by replacing them with operatives tending power looms. Nor did the strike even prove a helpful precedent. Despite further wage reductions, there was no significant rise in political activism among Slater and Merino operatives after 1827, no rush to participate in workingmen's conventions or the Ten-Hour Movement during the 1830s and 1840s, and no further strike among any local textile workers until 1858—and this second turnout was as fruitless as the first. . . . In an important sense, the operatives' response to industrialization which we have considered to this point, while far from inconsequential, appears to have left mill masters with the upper hand.

But there is more to say. A close reading of Slater and Merino records reveals one response that did force significant compromises from management. It is a response thus far glimpsed only in passing: leaving.

All that we know suggests employees throughout the early New England textile industry were transient. But so, of course, were most Americans. A host of investigations have disclosed significant patterns of geographic mobility beginning at least in the mid-eighteenth century and continuing on past the Civil War. In itself the restlessness of Slater and Merino employees (a necessary corollary of their short work stints) is thus not surprising. Still, the level of movement is remarkable. As Figure 1 indicates, aggregate arrivals and departures of East Village operatives, while varying widely from year to year, dipped below 100 percent of the average annual work force only two times before 1840. Nor did this turnover merely register movement through the payrolls: for just as most employees traveled long distances to reach these compounds, so most—around 80 percent—moved beyond nearby communities after leaving the Slater and Merino rosters.

For our purposes, however, the key rates disclosed by Figure 1 are voluntary departures. While only estimates, these data indicate that exits reflecting the workers' own decisions were numerous. Except for the 1816–20 depression, when operatives clung to jobs they had, at least 45 percent of the East Village average annual work force evidently chose to leave. Samplings from the Merino records yield even higher estimates: 116.4 percent in 1823, 108 percent in 1830.

Besides its volume, other structural aspects of this mobility warrant attention. First, transiency varied somewhat with skill levels and sex. Both skilled mule spinners and women power-loom weavers had below-average voluntary departure rates. The differences were not systematic, however, and were never greater than 20 percent.

Second, transiency ranks among the operatives' more private reactions to industrialization. We have already suggested that movement could undercut ties within the villages; what requires notice here is that workers typically left by themselves or with just a few others. Even families rarely left together. A sampling of children (between eight and sixteen) and fathers showed half of the former and most (56 percent) of the latter left kin behind when they departed. And many arriving workers had left relatives in other factories. This dispersal, or course, did not signal the breakdown of domestic relations any more than did the daily separation of parents and children within the villages. We find, after all, that compared to the unattached employees, workers with kin remained 50 percent longer in these mills, and upon leaving were 30 percent more likely to return; that some household members did travel together; and that scattered relatives often remained in contact and often journeyed to rejoin one another. We should also bear in mind that antebellum Yankee

FIGURE 1
AGGREGATE TURNOVER AND ESTIMATED VOLUNTARY DEPARTURE RATE, SLATER EMPLOYEES, 1814–40

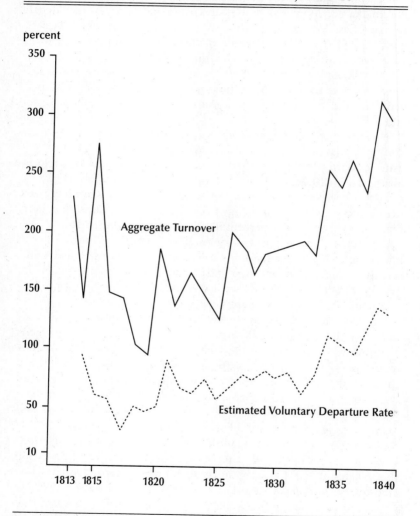

Data are for East Village alone, 1814–27; East Village and North Village, 1828–40. Data are unavailable for South Village.

youngsters commonly began a cycle of shifting to and from their homes—seeking schooling and sampling jobs—around twelve or thirteen. Nonetheless, the mobility of family operatives offers some structural indication that policies and pressures of the industrial regimen at least occasionally attenuated domestic bonds. For only among other hard-pressed wageworkers did fathers so frequently leave their families. And while less anomalous, departures of children always implicitly threatened terminal separation: "My daughter . . . about 12 . . . left the service of . . . the Cotton Factory at Waterford; since that time, no intelligence . . . has been received respecting her."

But why did family members leave? Indeed, why did any operative leave? Those using millwork as a temporary expediency departed when their expectations matured. Others left simply because they were accustomed to movement. Or, in rare instances, they left because they had saved enough to buy a business or farm. Or, especially among fathers lacking regular berths and perhaps feeling ineffectual in the villages, they left because they found better work situations elsewhere. Or especially among children who could expect neither training nor bequests from their parents if they stayed, they left because factory labor was intolerably tedious.

Operatives had left factories for such reasons even in the 1790s, and Slater and Merino workers reflected these promptings right through 1840. Gradually, however, in a manner paralleling other developments we have cited, another motive developed. As mills grew more numerous across New England, as there emerged among Slater and Merino employees cadres of operatives committed to long stretches of factory work, and as these operatives were subjected to stiffer demands, some workers began using movement, not to leave textile work, but to improve their situation within it. Obviously, this was a strategy for prosperous times. Depressions, as already noted, reduced mobility of operatives; and those who did move during slumps generally accepted any available opening and even angled for multiyear contracts. Yet against this we must contrast a mounting inclination of veterans to use good years as hunting seasons for better berths. Again, there were precedents: Slater had lost skilled men to another mill as early as 1802. But by the 1820s and 1830s the pattern was commonplace, and had broadened to include women and youngsters. In the East Village in 1834: "[M]ore [power-loom weavers] have given their notice to Leave to go to . . . where they can do better . . .”; in the Merino Village in 1841: workers are “leaving our employ more wages wanted.” Nor was maximizing income the operatives' only priority. They moved to secure better working facilities (“faster water”), more compatible supervisors, or more flexible “rules and regulations.” Indeed, among workers who rarely voted and whose other forms of resistance had only moderate effect, mobility may well have emerged as the principal means of rejecting “corrupt” dependency on management—of asserting independence and freedom.

But operatives did more than merely seize existing opportunities. They also used movement, or the threat of movement, to bid up the value of their services to create better jobs for themselves. They could do this because mobility presented difficulties for factory masters. While ideologues argued that turnover proved America had no permanent proletariat, managers found the phenomenon burdensome. The task of assigning incoming workers to suitable jobs, preparing lodgings, and maintaining current records taxed administrative facilities. And the stream of demands for terminal wage payments created frequent shortages of cash. Most serious, however, was that transiency aggravated the labor shortage these managers confronted, for it meant rosters had to be repeatedly replenished. . . . “I have sent out in various directions after weavers,” moaned an East Village agent, “but have not as yet had the Good Luck to get any.”

Here was the workers' leverage. In good times, factories wishing to retain hands were frequently maneuvered into bidding against other establishments. So William Richmonds used an offer from the Merino Village to chivy his Southbridge employer into “paying him his price.” By the same token, mills needing workers, and wishing to hire veterans, were often challenged to improve on bargains operatives already had: “I am [given] fair pay . . . where I am now,” a prospective Slater employee wrote in 1827, “[and it] would not be an object for me to change places unless I can receive as pay one dollar pr. day and board.” . . .

What, finally, do we make of these developments? How should we characterize the way employees and employers in the Slater and Merino villages came to deal with one another? No single formula is entirely adequate. But it is difficult to ignore signs that what we are chronicling is, fundamentally, the emergence of class. It is significant in this context that during the 1820s and 1830s operatives were increasingly perceived from outside the factory villages as a separate, ominous social grouping. Despite industry's claim to protect and improve its employees, New Englanders became steadily more convinced that millworkers deviated sharply from Yankee norms. The very term "operative" achieved currency—probably by the 1830s—to distinguish these wage laborers from other workers. And outside the Slater and Merino mills we find local townspeople in the early 1830s concluding that, despite their own chronic mobility, the "floating and transient" character of textile operatives was most alarming.

But the more significant indication of class was the social system developing within the mill compounds. By 1840 the net result of all the conflicts and compromises was a clear demarcation between the interest of employees and employers. One side wished to maximize output and minimize labor costs; the other side sought a regimen permitting the best price and the greatest independence possible. When every allowance is made for paternalism and concern on the one hand and deference and obedience on the other, this opposition is the axis around which the Slater and Merino mills came to revolve. . . .

Thomas Dublin

FACTORY EMPLOYMENT AS FEMALE EMPOWERMENT

Like Thomas Jefferson, the men who established the celebrated cotton mills in Lowell, Massachusetts, feared that manufacturing might breed moral corruption. To avoid this outcome—and to save on labor costs—they recruited young women from the New England countryside to work in the factories, and they built boardinghouses and churches to preserve the virtuous character and reputation of their labor force. Yet the work day was long, and the work itself was often tiring and monotonous. Why

From Thomas Dublin, *Women at Work: The Transformation of Work and Community in Lowell, Massachusetts, 1826–1860*. Copyright © 1979 by Columbia University Press. Reprinted with permission of the publisher.

did large numbers of young rural women flock to the mills during the 1830s and 1840s? In the following analysis, Thomas Dublin draws on both quantitative and qualitative evidence to explore the reasons that the so-called Lowell mill girls found factory employment liberating in comparison to life on the family farm. Dublin is a professor at Binghamton University. This selection is from his prize-winning book *Women at Work*.

The richest available evidence on the composition of the mill work force in the mid-1830s is contained in the labor records of the Hamilton Manufacturing Company of Lowell. Hamilton records enable one to determine the sex, nativity, place of residence, literacy, occupation, wage rates, and overall earnings of mill employees. The records must be sampled, however, as the survival of almost complete payroll records over the period 1830–1860 means that there are on the order of 400,000 individual monthly payroll entries. Thus the single payroll months of July 1836, August 1850, and June 1860 were chosen for detailed study. . . .

The work force of the Hamilton Company in July 1836 was overwhelmingly female. More than 85 percent—881 of 1030—of those employed in the company's three mills were women. Less than 4 percent of the work force were foreign-born. As Table 1 indicates, the proportion of immigrants among men, 6.1 percent, was considerably greater than the corresponding figure among women. The overall total of immigrants was very small; the Irish, numbering 20 in all, comprised the largest single group.

TABLE 1

ETHNIC MAKEUP OF THE HAMILTON COMPANY
WORK FORCE, JULY 1836

Nativity	*Males*	*Females*	*Overall*
United States	93.9%	96.6%	96.3%
Ireland	2.0	2.4	2.3
England	2.0	0.3	0.5
Canada	2.0	0.8	0.9
Total cases	98	765	863
Missing cases[a]	51	116	167

Note: Columns may not add up to 100.0% due to rounding.
[a]Missing cases include individuals unlinked in company register books, and individuals successfully linked but for whom the clerk failed to record nativity.

Another factor unifying the female work force was its homogeneity in terms of age. Of females 10 years of age or older who were resident in Hamilton Company boardinghouses in 1830 and 1840, more than 80 percent were between 15 and 30 years of age. Company records suggest that only about 3 percent of Hamilton workers were children under 15 years old. Thus children were a small and not very significant part of the work force of the early Lowell mills. Women in their teens and twenties dominated the work force of the Hamilton Company in these years. . . .

To limit the analysis to Lowell, however, is to gloss over the fact that the work force was the product of a rural-urban migration that linked the factory town to numerous villages in the surrounding countryside. Tracing women workers back to the families and communities from which they came will more clearly place the Lowell work force in a broader context and contribute to a fuller understanding of the meaning of the mill experience in the lives of women workers.

Here again the register volumes of the Hamilton Company provide a starting point for the analysis. These volumes recorded the entrances and departures of operatives, noting their nativity as well. Seven hundred workers entered the Hamilton mills in the first six months of 1836, and New Hampshire towns predominated among those sending large numbers into the company's employ. Excluding Lowell itself, twelve of the fourteen towns that sent the largest numbers of workers to Hamilton were found in New Hampshire, five of these in central Merrimack County. From the communities in Merrimack County that supplied so many workers to Hamilton, I selected three towns with particularly complete published vital records—Boscawen, Canterbury, and Sutton—for detailed examination. . . .

While all three towns were primarily farming communities, there were differences among them. Boscawen and Canterbury were river valley settlements, located just across the Merrimack River from one another. They had lush, flat farm land periodically enriched by deposits from spring flooding, while in sharp contrast, Sutton was a hill town, marred by steep hills that minimized the prime farmlands. As a result sheep and dairy farming were more important in the Sutton economy than in the other two towns. Sutton was also a far poorer community, as evidenced in the low property valuations of taxpayers in 1830. The mean valuation of individual taxed property in that year for Sutton was $362, well below the comparable figures of $518 and $685 for Boscawen and Canterbury respectively.

Despite these differences among the towns, large numbers of young women from all three set out for Lowell and found employment in the Hamilton Company. Between 1830 and 1850 at least 75 women left Boscawen to work in the mills of the Hamilton Company, while 55 and 45 came from Canterbury and Sutton respectively. In contrast to the total of 175 women recorded in company register volumes, only 9 men from these communities came to work at Hamilton, although larger numbers worked elsewhere in Lowell as city directory and marriage records make clear.

The women began employment at the Hamilton Company primarily in the 1830s, particularly in the first half of that decade. Table 2 indicates the distribution of their first entrances into the mill work force at Hamilton.

Women from these three New Hampshire towns were a representative cross section of the female work force at Hamilton. Since almost 80 percent of the women entered employment before 1840, it is reasonable to compare the group with women employed at Hamilton in July 1836. In terms of the rooms they worked in, their age and marital status, and the length of their careers, they did not deviate significantly from the work force as a whole. . . .

TABLE 2
FIRST ENTRANCES OF NEW HAMPSHIRE WOMEN
AT HAMILTON, 1827–1850

Entrance Date	Proportion (%)
1827–1834	47.7
1835–1839	30.8
1840–1844	12.8
1845–1850	8.7
Total cases	172
Missing cases	3

Note: Although the sample consisted of women recorded in register volumes between 1830 and 1850, a few actually entered earlier, necessitating the 1827 beginning date for the table.

Few children or older women came to the mills from these three rural communities. The mean age for beginning work at the company was 19.8, and women on the average completed their careers at Hamilton when they were 22.4 years old. Table 3 provides data on the age distribution of New Hampshire women at the beginning of their employment at Hamilton. . . .

About 80 percent of the women were between the ages of 15 and 29 when they began work at Hamilton. The proportion under 15, 14.3 percent, seems on the high side, but this age distribution catches the group at first entrance into the mills. By the time of their departures, only 4.5 percent of the women were under 15 years of age.

The data on age suggest that mill work attracted young women seeking employment for a brief period before marriage, and the evidence on marital status confirms this supposition. Almost 97 percent—124 of the 128 with usable marriage linkage—were single, never married at the beginning of their careers at Hamilton. At the end of their employment, fully 93 percent remained single. In terms of actual numbers, only 5 married women and 3 widows were included in this group of mill workers. . . .

Mill employment represented a stage in a woman's life cycle before marriage; this was demonstrated by the fact that the vast majority of operatives did marry after their sojourn in Lowell. Of the 115 women for whom adequate data survive, 98 married. About 15 percent—17 of 115—definitely did not marry, either because they

TABLE 3
AGE DISTRIBUTION OF NEW HAMPSHIRE WOMEN
AT FIRST ENTRANCE AT HAMILTON

Age Group	Proportion[a] (%)
Under 15	14.3
15.0–19.9	46.2
20.0–24.9	25.2
25.0–29.9	9.2
30.0 and over	5.0
Total cases	119
Missing cases	56

[a]Column may not add up to 100.0% due to rounding.

died at a relatively young age—one while working at Hamilton, for instance—or because they chose to remain single. Despite the claims of some contemporary critics of the mills, it is clear that mill employment did not disqualify young women for marriage.

These women came to the mills, of course, as individuals, but they also brought along with them a social position and cultural outlook from their home towns. Nominal record linkage, which provides evidence on the age and marital status of women workers, also enables the historian to place them and their families within the economic and social structure of their home towns. What kinds of generalizations may be made about the families of women operatives? What sort of place did they occupy in their rural communities? And how did millhand daughters fit within their families? It is possible to move beyond the solely individual focus and examine the women and their families within a broader context.

The vast majority of women came from farming families. Almost two thirds of their fathers traced in the 1850 manuscript censuses of these three towns—21 of 32—were listed as farmers by census enumerators. This proportion was slightly higher than that for all male household heads in the three communities. The remainder of the fathers of millhands filled a variety of skilled occupations—blacksmith, stonemason, and wheelwright among others. The occupations of the fathers suggest that the women came from rather typical rural families.

Tax inventories reinforce this conclusion. In all, the parents of 62 women workers were successfully linked to tax inventories for Boscawen, Canterbury, or Sutton for 1830. The composition of this group of linked parents and their property holdings indicate that the women were drawn from almost the entire range of families in these towns. Five of the 62 linked parents were widows, 8 percent of the group as a whole. Looking at the data in another way permits a somewhat different perspective. For the three towns taken together, 11 percent of tax-paying female heads of households had a daughter working at Hamilton; among males the comparable figure was 7.7 percent. Even though female-headed families were somewhat more likely to have a daughter working in the mills, more than 90 percent of linked operatives came from typical male-headed households. The female millhand supporting her widowed mother is hardly as common in actuality as contemporary sources suggest.

Property valuations of the fathers of operatives place them in the broad middle ranges of wealth in their home towns. None of the linked fathers was propertyless in 1830 or among the very richest in their communities. Table 4 compares the distribution of taxable property among linked fathers with that of all male household heads.

If those fathers linked in tax inventories are representative, then it is evident that women workers did not come from families near destitution. Fully 86 percent of linked fathers had property valued at $100 or more; for all male household heads in these towns the comparable proportion was less than 80 percent. On the whole, however, the typical millhand father was less wealthy than other taxpayers around him. The median property holding of millhand fathers in 1830 was only $338, compared to $459 for all male household heads taxed in the three towns. . . .

Still the evidence undermines any argument that sheer economic need drove large numbers of women into the Lowell mills in the period 1830–1850. At least the economic needs of the families of operatives could not have been a compelling force. Some women, perhaps the 8 percent whose fathers had died, may well have worked in the mills in order to contribute to the support of their families.

TABLE 4

ASSESSED PROPERTY VALUATIONS OF FATHERS OF HAMILTON OPERATIVES, COMPARED TO MALE HOUSEHOLD HEADS, BOSCAWEN, CANTERBURY, AND SUTTON, 1830

| | Proportions[a] | |
Assessed Value of Property	*Millhand fathers*	*Male household heads*
$0	0.0%	5.1%
1–99	14.0	15.3
100–499	43.9	32.8
500–999	26.3	27.8
1000–1999	15.8	13.7
2000+	0.7	5.1
Total cases	57	746

[a]Columns may not add up to 100.0% due to rounding.

The evidence strongly suggests that most young women themselves decided to work in the mills. They were generally not *sent* to the mills by their parents to supplement low family incomes but went of their own accord for other reasons. When we also consider the distance separating mill operatives from their families, the probability is strong that it was the women themselves who decided how to spend their earnings.

The correspondence of a number of operatives supports this view. Mary Paul, of Barnard, Vermont, began work in the Lowell mills at 15 or 16 in November 1845. Before going to the mills she had worked briefly as a domestic servant and then lived with relatives a short distance from her home; at that time she wrote seeking her father's permission to go to Lowell. In this letter she revealed the basic motivation that prompted her request: "I think it would be much better for me [in Lowell] than to stay about here. . . . I am in need of clothes which I cannot get about here and for that reason I want to go to Lowell or some other place." After getting permission, Mary Paul worked in Lowell off and on for at least four years. In 1850 she lived briefly with her father, but then went on her own again, this time working as a seamstress in Brattleboro, Vermont. She evidently felt some guilt at not contributing to her father's support. In an 1853 letter she wrote, "I hope sometime to be able to do something for you and sometimes feel ashamed that I have not before this." But there were obstacles which she noted:

> I am not one of the *smart* kind, and never had a passion for laying up money, probably never shall have, can find enough ways to spend it though (but I do not wish to be extravagant). Putting all these things together I think explains the reason that I do not 'lay up' anything.

She expressed the wish that sometime she could live with her father and provide for him but always fell back on the argument that sent her to Lowell in the first place: "I . . . must work where I can get more pay."

Sally Rice of Somerset, Vermont, left her home in 1838 at the age of 17 to take her first job "working out." Her work and her travels took her to Union Village, New York, where she supported herself on farm work, and led eventually to Thompson, Connecticut, where she found employment in a textile factory. That she was working for her own personal support and not to assist her family is evident in a poignant letter she wrote to her parents from Union Village in 1839 rejecting her familial home:

> I can never be happy there in among so many mountains. . . . I feel as though I have worn out shoes and strength enough riding and walking over the mountains. I think it would be more consistent to save my strength to raise my boys. I shall need all I have got and as for marrying and settling in that wilderness, I wont. If a person ever expects to take comfort it is while they are young. I feel so. . . . I have got so that by next summer if I could stay I could begin to lay up something. . . . I am most 19 years old. I must of course have something of my own before many more years have passed over my head. And where is that something coming from if I go home and earn nothing. . . . You may think me unkind but how can you blame me for wanting to stay here. I have but one life to live and I want to enjoy myself as well as I can while I live.

Sally Rice left home to earn "something of my own," which was obviously not possible in the family economy of her father's farm. The more fertile farm lands of neighboring New York created a demand for agricultural labor and offered wages high enough to attract Sally Rice away from the "wilderness" about Somerset. The wages in the textile mills of central and southern New England soon proved an even greater lure for this farmer's daughter eager to earn her own money.

Earning wages to provide for a dowry seems to have been Sally Rice's primary motivation for leaving home in 1838. Mill employment appealed to her principally because its wages were higher than those for farm laborers or domestic servants. She did not consider mill work a long-term prospect but intended to remain there only briefly: "I should not want to spend my days in a mill unless they are short because I like a farm too well for that." Finally, in 1847, probably with a sufficient dowry laid up, Sally Rice married the brother of a fellow operative and settled in Worcester, Massachusetts.

If clothes and a dowry provided the motivation for Mary Paul and Sally Rice to leave home and work in textile factories, a desire for education stimulated the efforts of one mill worker in Clinton, Massachusetts, in 1851. One Lucy Ann had her sights set on using her wages to attend Oberlin College. In a letter to a cousin she wrote: "I have earned enough to school me awhile & have not I a right to do so, or must I go home, like a dutiful girl, place the

money in father's hands, & then there goes all my hard earnings."
If she had to turn her wages over to her family she would consider
them a "dead loss" and all her efforts would have been "spent in
vain." Clearly mill employment could be turned to individualistic
purposes. As Lucy Ann summed up her thinking: "I merely wish to
go [to Oberlin] because I think it the best way of spending the
money I have worked so hard to earn." . . .

The view of women's motivations that emerges from analysis of
their social origins and correspondence with their families stands in
sharp contrast to contemporary writings, especially to the *Lowell
Offering,* an operatives' literary magazine of the period. In the repeated "factory tales" published in the *Offering,* writers stressed the
selfless motivations that sent women into the mills. Characters in the
stories were invariably orphans supporting themselves and younger
brothers and sisters, or young women helping to pay off the mort-
gage on a family homestead or to send a brother to college, or
widows raising and supporting families. Never, in the fiction at least,
did an operative work in the mills in order to buy "new clothes" or
to get away from a domineering father, though in real life these
motivations must have been common enough. The more idealistic
themes of the *Offering* presented the best possible case against those
who argued that women should not work in the mills at all. The data
on the social origins of workers, together with their letters, tell a
rather different story.

Mill work should not be viewed as simply an extension of the traditional family economy as work for women moved outside the
home. Work in the mills functioned for women rather like migration
did for young men who could see that their chances of setting up on
a farm in an established rural community were rather slim. The mills
offered individual self-support, enabled women to enjoy urban
amenities not available in their rural communities, and gave them a
measure of economic and social independence from their families.
These factors made Lowell attractive to rural women and led them
to choose to work in the mills. The steady movement of the family
farm from a subsistence to a commercial basis made daughters relatively "expendable" and gave fathers who otherwise might have
guarded the family labor supply reason to allow them a chance on
their own.

IMAGES OF INDUSTRIALIZATION: THE TECHNOLOGICAL TRANSFORMATION

In 1790, British immigrant Samuel Slater constructed a small-scale system of mechanized cotton spinning at a site on the Blackstone River in Pawtucket, Rhode Island—an event often characterized as the start of the Industrial Revolution in America. In 1793, Slater and his partners opened a new, more substantial cotton mill nearby, a structure that still stands today. The engraving above depicts "Old Slater Mill" as it appeared ca. 1810. (Rhode Island Historical Society)

LAUNCH OF THE STEAM FRIGATE FULTON THE FIRST, AT NEW YORK, 29.th OCT. 1814.

Changes in the technology of production were paralleled by changes in the technology of transportation. Beginning in the 1780s, a number of inventive Americans, including John Fitch, James Rumsey, and John Stevens, Jr., competed to develop a steamboat that could operate safely and efficiently on American rivers. Robert Fulton achieved fame and fortune with his introduction of the *North River Steamboat,* later known as the *Clermont,* on the Hudson River in 1807. Pictured above is the launching in 1814 of the steam frigate *Fulton the First,* the nation's first steam-powered warship, along with a letter by Fulton describing the vessel. (Peabody Museum)

The most celebrated industrial community in early nineteenth-century America was Lowell, Massachusetts, which grew from a small rural village into a major manufacturing center between the early 1820s and 1850. The textile mills at Lowell were huge by the standards of the day, and they employed mainly young women drawn from the New England countryside to operate both spinning and weaving machinery. The daguerrotype above shows a Lowell mill operative at her loom at mid-century. (Museum of American Textile History)

An important factor in the acceleration of American industrialization during the middle decades of the nineteenth century was the growth of the machine tool industry, which produced specialized machines used to make other machines. Yet even in highly mechanized industries, certain phases of the production process commonly required the use of hand tools by workers who possessed a high degree of manual skill. Pictured above is a machinist's apprentice with a file and gear. (Matthew Isenbury Collection)

REGULATING THE HAMMERS.

Early industrialization entailed not only mechanization but also greater specialization within the work process. One industry that utilized both new technologies and a more elaborate division of labor to boost output without sacrificing quality was piano making. This drawing, selected from a series published in *Frank Leslie's Illustrated Newspaper* in 1859, shows a workman regulating piano hammers at the Chickering factory in Boston, Massachusetts. (Smithsonian Institution)

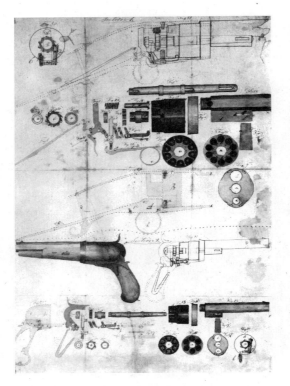

One of the most famous examples of "Yankee ingenuity" in the nineteenth century was the Colt revolver. Sam Colt received a patent for his original repeating firearm in 1836, but did not achieve commercial success until he was awarded a government contract during the Mexican War (1846–48). Thereafter, business boomed. Colt and his guns won international acclaim at the Crystal Palace Exhibition in London in 1851, and he later testified before the British Parliament about the merits of the "American system of manufacture." The illustration above is Colt's first patent drawing. (Connecticut State Library)

III

The Transformation of the Craft Production

Gary J. Kornblith

THE ENTREPRENEURIAL ETHIC

Among the most acclaimed social figures in industrializing America was the "self-made man" who succeeded in business on the basis of personal character and determination, rather than inherited wealth or family ties. Among those commonly depicted as self-made men were innovative master artisans who pioneered the transformation of traditional handicraft trades into modern capitalistic industries. The following article, written by the editor of this volume, focuses on the career of Boston piano maker Jonas Chickering. Designed as a case study in nineteenth-century artisanal entrepreneurialism, the article pays particular attention to the motivations for, and social meaning of, Chickering's technical, organizational, and financial achievements.

The piano-forte has grown up and come to maturity in this country under the care and direction of Mr. Jonas Chickering," wrote music educator Lowell Mason on the occasion of Chickering's death in 1853. Over the previous thirty years, Chickering had emerged as America's premier piano maker by adopting production strategies that paralleled innovative developments in several other trades: the expansion of a wage-earning work force, the subdivision of the manufacturing process into highly specialized tasks, the use of new materials and new technologies, and the design of relatively standardized products appropriate for sale to a national clientele. The results earned Chickering widespread critical acclaim and an unrivaled share of the American market for pianos. Of an estimated 9,000 pianos produced nationwide in 1852, approximately one in every nine was manufactured by Chickering's Boston-based firm. "The improvements in travelling by rail and by steam," Mason observed, "are hardly greater than has been the growth and development of the instrument under the *administration*—as we

From Gary J. Kornblith, "The Craftsman as Industrialist: Jonas Chickering and the Transformation of American Piano Making," *Business History Review*, Autumn 1985 (footnotes omitted). Copyright © 1985 by the President and Fellows of Harvard College. Reprinted by permission of Harvard Business School.

believe the piano-forte manufacturers will permit it to be called—
of Mr. Chickering. . . ."

Like other prominent piano makers of his generation, Jonas
Chickering came to the trade by way of cabinetmaking. Born in
1798 and raised on a farm in New Ipswich, New Hampshire, he was
apprenticed at the age of seventeen to local cabinetmaker John
Gould. Over the course of three years, Chickering learned the basic
techniques of furniture construction, and after gaining his freedom
in 1818, he headed south to Boston, where he found employment
as a journeyman in the cabinetmaking establishment of James
Barker. Even before leaving New Ipswich, however, Chickering displayed an interest in music and musical instruments. . . . Once in
Boston, he joined the Handel and Haydn Society, a local choral
association, and according to the recollections of contemporaries, he
was also "seen playing a clarinet in the streets, to the accompani-
ment of bass-drum, &c., the old-fashioned military music of the
day." In 1819, he drew upon his vocational training to follow his
avocational bent and went to work for piano maker John Osborn.
. . . Osborn's . . . operation . . . was renowned for the high quality
of its products, which won acclaim in New York and Philadelphia as
well as Boston. Chickering learned piano making from a true master
of the trade. . . .

Chickering worked for Osborn as a journeyman for four years,
during which time Osborn took as his partner James Stewart, a British immigrant who had previously set up shop in Baltimore and
Philadelphia. . . . Notwithstanding the positive reception accorded
their instruments, Osborn and Stewart soon severed their business
connection. . . . While Osborn resumed operations as a lone proprietor, Stewart sought a new partner. He approached Chickering, and
on 15 February 1823, they opened a small shop on Tremont Street
near King's Chapel. Three months later they sold the first Stewart
& Chickering piano, a square, for $275.

The prospects for success looked promising. Not only were both
partners highly skilled craftsmen, but local demand for pianos was on
the rise. Boston's rich were getting richer, and their growing wealth
was reflected in more elaborate forms of social display. . . . For three
years Stewart and Chickering collaborated successfully to take advantage of this economic opportunity. Assisted by at least one apprentice
and probably a few other workmen, they produced fifteen pianos in

1823, twenty-two in 1824, and twenty-nine in 1825. With prices ranging from $200 to $350 for the typical square models and from $450 to $700 for the more unusual uprights, the firm's gross revenues rose from approximately $4,300 the first year to nearly $8,000 the third. But by 1826 collaboration had yielded to contention. After a dispute over his use of business funds for personal purposes, Stewart withdrew from the partnership and departed for London. At the age of twenty-eight, Chickering became sole owner of the small but prosperous piano manufactory.

He proved an enterprising proprietor. Following a decline in 1826, the firm's annual output climbed steadily over the next three years and reached forty-seven instruments in 1829. In the light of this progress, Chickering moved his shop to larger quarters at 416 Washington Street. As a businessman as well as a craftsman, he was beginning to make his mark on the trade.

To make a greater impression, he needed access to more capital. At a time when banks were reluctant to lend to artisans, he found a financial patron and congenial partner in John Mackay, a former sea captain and long-time merchant of musical instruments. . . . Early in 1830 Chickering and Mackay joined forces. Within less than a decade the firm of Chickering & Company, as it was styled in the mid-1830s, rose to a preeminent position among piano manufacturers in the United States.

From the beginning Chickering and Mackay divided up managerial responsibilities in accordance with their respective backgrounds and expertise. Chickering concentrated his attention on the manufacturing end of the business, and he acted quickly to increase the firm's productive capacity. In 1831 the firm employed a work force of approximately twenty men and produced 177 pianos—roughly one-third the total number made in Boston and more than three times the firm's output two years before. As he increased the quantity of instruments manufactured, Chickering also expanded the variety. To the firm's regular line of square pianos and occasional upright models, he added a series of horizontal grands. By the mid-1830s, the firm's output had grown to about 350 pianos per year, of which one-sixth were grands. . . . Among the foremost difficulties confronting American piano makers at the time was the instrument's susceptibility to atmospheric variation, especially changes in moisture and temperature that resulted in tonal distortion. Chickering first

attempted to solve this problem by using sturdier woods and season-
ing them for longer periods of time. Then in 1837 Alpheus Babcock,
Mackay's former partner, came to work for the firm. Twelve years
earlier Babcock had received a patent for a metal piano frame, cast in
one piece, and now Chickering began placing a full iron frame into
some of his more expensive instruments. The resulting pianos were
at once more durable and more sonorous. Not only did the iron
frame provide protection against an irregular climate, but—more significantly—it permitted the application of greater tension to the
strings. In 1840 Chickering was granted a patent for the distinctive
features of his iron frame, and within a few years he was using it in
most of the firm's instruments.

While Chickering transformed the way in which pianos were
made, Mackay transformed the way in which they were sold. Without
ignoring the local market—the firm's Boston sales grew four times
faster than the city's population during the early 1830s—he moved
aggressively to establish a network of business agents in major cities
throughout the United States. By 1835 he had enlisted piano dealers
in Providence, New York, Baltimore, Washington, Norfolk, Augusta,
Savannah, Charleston, and New Orleans, and with their help the firm
penetrated markets previously beyond its range. Whereas in 1830
three-quarters of the firm's output was sold to customers residing in
Massachusetts, in 1835 well over half of its production was sent out
of state. When combined with Chickering's improvements in the
manufacturing process, Mackay's creative marketing strategy enabled
the enterprise to take advantage of the accelerating transportation
revolution and reach consumers nationwide.

Encouraged by their commercial success, Chickering and Mackay
between 1837 and 1838 erected a new manufactory at 334 Washington Street. Assessed at $30,000 and worth at least twice that
amount, this edifice stood six stories high and was designed to ac-
commodate around one hundred workmen. . . .

Death cut short Chickering and Mackay's partnership in 1841,
when Mackay vanished at sea while on a voyage to Rio de Janeiro to
procure quality woods. Under the terms of his will, his interest in
the business passed to his son William, who had joined the firm as a
junior partner two years before. Chickering proceeded to buy out
the younger Mackay for a price reportedly "counted in hundreds of
thousands of dollars," payable over several years. While the trans-

action saddled Chickering with a substantial long-term debt, it enabled him to resume sole control of the enterprise. . . .

In 1843 Chickering received a patent for his "peculiar method of constructing the metallic frame of a grand piano, by casting the same with a series of bars, in combination with an inclined front plate and vertical ledge and curved side plate." This technique, he contended, enhanced the tone of the instrument, and the following year judges at a local industrial exhibition awarded Chickering a gold metal for the "unquestionable . . . preeminence" of his entries. . . . Nor was this opinion simply local prejudice. At the Crystal Palace Exhibition in London in 1851, Chickering won a Prize Medal for his square piano, and according to the official report, "the Jury [thought] highly of his grand pianoforte" as well.

While Chickering's skills as a craftsman enabled him to make pianos of world-class quality, his aptitude as an entrepreneur enabled him to produce them in unprecedented numbers. The manufacturing schedule of the seventh federal census provides a statistical sketch of the firm's operations in 1850. On the basis of a fixed capital investment of $100,000, the firm generated an annual output of 1,000 pianos, conservatively valued at $200,000. . . .

Behind the census statistics lay a complicated manufacturing process spread over three cities and encompassing a highly advanced division of labor. Fortunately, a detailed account written by Oliver Dyer, co-publisher of the *Musical World and New York Musical Times,* permits a closer view of the steps involved in the making of a Chickering piano at midcentury.

"In the first place," Dyer reported after a visit to Chickering's manufactory on Washington Street, "we found that the lumber used in making pianos, and which consists, for the most part, of oak, rock-maple, pine and spruce, come from Maine, New Hampshire and New York." The oak and rock-maple were used for the structural case, the spruce for the sounding board, and the pine for "a variety of purposes too numerous to mention." So essential was the proper selection of these woods that Chickering took personal charge of their procurement. "He purchases vast quantities at a time," Dyer explained, ". . . and he always has from fifty thousand to seventy-five thousand dollars worth of rough wood, or lumber, on hand."

After being cut into appropriate sized pieces, the oak and rock-maple were transported to an establishment under contract to Chickering in Lawrence, Massachusetts. There they were "stuck up to season," first for about two years outdoors and then for another couple of years "under cover." "After the wood has been thus dried and redried," Dyer reported, "it is sawn, and plained [*sic*], and turned into the right dimensions and shapes for the foundation of the cases, legs, etc." Once this water-powered operation was completed, the parts were placed in "the 'drying room,' *and dried, or seasoned, for the third time.*" "Thus, it appears," Dyer concluded, "that, after a tree is cut down and sawn into lumber, it has to undergo a probation of some six years, before it is admitted into one of Chickering's pianos."

Upon removal of the wood from the drying rooms, the cases were assembled and sent by rail to a veneering factory owned by Chickering at Franklin Square in Boston. This sizable establishment employed "one hundred men . . . in veneering the cases, in carving, and other ornamental work." Their skilled labor transformed utilitarian hardwood structures into fashionable pieces of rosewood or mahogany furniture.

While the cases evolved toward their final form at the Franklin Square factory, the manufacture of the keys was under way at a separate plant in Lancaster, Massachusetts. The veneered cases and the keys converged at Chickering's main factory on Washington Street, where the pianos were ultimately completed. According to Dyer, the "finishing" operation began with the placement into the case of a spruce sounding board that had been *"thoroughly seasoned"* at the Washington Street plant. Then came the insertion of the cast iron frame, which had been manufactured at Cyrus Alger's foundry in South Boston. Next the instrument was sent to the varnishing room and thereafter to "the 'finishing-room' *par excellence*." Here one set of workers strung the piano, and another group installed the action. "The tuners follow[ed] and 'put the instrument' in tune." It was then "carefully inspected and regulated by a Mr. Brown, an experienced workman, who ha[d] done nothing else for a number of years." Finally, it was "examined by Mr. Chickering himself, who remedie[d] any trifling errors . . . ; but, if he detect[ed] an important defect, he sen[t] the instrument back to the department in which the error [had] occurred, and ha[d] it at once perfected." Thus, like traditional master craftsmen operating on a much smaller scale, Chickering retained a decisive degree of personal control over the product to which he attached his name.

Yet the Washington Street factory was not simply a craft shop writ large. The work force of approximately one hundred men was organized into over twenty separate departments, each devoted to a different step of the manufacturing process. . . . Whereas at the time of Chickering's entry into the trade apprentices and journeymen had regularly been taught all aspects of piano making, at midcentury the workmen he employed were usually trained in only a small part of the production process. Consequently, with the conspicuous exception of his sons—at least two of whom enjoyed the benefits of a regular apprenticeship under his supervision—Chickering's employees lacked the range of knowledge to become masters in their own right and could expect to remain wage earners for the duration of their careers within the trade.

Yet apparently Chickering had little difficulty mustering the necessary work force. . . . An estimated 15 percent of the firm's employees in 1840 were still on the payroll over a quarter century later—a high rate of persistence in comparison with figures for contemporary textile operatives.

At least two factors encouraged worker loyalty: relatively good pay—according to the census, the average wage of Chickering's employees in 1850 was $45 per month, or nearly $1.75 per day—and Chickering's style of management. While he did not work alongside his employees on the shop floor, neither did he retreat into the confines of the counting room. According to the accountants of various contemporaries, a visitor to the Washington Street factory was likely to find Chickering, dressed in a craftsman's apron, designing instruments or covering hammers in his private workshop. Or he might be showing customers a piano in the salesroom. By contrast, he left day-to-day management of the counting room to a subordinate. Yet Chickering exercised ultimate command over the firm's energetic marketing strategy. . . . To promote the firm's sales nationwide, he extended the network of agents established by Mackay and encouraged the widespread use of advertisements in music journals and the general press. . . .

Over the course of thirty years, Chickering had become, in the truncated prose of a Mercantile Agency correspondent an "upright, gd. bus. man." His success brought him both fame and fortune. In 1848 he ranked among the two hundred wealthiest taxpayers in Boston. Three years later the authors of *The Rich Men of Massachusetts* estimated his total worth at $300,000. . . .

Recent studies of antebellum artisan culture have tended to portray the promoters of early industrialization within the trades as opportunists who betrayed the cooperative ethos of handicraft production for the sake of private gain. But the historian must also be careful not to reduce the drama of the Industrial Revolution to a morality play. For many master artisans, there was no inherent contradiction between the "modern" goal of maximizing one's profits and the "traditional" goal of perfecting one's craft. Chickering, in particular, accomplished both ends simultaneously through the application of new technology and an advanced division of labor in the manufacturing process. His firm's products were not only highly marketable commodities but also superior musical instruments.

Stories of Chickering's benevolence contributed to his public reputation. Active in a variety of Boston's voluntary associations, he was credited with saving the Handel and Haydn Society from financial ruin after assuming its presidency in 1843. . . . But he was most highly esteemed for his acts of personal charity. He helped aspiring musicians launch their careers by making his facilities available to them at no cost and by subscribing generously to their concert series. . . . Just as he combined the functions of craftsman and capitalist, so he conjoined the roles of beneficiary and benefactor of the musical arts. . . .

Public response to Chickering's death [on 8 December 1853] testified to the high regard in which he had been held during his lifetime. . . . The mayor ordered that church bells be rung throughout Boston on the day of Chickering's funeral, and over eight hundred people joined in the procession honoring the deceased piano maker. Among those participating in the funeral ceremonies were prominent representatives of the Brahmin elite, including Governor Robert C. Winthrop . . . ; members of the several voluntary associations to which Chickering had belonged . . . ; local musicians; and the proprietors and employees of the city's piano-making establishments.

The participation of workers is noteworthy. It suggests that whatever their complaints about the changes Chickering had introduced in the piano trade, they respected and admired the man and his entrepreneurial achievements. The high level of persistence among Chickering's work force and the absence of a recorded strike or labor dispute at his firm since its inception lend credence to this interpretation. . . .

By all accounts, Jonas Chickering was an extraordinary individual who made a unique contribution to the development of American piano making. Yet, as a growing body of historical literature demonstrates, Chickering was not alone in making the transition from craftsman to industrialist; in important respects he may have been a representative figure. Motivated not only by the drive for monetary gain but also by the dream of technical perfection, he turned his shop into a factory and his craft into an industry. Equally important, as a person trained under the old productive order, he conferred legitimacy on the new. By infusing industrial capitalism with the authority of craft tradition, he and other artisan entrepreneurs obscured the emerging conflict of interest between capital and labor, and made innovation more palatable to workers and consumers alike. As a result, support for technological change and economic development cut across class lines, and there emerged a broad-based coalition in favor of the Industrial Revolution in America.

Sean Wilentz

THE BASTARDIZATION OF CRAFT

While advocates of American industrialization celebrated technological progress and the promise of economic growth and social mobility, critics decried the degradation of craftsmanship, the deterioration of traditional social bonds, and the growing gap between rich and poor. In the following selection, Sean Wilentz analyzes how "metropolitan industrialization" unfolded in New York City during the second quarter of the nineteenth century. Evaluating changes largely from the critics' point of view, Wilentz concludes that the reorganization of craft

production undermined artisanal pride, lowered earning power, and reduced workers' independence, even in trades that escaped large-scale
mechanization. Wilentz is professor of history at Princeton University.
This selection is drawn from his prize-winning book *Chants Democratic.*

Between 1825 and 1850, New York became the most productive
manufacturing city in the United States—the metropolitan center of
a manufacturing complex that reached as far south as Delaware and
that by the late 1840s was probably the fastest-growing large industrial area in the world. These extraordinary developments utterly
changed the city's crafts, but in ways very different from those
evoked by the usual images of early industrial growth. Huge firms
absorbed thousands of craft workers—but did not eradicate the
city's small producers. New, highly sophisticated steam-powered
machines thundered in the factory districts—but most of New
York's largest manufacturers intensified the division of labor already
underway rather than invest in labor-saving machinery. Although a
few, rapidly growing trades dominated the city's manufacturing
economy, hundreds more remained, leaving New York with a manufacturing sector of almost baffling diversity. . . .

The [diversity] of the early industrial metropolis should not de-
ceive us: a revolution, and not just an expansion of production, took
place in New York's workshops—a revolution that *Hunt's Merchants'
Magazine* described in 1849 as very much "in keeping with the spirit
of the age." It was a revolution already begun in 1825; although it
would continue into the Gilded Age and beyond, by 1850 it had
transformed the very meaning of labor and independence in the
city's largest trades. . . .

"Overturn, overturn, overturn! is the maxim of New York,"
Philip Hone wrote in his diary in 1845. "The very bones of our ancestors are not permitted to lie quiet a quarter of a century and one
generation of men seem studious to remove all relics of those who
precede them." . . . Such thoughts did not come to New Yorkers
twenty years earlier, when Hone and his colleagues had only begun
their careers; the pathos of Hone's entry lies in his inability to com-
prehend how his own achievements had helped prepare the way for
a new, more aggressive order. Something had happened in twenty
years to change the very ethos of the city. That something was tied
to commerce, but it touched every aspect of New York life. . . .

The rising dominance of antebellum New York over American trade and finance is still staggering to contemplate. The trade statistics only hint at this growth; so thorough was Manhattan's consolidation of commercial capital and transport routes (first the canals, then the railroads) that one observer was led to suggest, "The great city of New York wields more of the destinies of this great nation than five times the population of any other portion of the country." . . . With this rapid acceleration of New York trade and with the stunning prosperity of the city as a whole came a further deepening of economic inequality and a general deterioration of living conditions in the poorer and middling neighborhoods, especially in the central Fourth and Sixth wards and along the East Side. The statistics on wealth in the 1820s and 1840s mark the steady redistribution to the top, a phenomenon common to all expanding commercial capitals; the grimmer toll of over-crowding, disease, filth, and mortality in New York's poorer and working-class districts reveals the human cost, in a city that ranked second to none as a disaster of laissez-faire urban development. . . . Above all, there was the sheer crush of numbers, as rural migrants and poor immigrants flooded into the port. Between 1825 and 1850, New York's population grew over threefold, making its rate of growth since 1800—750 percent—one of the highest in the world, twice as high as Liverpool's, three times higher than Manchester's, higher than that of all the jerry-built catastrophes of Dickensian lore. Until about 1830, the increase was fed primarily by newcomers from New England and the city's immediate hinterland, by British Protestants, and by a small but growing stream of Irish Catholics and Germans. The tide shifted in the 1830s and shifted again even more sharply in the 1840s with the arrival of tens of thousands of Germans and famine-plagued rural Irish. In just over twenty years, from the early 1830s to the mid-1850s, New York changed from a major seaport where the vast majority of citizens were native born to a metropolis where more than half of the population had been born abroad and where more than four-fifths of the immigrants had come from either Ireland or Germany.

This demographic explosion, coupled with the expansion of the port, set the terms for the emergence of New York's working class. The quickening tempo of trade and finance greatly enlarged the number of white-collar clerkships, entrusted mostly to local sons and fresh arrivals from the American countryside who had contacts among the resident merchants. Alongside this new male office-worker group, the number and proportion of unskilled jobs—for dockworkers, draymen, porters, cartmen, day laborers of every kind—rose preciptously, while the growth of middle-class wealth widened the demand for female domestic servants, numerically the city's largest occupation at midcentury. These were the jobs for the city's blacks and the immigrant poor, especially the Irish: by the mid-1850s, more than half of the city's male Irish workers were day laborers or cartmen and about one-quarter of *all* the Irish females in the city were domestic servants.

Less readily understood was the expansion of local manufacturing production, an expansion that left manufacturing and craft workers as the largest sector of New York wage earners. At a glance, commercial New York was an even more unlikely manufacturing city in the 1840s than it had been twenty years earlier. Rents in the central districts, already considered high in the 1820s, spiraled with the development of mercantile and transport facilities and with the squeeze for residential space, thus discouraging the building of factories and large central shops in all but a few trades. Manhattan's lack of any harnessable source of waterpower was even more glaring in the 1840s—the great age of American waterpower—than before. The inflow of easily transported manufactured goods from Britain, New England, New Jersey, and the Delaware Valley rendered superfluous the manufacture of numerous goods in New York. In all, New York, like London, might well have seemed, in J. L. Hammond's phrase, a city that would be passed over by the storm clouds of the industrial revolution. But New York, also like London, had its ever expanding population—amounting to both the largest and most diverse consumer market and the largest concentration of surplus wage labor in the United States. Not only were workers needed to feed, house, and clothe these swarms, no matter how meanly; New York, with its immense labor pool, its credit facilities, its access to prefinished materials from Britain and New England, and its transportation lines, was a superb site for producing finished consumer goods, for local consumption or shipment elsewhere.

The interaction of these limits and incentives to manufacturing led to a uniquely metropolitan pattern of early industrial transformation. . . . The chief distinguishing feature of early metropolitan industrialization may be easily summarized: while manufacturing workers remained the largest group of New York wage earners, the established light handicraft industries—especially the consumer finishing trades—along with the building trades remained the most important sectors of the manufacturing economy. There were some important exceptions, those capital-intensive industries for which close proximity to specialized metropolitan markets was imperative, above all iron molding and casting. Other new, heavy urban industries—gas production, fine toolmaking—settled along the East River and at the edge of town; several older ones—brewing, distilling, sugar refining—all flourished and grew with the city's population. Yet while these industries fostered the rise of a significant factory sector in New York, far in advance of most American cities, and while they were important to the metropolitan economy, they employed no more than 5 percent of all New York manufacturing workers and only about 2 percent of all the gainfully employed in the 1850s. As in the Jeffersonian period, the typical manufacturing worker in antebellum New York was not an iron molder or a brewery worker, but a tailor (or tailoress), a carpenter, a shoemaker, a baker—to name only the largest occupations.

Beyond the central importance of the crafts, the main lines of metropolitan industrialization before 1850 were more tangled. In general, manufacturing growth in New York, as elsewhere, entailed a steady increase in the size of individual enterprises, which soon dwarfed the infant manufactories of 1820; in all, in 1850, 588 enterprises hired more than twenty workers each; these firms, in turn, employed most of the manufacturing work force. But these figures can be misleading if we equate the rise of large firms with the construction of large factories and the eradication of the city's small producers; in only one major metropolitan craft, printing, did the transitions of the 1830s and 1840s entail swift mechanization. Here, three additional features of early metropolitan industrialization complicated the pattern. First, the luxury and custom trade remained an important one in all branches of consumer production; New York, after all, boasted the wealthiest elite market in the country. . . . In these branches of even the most rapidly industrializing trades, the artisanal conventions and small-shop production continued. Second, some entire trades grew enormously without significantly changing their production processes. These included those crafts that were tied exclusively to the local consumer market—above all the food preparation trades—as well as those maritime trades that still required highly skilled hands. Finally, and most important, most of the city's leading craft entrepreneurs, in line with the limits and incentives of the port, relied on an intensified division of labor and one or another form of out-of-shop contracting—innovations usually treated by historians as "transitional" or "proto-industrial" in character—to cut their costs and to multiply output. These arrangements varied from trade to trade, from urban outwork to garret-shop contracting, but the logic was always roughly the same: manufacturers, having subdivided their work into its minute details, relied on one of several kinds of underpaid worker—debased artisans, garret-shop hands, or outworkers—to perform as much of their labor as possible. . . . By 1850, this process of subdivision and subcontracting had advanced to the point that most of the city's leading trades could barely be called crafts at all, even though some workers still clung to the appellations "mechanic" and "journeyman." In their place arose a bastard artisan system, one that would remain at the heart of New York manufacturing, even after the introduction of machines to some of the consumer finishing trades, . . . well into the twentieth century.

It was the ascendancy of this bastard system, along with the multiplicity of New York markets and the precocious mechanization of select sectors of the manufacturing economy, that was chiefly responsible for the proliferation of so many different kinds of work settings throughout Manhattan between 1825 and 1850. Of these, the factories remained of secondary importance; indeed, although a few New York trades mechanized very early, factory production was virtually nonexistent in New York in 1850 outside of the heavy industries, some small segments of the building trades, and in the book and periodical branches of the printing trades. In these places only did New York workers experience some approximation to the conditions of Lowell and Manchester, with their strictly enforced work rules, the constant surveillance of the patrolling foreman, and the unending din of the power machines. Even then, it was only an approximation: although the factories employed hundreds of hands, many, possibly a majority, were either highly skilled workers (for example, the most skilled compositors in the printing plants) or strictly manual laborers (for example, packers and delivery men); by no means did they constitute an undifferentiated mass of semiskilled factory operatives.

Related to the factories but far better suited to New York's cramped conditions were the city's small mechanized workshops, which gathered between three and twenty workers each, to labor (if only part-time) on machinery ranging from the most primitive power saws to elaborate distilling equipment. A few of the city's breweries and distilleries were in this category, as were some printing and engraving firms; the overall proportion of these enterprises, however, was small, and the proportion of wage earners who worked in them even smaller. Unfortunately, we know next to nothing about how work proceeded in these places—but it certainly would be mistaken to regard them, as a group, as either mini-factories or the most exploitative workshops. Most employed fewer than fifteen workers each. Apart from the primitive strapping shops in the building trades, most tended to pay wages above the average for manufacturing workers. Above all, most were in the newer trades created by the industrial revolution—machine making, precision toolmaking, and the like—and were geared to specialized, flexible markets and not to mass production. Despite the presence of labor-saving machinery, a great deal of the work in these firms required the highest degrees of skill; indeed, wage earners in some of these trades remained among the most skilled workers in the country until well into the second half of the nineteenth century, even after production had moved into factories.

The manufactories and outwork manufactories were the headquarters of the bastard artisan system. The manufactory may be thought of as a machineless factory—defined here as a concentration of more than twenty workers, each of whom performed the old handicraft tasks in a strictly subdivided routine. As in the factories, manufactory work was closely supervised: the difference was that manufactory workers were literally debased artisans, men (for the most part) who completed only a portion of the labor that skilled journeymen used to do on their own. The outwork manufactories—the largest employers in the city—operated differently: only the most skilled jobs were completed on the premises (although again, as in the manufactories, in a subdivided regime); the bulk of the semiskilled assembly work was put out, either to contractors or directly to outworkers. The census records do not reveal the ratio of "inshop" workers to outworkers in these enterprises, but a few existing reports on major clothing firms suggest that it was extremely low, perhaps one "inside" hand to every fifty outworkers. A conservative estimate suggests that while almost half of the city's craft workers were employed in outwork manufactories, only about 5.0 percent were "in-shop" workers; the rest—46.3 percent of all the city's craft workers—were outworkers.

It was in the remaining work places—all small, all unmechanized—that most craft workers actually earned their livings. The small neighborhood shops—still the largest group of *shops* in New York in 1850—included the remaining custom firms in the most rapidly industrializing trades (fine shoemaking, independent custom tailoring) as well as those firms in trades relatively unaffected by bastardization and dilution of skill, like blacksmithing and butchering. Garret shops were slightly larger and were usually tied to the bastard system. Watched over by small masters and former journeymen, most garret workers either completed outwork for the manufacturers or prepared a single line of product to be sold off in bulk to wholesalers and local retailers. In either case, they worked in a divided regime according to piece rates set by the garret masters, who in turn adjusted their wages to suit the rates set by their patrons. Finally, there were the outworkers' homes—manufacturing sites unrecorded as such in the census—where entire families and groups of friends toiled at the assembly jobs handed to them by the manufacturers or contractors.

This, then, was the New York manufacturing cityscape at mid-century, with its immense diversity of scale and its complex middle range of journeymen, contractors, small masters, and independent producers bridging the gap between the largest manufacturer and the lowliest outwork hand. It was not, contrary to the most cataclysmic images of the early industrial revolution, a setting where all opportunity had been destroyed by invading merchant capitalists— where all artisans were plunged into the ranks of proletarianized wage labor. As Frederic Cople Jaher has pointed out, New York's commercial bourgeoisie had very little to do directly with the expansion of local manufacturing, apart from providing craft entrepreneurs with credit. Rather, with some important exceptions in the clothing trades, it was the city's leading master craftsmen who, after transforming their own operations or rising through the ranks of another's, came to dominate the manufacturing elite. Some did spectacularly well, meriting inclusion in lists of the city's wealthiest men; other masters made solid, if not outstanding, fortunes. . . . As for the journeymen, not all were consigned to perpetual dependence, even in the most bastardized trades; the minuscule capital requirements necessary to set up as a contractor or a small master in the most debased crafts probably made it easier than ever, at least in principle, for journeymen to strike off on their own. Those who remained wage earners could, at least theoretically, vie for the more privileged posts in the custom shops and outwork manufactories.

Balanced against these abstract opportunities were the harsher realities of manufacturing work and the market for most craft workers and small masters. Access to capital, although widened greatly in the antebellum period, was not equal; nor was "upward mobility" a matter of succeeding in a free and impartial market. Bank committees closely scrutinized all requests for credit and discounted paper and naturally served those they knew to be good risks. . . . Not surprisingly, the distribution of capital among the city's masters in 1850 was extremely uneven. The deteriorating situation of the mass of craft workers, meanwhile, may be approached indirectly by examining some rudimentary statistics. First, there can be little question that average real wages fell in the city's major trades in the 1830s and 1840s. The entire logic of the bastard artisan system was based on the premise that employers could expand production by reducing their wage bills. While a small elite of workers was well paid, most men and virtually all women worked at piece rates that brought mediocre—for some, abysmal—incomes. The wage figures recorded in the census of 1850 suggest the overall effects of this downward pressure. In 1853, a report in the New York *Times* estimated that the minimal budget for a family of four (with the barest allowance for medical expenses) came to $600.00 per year. . . . According to the 1850 census, however, the average annual income for male workers in the trades was almost exactly $300.00. . . . Even male workers in the best-paid of the major trades earned on the average only close to the estimated family minimum. . . .

But these figures are suggestive at best; even if they were more precise, they would not disclose how metropolitan industrialization transformed the social relations of production, transformations that affected everyone—large employers, small masters, and every variety of wage earner—in different ways. . . . No two New York crafts industrialized in exactly the same manner or at the same pace; some barely changed at all. It was this lack of uniformity in the social experience of New York's workers and employers that distinguished the metropolis from the most famous early industrial towns before 1850. It would prove a critical factor in shaping the contours of metropolitan class formation and class conflict in the 1830s and 1840s.

Robert B. Gordon

REALIZING THE IDEAL OF INTERCHANGEABILITY

American armories were the first in the world to produce firearms with truly interchangeable parts, a technological feat that greatly facilitated repairs under battlefield conditions. After this achievement gained widespread attention at the Crystal Palace Exhibition in London in 1851, the British Parliament dispatched investigators to the United States to identify the unique features of the so-called American system of manufacture. The investigators reported that American armories employed special-purpose machinery in place of traditional manual methods of gun making. Until recently, most scholars have concurred in this assessment. Using archaeological methods to analyze surviving nineteenth-century firearms, Robert Gordon offers a different interpretation. By his account, credit for interchangeability belongs properly to highly skilled artificers using hand tools and gages. Gordon is professor of geophysics and applied mechanics at Yale University. He is the coauthor, with Patrick M. Malone, of *The Texture of Industry: An Archaeological View of the Industrialization of North America* (New York, 1994).

In 1884 Charles Fitch described interchangeable manufacture as a *mechanical ideal* accomplished by American inventors, entrepreneurs, and mechanicians who in fifty years had transformed the United States from an agricultural nation dependent on imported manufactured goods into a country that was exporting sophisticated production machinery to European customers. . . . The evolution of interchangeable manufacture continues to interest historians because it is one of the roots of American success in large-scale manufacturing. Moreover, because interchangeability implies reliance on machines, they regard it as underlying the removal of traditional artisan skills from the production process. . . .

I wish to challenge the notion that the precision of machines replaced the mechanical skills of artificers in the 19th century. To do this, I will use material evidence to show how representative products were made. Then I will define what I mean by skill and ask how much of the realization of the mechanical ideal was dependent on the performance of the artificers who used the new methods and to what degree the mechanical ideal was built into the new machinery instead of the abilities of the artificers. I will argue that the new methods of manufacturing metal products introduced in the 19th century not only fully engaged the traditional mechanical skills of artificers but also made new demands on their skills. The development and learning of these skills took many years and was, in fact, the factor that limited the progress of the new technology.

The role of the artificer's skills has been overlooked in previous research not perhaps for want of scholarly interest but for want of evidence. Documentary sources reveal little about what was required of the artificers engaged in manufacturing in the 19th century. The problem must be approached by archaeological methods. The surviving examples of 19th-century products are a source of information about the work of those who made them; they give us a kind of direct contact with the individual artificers that cannot be attained in any other way. . . .

Many of the surviving examples of 19th-century manufactured goods could serve our purpose, but most suitable would be a manufactured product of some complexity, difficult to make, meeting demanding service requirements, and produced in large quantities at a place where new manufacturing technology was devised and for which documentary evidence has survived. Examples should be datable and there should be no major design changes in the time interval under consideration. Possibilities include clocks, cylinder locks, sewing machines, edge tools, railway equipment, textile machinery, and artillery, but military small arms best fit the above criteria. Although overrepresented in discussions of the history of manufacturing technology, they nevertheless have some important advantages for our purposes. Arms collectors have identified date and place of manufacture for many museum specimens. The lock mechanism, stock, and barrel of the military small arms made in the United States, principally at the Springfield Armory, changed little in basic design until the bolt-action rifle was adopted in 1892. Small arms also were made in the first part of the 19th century by a number of contractors, whose work can be compared to that done at Springfield.

There are about twelve essential parts in a percussion lock (illustrated in Figure 1) and a few more in a flintlock, and it is helpful to pick one part that can be studied in detail. I have chosen the tumbler (marked *T* in Figure 1). It has a complex shape and is subject to large forces as the lock operates. The hard service to which tumblers were subjected in use is evidenced by the breakage rate in the middle of the 19th century, about 2 percent per year. . . .

An artificer will encounter several difficulties in making a tumbler. The profile is an irregular curve, but flat, square, and round surfaces also have to be formed; a deep hole has to be drilled and tapped; and the part has to be heat treated to the requisite degree of hardness and toughness. Examination of the finished product will show how these manufacturing problems were handled. . . .

In the 19th century the exterior parts of small arms were usually polished after they were shaped, but the interior surfaces usually retain the markings left by the last metal-cutting operation performed on them, the one that brought the part to its final dimensions. . . . Different types of tools used to shape metal or wood leave distinctive surficial markings on the workpiece. . . . I will describe the surficial markings on two of the tumblers studied and then note important differences observed on the other examples.

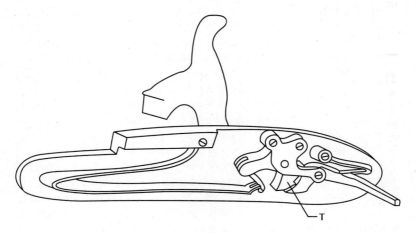

FIGURE 1. The mechanism of a percussion lock. The tumbler is marked *T*. There was little change in the design of this mechanism throughout the 19th century.

M1812 Musket Made Circa 1820

This musket was made at the Whitney Armory after Eli Whitney had gained twenty years' experience in the manufacture of firearms. . . . The edges of the tumbler were formed by transverse cuts with a coarse file, probably without a filing jig since the curves are not well blended and the tilts of the edge are not all in the same direction. The final finish on the top edge was made by curved strokes with a fine file; the areas that are more difficult to reach retain coarse file marks. The face of the tumbler on the pivot side shows no machine marks; file cuts in various directions were used to form this face. The face on the arbor side shows the characteristic marks of hollow milling. The cutter used chattered badly, producing deep gouges. At least two hollow mills were used; one formed the shoulder and the arbor, the other the relief on the face. The latter is a more demanding task, and the performance of the milling machine was poorer. The cylindrical surface of the arbor was formed by the hollow mill, but the flats that engage the square hole in the cock were filed. The pivot was made by transverse strokes with a hand file rather than by milling. Each stroke has left a facet on the surface of the pivot. . . . (The arbor and pivot are off center by .030 inches.) . . .

M1841 Rifle Made 1851

The M1841 rifle was made by a number of contractors, including the Whitney Armory, which was then under the management of Eli Whitney, Jr. . . . The quality of the mechanical work on the 1851 tumbler is greatly improved over that of 1820. . . . Four types of surficial markings resulting from the use of coarse and fine files with longitudinal and transverse strokes can be recognized around the edge of this tumbler. Both faces were formed by hollow milling, probably with a double milling machine. An additional hollow mill with a larger hole was used to make the shoulder on the arbor side. The accuracy of the work was sufficient to form a shoulder only 0.008 inch high, but the surface finish attained was poor and it was cleaned up with a file. Circular grooves with a slight inclination due to the feed rate of the mill are observed on the arbor and pivot and were probably made by the same milling operation that was used to form the faces. The flats were filed with transverse strokes.

Except for the milling of the pivot, no more machine work to final gage is present on the 1851 tumbler than on the 1820 example, but the quality of the handwork is enormously improved. The use of the hand file for the final shaping of the profile of the tumbler shows that the machines in use in 1851 at the Whitney Armory were not capable of finishing a product that would be to gage; handwork was required.

Springfield Armory

Both faces of a tumbler made in 1803 were found to be hollow milled; it is filed on all except the arbor face, and the quality of the file work is somewhat better than on the Whitney 1820 example. An example for 1812 was made by the same methods as that for 1803, but the quality of file work is much lower. The number of artificers at the Springfield Armory doubled between 1808 and 1810. The decrease in quality suggests that the learning time for this work was at least two years. There is a marked improvement in the appearance of Springfield tumblers by 1830; the example studied has been filed in the same places as the earlier examples, and the inner edge of the pivot has been damaged by careless filing, but the filed faces are more nearly parallel, and the crown and slant of the edges are reduced. A tumbler for the same model musket made in 1839 is similar in appearance, but there has been a further improvement in workmanship, illustrated by the absence of damage to the edges of the pivot caused by the filing of the pivot face. Equivalent areas on the 1830 and the 1839 tumblers show similar patterns of file strokes, although within these areas there are differences in the angles and uniformity of the strokes. This suggests that a generally accepted way of doing the job had been established but that the details of carrying it out were left up to the individual filer.

The first indication of a difference in the machine work on the Springfield tumblers is found in the example for 1844, where it appears probably that clamp milling was substituted for hollow milling to form the cylindrical surfaces of the arbor and pivot. This change came at a time when the armory was making substantial additions to its machine-tool inventory. A tumbler for the same model musket (1842) made in 1852 is very similar and has the same pattern of filing marks but is not numbered. This shows that the practice of assembling locks by groups of parts had been dropped and that a generally accepted procedure for filing was in place. The tool marks on the examples for 1873 and 1884 are nearly identical. The upper, front, and bottom edges of these tumblers are described as being milled after forging, but the surficial markings show that these surfaces were brought to their final dimensions by filing. This includes the notch, which we know to have been jig filed. The quality of the file work is very high; the crown of the edges is barely detectable and the edges are perpendicular to the faces. The need to file the edges of the tumbler shows that as late as 1884 the milling machinery was still not capable of bringing tumblers to gage dimensions. How good the filers were at this task will be shown in the discussion on dimensions.

Other Armories

Examination of tumblers of M1841 rifles made by Harpers Ferry, Tryon (Philadelphia), Robbins & Lawrence (Windsor, Vt.), Remington, and Whitney shows that the same set of manufacturing operations was used on all of them and that these operations were the same as those used at the Springfield Armory for the M1842 musket (except that there is no evidence of clamp milling of arbors and pivots outside of Springfield). . . . Since it is unlikely that each maker independently reached exactly the same conclusions about the best way to go about making a tumbler or that such details of method were imposed by contract terms, the exchange of ideas through the network of mechanicians must have been very effective in diffusing an accepted "right way" to do this job.

Reproducibility of Dimensions

Figure 2 shows the dimensions that were measured on the tumblers. In addition, the squareness of the edges to the faces and the amount of crown on the edges of each tumbler were examined, and as many

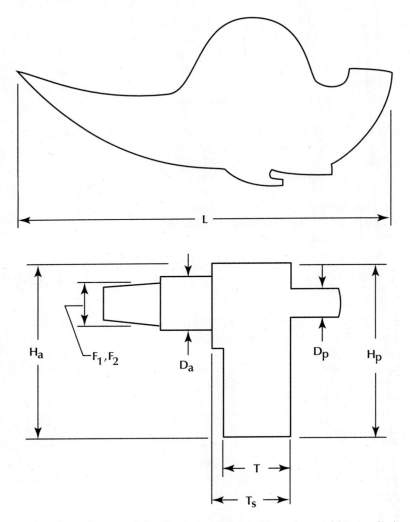

FIGURE 2.   Diagram of the dimensions measured on the tumblers studied. Any difference between H_a and H_p shows that the edges are not square to the faces. F_1 and F_2 are the widths of the inner ends of the two pairs of flats.

of the dimensions as could be determined on each tumbler listed in Table 1 were measured. The mean of all the measurements of each dimension on all the examples of a given model lock was calculated.

TABLE 1
LIST OF TUMBLERS EXAMINED

Model and Maker	Date of Manufacture
M1795	
Springfield	1803
Springfield	1812
M1812:	
Whitney	ca. 1820
M1816:	
Springfield	1830
Springfield	1839
M1842	
Springfield	1844
Springfield	ca. 1850 (2 examples)
Springfield	1852
Harpers Ferry	1844
M1841:	
Harpers Ferry	1851
Tryon	1845
Robbins & Lawrence	1850
Remington	1853
Whitney	1851
Whitney	1854
M1855:	
Springfield	ca. 1855 (2 broken examples)
Tower (London)	1862
M1873:	
Springfield	ca. 1873
M1884:	
Springfield	1884

Note: The locks for the M1873 and M1884 are identical.

The average of the deviations of each dimension from the mean of all the measurements of that dimension on each model of lock is a measure of the consistency of size and shape attained in the manufacture of the tumblers. The calculated average deviations are shown in Figure 3. The individual data points represent averages of from sixteen to forty-five measurements, depending on the number of examples available. The results show that there is a continuous improvement in the consistency of the dimensions along what may be described as a learning curve. By about 1880 the average deviation becomes less than 1/1000 inch. . . .

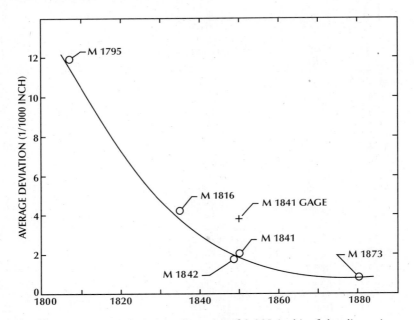

FIGURE 3. Average deviations (in units of 0.001 inch) of the dimensions of the tumblers for each model of lock examined from the mean of each dimension for that model. If all the tumblers of a given model were identical, the deviations would be zero. The average deviation is a measure of the degree to which the tumblers of a given model vary among themselves. The numbers of measurements averaged for each datum point are: M1795, 17; M1816, 14; M1841, 45; M1844, 30; and M1884, 16. The average departure of the measured dimensions from those set by the inspector's gages for the M1841 rifle is shown by the cross. It is slightly greater than the deviations of the tumblers among themselves.

Before proceeding to an interpretation, I will summarize the material evidence. The tool marks and dimension measurements show that by 1850 artificers using hand files had learned to bring rough forged and machined parts of complex shape to final dimensions specified by gages to an accuracy of a few thousandths of an inch in routine production. This was achieved by artificers at the national armories and at the works of private contractors from Philadelphia to Windsor, Vermont. They achieved higher standards of accuracy than could be attained with machine tools throughout most of the

19th century. A generally accepted method of doing this handwork was followed at all of the armories. . . .

The material evidence . . . shows that bringing lock parts to gage required handwork with a file at least through 1884. The dimensional tolerances and the quality of workmanship achieved by the artificers improved continuously along a learning curve. The improvement in product quality attained was primarily due to the superior mechanical skills developed among the artificers who made the lock parts, although better organization of the work and manufacturing procedures helped facilitate development of these skills. Clearly, the skills required to achieve interchangeability in the new system of manufactures was not "built into the machines" but remained in the hands of the artificers. . . .

I like to describe the skills required of mechanical artificers in terms of four components: dexterity, judgment, planning, and resourcefulness. *Dexterity* is the ability to manipulate tools with facility, and *judgment* is the capacity to gage size and shape by eye and goodness of fit between mechanical parts by feel. *Planning* and *resourcefulness* relate to decisions an artificer must make in organizing the way in which a task is to be undertaken and in responding to the unanticipated complications that inevitably crop up owing to inhomogeneity of the materials used or wear of the tools or machinery employed. All these elements of skill were required of artificers making small arms, but the relative importance of the four components changed throughout the course of the 19th century. . . .

As manufacturing methods developed through the 19th century there was less call for planning skills but heavier demands on the artificer's dexterity and judgment. Superior mechanical skills were developed and disseminated among a growing number of artificers. The mechanical requirements and the methods of attaining them were established early in the century, and after that there was little change in the basic methods of making parts for lock mechanisms other than increased use of machine tools for the heavy labor of roughing cuts, which allowed filers to concentrate on the final, precise shaping of parts to gage. There was a continuing improvement in the quality of work done with hand tools. The rate of progress in the attainment of interchangeable manufacture in the first two-thirds of the 19th century may have been limited as much by the rate of learning and transmission of the requisite mechanical skills among artificers as by the rate of invention of mechanical appliances to aid their work. . . .

A mechanical ideal was indeed achieved in 19th-century American manufacturing, but it was not the one proposed by Fitch. It was the superior standards of workmanship and mechanical skill of American artificers.

IV

The Emergence of
the Metropolis

Stuart M. Blumin

URBAN LIFESTYLES AND MIDDLE-CLASS FORMATION

As Thomas Jefferson and other founders of the Republic had anticipated with trepidation, the development of manufacturing was accompanied by the growth of urban population. Most Americans continued to live in rural areas throughout the nineteenth century, but an ever-increasing proportion resided in cities, and leading cities like New York grew at extraordinary rates. Although urbanization brought more and more people together in central locations, it did not produce social homogenization. On the contrary, the hallmark of the nineteenth-century American metropolis was its diversity, including segmentation along class, racial, ethnic, and gender lines. In the following selection, Stuart Blumin examines how men and women of the emerging urban middle class effectively set themselves apart from the very rich on the one hand and manual workers and the urban poor on the other. Blumin places particular emphasis on the organization of urban space, patterns of consumption, and the cultural leverage of women in middle-class homes. Blumin is professor of history at Cornell University. This selection is from his book *The Emergence of the Middle Class.*

> Things are in the saddle,
> And ride mankind
>
> > —R. W. Emerson, "Ode Inscribed
> > to W. H. Channing," 1847

Emerson's complaint was not a new one among thoughtful Americans, but it had acquired a new urgency in the Jacksonian era, when rising personal incomes and an expanding array of consumer goods (and of attractive downtown retail shops) produced striking changes in the habits and life-styles of large numbers of urban Americans, unleashing what one recent historian of New York City has called "a revolution of expectations regarding luxuries and comforts." Some city people forthrightly pursued an extravagant way of life during these

From Stuart M. Blumin, *The Emergence of the Middle Class: Social Experience in the American City, 1760–1900.* Copyright © 1989 by Cambridge University Press. Reprinted with the permission of Cambridge University Press.

years, pushing aside the once influential doctrine that associated virtue with plain living. A larger number, no doubt, retained that doctrine . . . even while redefining the meanings of simplicity and comfort in accordance with new conditions. In the words of one contemporary:

> Time was when it was sufficient for a comfortable liver to have half a house, or to have one spare front-room for company: now, the same man must have a whole house, and the first story must be thrown into parlors. Not *very* long since, one servant, for general purposes, was all that was deemed necessary: now, the requirement is extended to two certainly, with special aid for extra occasions, and a nurse for the little ones. . . . It is not many years since the class spoken of were only occasionally favored with a piano: now, that instrument must be set down as a requisite to parlor equipment. The same is true of the dietetic department, of our social entertainments and modes of dressing—great changes have occurred with our so-called advancing civilization.

Recent historians have made it clear that "the class spoken of" was the urban middle class, whose members experienced a domestic revolution during these years that went beyond the acquisition and furnishing of a larger and more elegant home (completely separated, we might add, from the male household head's place of business) to the sanctification of the home and of domestic affairs, the redefinition of gender roles within the home, and the reformulation of strategies of child nurturance and education, the whole constituting . . . not merely a middle-class phenomenon but a phenomenon critical to the formation and perpetuation of the middle class. . . .

Did consumption contribute to class distinctions in this era, or did it tend to dissolve the boundaries that were taking shape in the urban workplace? The most dramatic changes in the production of consumer goods were those that made ordinary goods cheaper. Hence, those mechanics who were able to find work fairly often, and who maintained their skill levels in the face of industrialization, were able to take advantage of significant price reductions in cloth, clothing, and a number of household goods that previously had been available only to people with larger incomes. Workers in the new furniture factories and specialized cheap furniture shops, for example, may have experienced new limitations of income and opportunity, but they and other workers benefited from the low prices of mass-produced furniture. . . . Carpets, too, once restricted to the well-to-do, plummeted in price after the introduction of power-loom weaving, and became accessible to all classes. . . . By 1860, reports Edgar W. Martin, "as good an eight-day clock could be obtained for $3.00 or $4.00 as would have sold for $20.00 before 1837, and a one-day clock could be sold at a fair profit for 75 cents." . . . Perhaps the most significant price changes were those introduced by the new ready-to-wear clothing industry. Clothiers usually did not advertise their prices during this era, but a few of the less expensive ready-to-wear clothing stores, such as Philadelphia's Phoenix Clothing Bazaar, listed prices for business coats ($4.25 to $8.00), vests ($1.00 to $3.00), and other items of respectable dress that were within range for a number of manual workers. In the same year (1860) Dickerson's hat store of Philadelphia advertised "fine dress hats" at $2.50, while an unnamed competitor offered the "cheapest silk hats" from a "one-price store" that was in the midst of a working-class neighborhood.

These final items suggest that workers may have emulated (or duplicated without seeking to emulate) middle-class styles of consumption, especially in clothing, which was certainly one of the most visible and status-relevant types of consumer goods. But the question of class-related styles of clothing in antebellum urban America is a difficult one to resolve. . . . Illustrations of workplaces and street scenes offer an interesting but limited and sometimes contradictory view of contemporary perceptions. Some views of factories and smaller workshops portray working men and women in plain and sometimes rough clothes, usually covered by an apron. Men's shirts are often white (or at any rate are light and uniform in color), but sleeves are usually rolled and shirt collars are absent or open. Men work hatless, or wear soft caps or hats, or the paper hats traditional to a few trades. Women wear plain, unadorned dresses, sometimes with an apron. Other views, however, depict workers who are better dressed, with closed collars, cravats, and vests for men, and lace-trimmed dresses for women. . . . These workers may have been fully qualified citizens of what *The Illustrated News* would call, a few years later, the "plain dark democracy of broadcloth."

It is probable, however, that most contemporaries perceived differences where we can see only similarities. Inexpensive clothes, clothes purchased in secondhand shops, and clothes worn for too

long a time created visible differences within the broadcloth democracy, even in the absence of differences in style. Moreover, depic-
tions of businessmen, clerks, prosperous shoppers, and pedestrians
in downtown retail districts convey a greater opulence of dress than
appears in any of the workshop views. Bowery b'hoys and other
working-class dandies may have tried to match this opulence, but
the effect was very different. Mose and the b'hoys wore black frock
coats, tall beaver hats, and silk cravats, but greased and curled "soap
locks" sticking down out of their hats, and black cigars sticking out
of their teeth, gave the b'hoys anything but a respectable appearance. Lize dressed "high" but, in George Foster's estimation, not
well, in bright, clashing colors "gotten together in utter defiance of
those conventional laws of harmony and taste imposed by Madame
Lawson and the French mantua-makers of Broadway." There is a
suggestion here not only of defiance but of parody as well—Mose
and Lize may have deliberately combined some of the elements of
middle- and upper-class dress to create a counterstyle that expressed
contempt for bloodless gentility. In any case, it certainly expressed
the high spirits of the young people of the "Republic of the
Bowery," and just as certainly did not express any desire on their
part to emulate the dress and mien of the middle class. In this they
succeeded, and in the very act of utilizing elements of middle-class
dress came closer than anyone else to developing a distinctively
working-class style. . . .

Workers who spent large portions of their income on food and
clothes (and unknown additional amounts on drink and entertain-
ment) had less money left over for renting and furnishing the kind
of household that, increasingly in this era, signified respectability.
. . . Boardinghouses absorbed many of the unmarried male workers
of the lower wards, and tenements—in former single-family dwellings, in cellars, in back-lot and courtyard buildings, and increasingly,
in new buildings built specifically as multiple-household dwellings—
absorbed most of those workers who had families. By 1864, according to a careful and well-known survey of the city's housing and
sanitary conditions, more than half a million New Yorkers lived
in tenements. Most were poor immigrants, and most tenements
were appallingly squalid, but some tenement dwellers were skilled,
American-born mechanics who were making the best of life in an

overcrowded city. Indeed, if the sanitary inspectors counted accurately, the bulk of the skilled native working class must have lived in tenements. . . .

Mechanics' tenements were not necessarily squalid. Several of the sanitary inspectors noted tenement buildings or even groups of buildings in which living conditions were healthy and clean, and even in some of the worst districts of the city, where the inhabitants were "of the laboring class, poor, imperfectly nourished, . . . uncleanly in their persons and habits, and grossly addicted to intemperance," and where the houses were "the usual three to six-story tenements, generally out of repair," there were also "many families of mechanics of more temperate habits, whose comforts are consequently greater." Moreover, in other cities, where the pressure on real estate was not as acute as it was in New York, fewer workers lived in tenement houses or in such densely crowded districts. In 1845, only one-quarter of Boston's families lived in buildings containing more than three families, while nearly a third lived in single-family dwellings. The 42% who shared a building with one or two other families probably included the major portion of the skilled work force. Philadelphia and Baltimore both accommodated to rapid growth by building row houses rather than tenements and by increasing the numbers of small houses and tenements in back alleys and courtyards. . . .

The better tenements of New York, and the workingmen's houses of Boston, Philadelphia, Baltimore, and other cities, provided skilled mechanics and their families with housing that may have been adequate in many respects, but that was neither spacious, attractive, nor very comfortable. The little back-alley houses of Philadelphia ordinarily contained only one room per story, and most were only two stories tall. Many mechanics lived in three-room tenements or houses, or in three rooms of a subdivided house, but there probably were few (except for carpenters and other construction tradesmen who built houses for themselves on cheaper land beyond the inner city) who could afford more than three rooms. These rooms were furnished with bedsteads, chairs, tables, and other articles from the inexpensive furniture stores, and their floors were often covered with carpets—an improvement, perhaps, over the sanded floors and sparsely furnished living quarters of most eighteenth-century mechanics. . . . This is hardly a catalogue of opulence, however, and even suggests that workers may have had to choose between a decently furnished home and evenings spent at the Bowery Theater. Few workers, moreover, enjoyed the comforts of indoor toilets or running water, although some of the newer New York tenements did, apparently, have a water spigot on each floor. . . .

Middling folk of the nonmanual sector lived much better than the mechanics, not only because more money bought more and better goods, but also because these men could afford to commute to work each day on the city's omnibuses, street railways, and ferries, and hence could rent or purchase larger and more attractive homes in the less congested and less expensive parts of the city. When Walt Whitman wrote of the "most valuable" middle class in 1858, it was to promote the construction of inexpensive houses in Brooklyn, and to observe as well as to encourage the flight of salaried New Yorkers across the river to both better and cheaper houses. *Frank Leslie's Illustrated Newspaper* made the same observation around the same time in a humorous sketch, "On the Inconvenience of Living in a Very Friendly Neighborhood." The narrator of the sketch is a "young clerk in a wholesale, down-town store, on a rising salary of— well, no matter what per annum." He rents a small house with a large backyard in Brooklyn for $200, where he lives with his wife and baby, happily, except for a too friendly neighbor who wants to borrow one thing after another, including at one point the couple's baby. The neighbor is also a nonmanual worker, a "drummer" for a New York dry goods establishment, and the two commute together each day. Edward Spann notes that there were large numbers of real clerks and "drummers" who, along with many of their employers, found good homes in Brooklyn and in other peripheral areas within and beyond the boarders of New York City—Mott Haven, Morrisania, and Fordham in what is now the Bronx, Yorkville on the upper East Side, and several less distant sections separating the wealthy area around Fifth Avenue from the working-class districts along the rivers. In one of these sections, stretching from Thirtieth to Forty-fifth street on the East Side, "handsome dwellings" rented for $300 to $400 per annum, beyond the means of the Brooklyn clerk, perhaps, but well within the budget of the "frugal family of four" described in *Hunt's Merchants' Magazine.* . . .

The removal of work from the homes of middling folk permitted the multiplication of parlors, bedrooms, and other purely domestic spaces, even in smaller houses inherited from the eighteenth century.

Newer houses, moreover, were often larger, and it is clear that businessmen and salaried workers who complained about rising urban housing costs, and who fled to Brooklyn and other less central districts in search of more satisfactory homes, were pursuing a rapidly changing standard of middle-class space and comfort. This changing standard is reflected in Gervase Wheeler's *Homes for the People,* one of several architectural books written during this era in response to the enormous demand for new home designs that accompanied urban growth and new concepts of domesticity. Wheeler offered plans for all levels of the urban and suburban market, including tenements and cottages for "those who have to calculate every item of house-keeping cost, and who, living by mechanical labor, have need of frugal employment of their means to bring up a family in respectability and comfort." His tenement design, the only realistic plan in the book for housing urban workers, specifies individual apartments of four rooms plus a water closet—a quite conventional allocation for a model tenement intended to upgrade the housing of urban workers, and one that totals 646 square feet of interior space, almost exactly the median of the estimated actual living space of Philadelphia artisans in 1798. In striking contrast to this continuity of perceived standards for city people "living by mechanical labor" are Wheeler's designs for the urban middle class. His city or suburban home "for those of moderate means" is a house of three stories and a basement, richly ornamented in a Gothic style, and totaling no less than 3,375 square feet on the three stories of living space. Costing from $3,000 to $3,500 to build in 1855, according to the author, this model home was clearly beyond the means of artisans earning $500 or $600 per year (or even of those who earned somewhat more) but was affordable to . . . the small nonmanual businessmen. . . . So, too, were several other suburban villas Wheeler designed of a similar size. These were much larger homes than those of late-eighteenth-century middling folk. They were, of course, models, not actual homes, but they are offered as practical, not visionary schemes, and are priced, sized, and related to specific clientele in a manner that could not have varied much from prevailing standards. . . .

The domestic influence of middle-class American women is by now a familiar theme in the historical literature of the nineteenth-century family. According to this literature, perhaps best exemplified by Nancy Cott's excellent study of the diaries and letters of one hundred "middle-class" and "upper-middle-class" New England women, the home, the traditional domestic tasks of women, and the particular task of childrearing over which women were acquiring nearly complete control, were increasingly sanctified during the early years of the nineteenth century and served increasingly as the foundation for the assertion of the moral superiority of women over men. Some historians have stressed the gains in personal esteem that finally accrued to the "separate sphere" of womanhood in the nineteenth century, including those that resulted from a more genuinely companionate marriage. Others, including Cott, contend that these gains were bought at the price of increasing confinement and continuing subjugation to male authority in all things other than those pertaining to childrearing, manners, and other matters of sensibility. All these contradictions and nuances within the canon of domesticity have been examined at length; yet at least three relatively neglected aspects of the reorganization of gender roles and influence deserve emphasis here. One concerns the nature and extent of male acquiescence. *Harper's* blithely noted that men were "perfectly content" to follow the female lead in domestic manners, but as late as 1857, a year after the article just cited, the same magazine could list a whole catalogue of continuing male abuses against decent social behavior. Some men no doubt did freely acquiesce in their wives' urgings to behave in a more genteel fashion, and surely there were large numbers who gave up spitting and took their feet off the furniture in response to their own desire for self-esteem and social status. But obviously there were others who did not choose to change their rough habits, just as some men did not defer to their wives in the raising of children. In some middle-class homes, in other words, the domestication of males . . . was a battle to be won, not a smooth and painless process of acquiescence to superior feminine sensibility.

A second facet of the emerging domestic canon, and one more closely connected to the central argument of this chapter, is the role of the specific *setting* of domestic relations, and of consumption and consumer goods, in shaping both the middle-class home and the reorganization of gender roles within it. As Karen Halttunen points out, it was the parlor, the most carefully and elaborately furnished room in every middle-class home and the space within the home where the family socialized with other people of its own choosing, that served as "the arena within which the aspiring middle classes worked to establish their claims to social status, to that elusive quality of 'gentility'." Halttunen's fascinating discussion of parlor etiquette, and of the elaborate theatrical performances that took place within the parlors of the 1850s and beyond, pertains most forcefully to the wealthiest and most socially ambitious middle-class families. But more ordinary middling folk also found that the parlor made demands on their deportment. "It is impossible to say," confesses Russell Lynes, "whether the stuffiness of the room dictated the increasing stiffness of manners or if the determination to behave genteelly made the room more uncomfortable, more formal, and more forbidding." Put another way, some men either found it more difficult, or found themselves less inclined, to spit on the Brussels carpet than on the sanded floors of earlier middling homes, to drape their legs over the new parlor sofa, or to tell loud stories while their daughters (or their hosts' daughters) were at the piano. The carpet, the sofa, and the piano, therefore, all artifacts of the new middle-class way of life, exerted their influence over middle-class modes of behavior, especially the behavior of men.

And it was partly through these consumer goods that women exerted their influence. Increasingly, as women assumed responsibility for the management of the home, the purchase of those goods that helped define the middle-class household (and refine male behavior) became a female function and prerogative. The point applies not only to durable goods but to food as well. Faye Dudden observes that during the 1850s the responsibility for marketing in middling homes shifted from the husband to the wife, and offers the interesting suggestion that this shift reflected in part the increasing desire and ability of the wife to exert control over the production of more refined and elaborate meals. (These were meals, one might add, that the wife might have compelled her husband to eat more slowly, and with a fork rather than a knife.) It is not clear that women gained complete ascendancy over the furnishing of the home—men's names dominate the list of piano purchasers in the 1855 city directory advertisement of J. E. Gould's Great Piano and Melodeon Emporium of Philadelphia—but contemporary discussions of shopping focused mainly on women, and almost certainly the woman's role in the selection and acquisition of goods was expanding along with the pace of acquisition itself. The retailer and the tradesman succeeded, according to *Harper's,* "by pleasing women." There can be little doubt that women played a significant role in the shaping of the middle-class home. In most cases it was probably a decisive one. . . .

By now it should be clear that the final aspect of the nineteenth-century domestic revolution that I wish to emphasize is its relationship to the formation of the American urban middle class. Virtually every historian of the emerging canon of domesticity . . . has recognized its middle-class character, or at the very least the middling social condition of those who left behind the documents on which our understanding is based. "The canon of domesticity," writes Cott, "expressed the dominance of what may be designated a middle-class ideal, a cultural preference for domestic retirement and conjugal-family intimacy over both the 'vain' and fashionable sociability of the rich and the promiscuous sociability of the poor." Mary Ryan has gone further than this by arguing that the *emergence* of a distinct middle class was closely connected with, and largely dependent upon, the development of the domestic ideal. "Early in the nineteenth century," she writes, "the American middle class molded its distinctive identity around domestic values and family practices." By midcentury these values and practices, particularly those concerning the rearing and education of children, had evolved into a set of specific strategies for securing the family's foothold in the developing middle class. First, "prescient native-born couples" began to limit the size of their families, "thereby concentrating scarce financial and emotional resources on the care and education of fewer children." Second, these same couples "initiated methods of socializing designed to inculcate values and traits of character deemed essential to middle-class achievement and respectability," values and traits not of the aggressive entrepreneur but of the "cautious, prudent small-business man" (thereby helping to define "the upper as well as the lower boundaries of the middle class"). Third, children were kept within their parents' household for longer periods, prolonging parental surveillance and material support. Fourth, these resident children were given greater amounts of formal schooling, a crucial tactic intended to help them secure positions in the expanding nonmanual work force. And finally, the young men who emerged from this middle-class "cradle" were encouraged to delay their marriages until they had secured their own middle-class positions, a tactic that also contributed to the perpetuation of the tactical sequence, because it encouraged the reproduction of small families. The implication of all this (and not merely the final tactic) is that the sequence was self-perpetuating—that, once implemented, these strategies would succeed in gaining or securing each family's position in the middle class, and established middle-class families would be the ones most likely to pursue the same strategies in subsequent generations.

I would add to Ryan's argument that consumption too was a family strategy, a more or less deliberate attempt to shape the domestic environment in ways that signified social respectability, and that facilitated the acquisition of habits of personal deportment that could set a family apart from both the rough world of the mechanics and the artificial world of fashion. . . .

Middling families, then, reasonably perceived their homes and their domestic strategies and habits to be distinct from those of manual workers, as well as from those of the fashionables who did not even aspire to the domestic ideal. If this was an achievement—and it was often described that way by contemporary writers—it was one that should be attributed largely to the women who shaped the middle-class home, sometimes with and sometimes without the cooperation of the men who provided the financial means. At least partly in response to the new ways in which middling women performed the roles of wife, mother, household manager, and consumer, the American urban middle class "molded its distinct identity." In this respect we may say that middle-class formation was a phenomenon that went beyond the realignment of work, workplace relations, incomes, and opportunities. Events on the other side of the retail sales counter, and in the "separate sphere" of domestic womanhood, were influential, perhaps even crucial, in generating new social identities. To this extent, middle-class formation was woman's work.

Christine Stansell

THE GEOGRAPHY OF VICE

Ironically, while industrialization yielded an unprecedented increase in wealth per capita, it made the existence of poverty more obvious for all to see, especially in metropolitan centers. Religiously inspired members of the emerging middle class took this evidence of social illness to heart, and many sought to rescue the poor from squalor by offering charity in the service of moral uplift. Rather than attempt a radical restructuring of society as a whole, most urban reformers tried to save poor people by converting them to middle-class cultural values. In her analysis of reform activity in New York City, Christine Stansell pays particular attention to the role of women in this social process. Through home visits and other personal contacts, middle-class women displayed sincere sympathy for poor women, at least those of "worthy" character. But in the end, Stansell argues, the reformers' feelings of sisterhood and their strategies of benevolence were deeply distorted by class loyalties and prejudices. Stansell teaches American history at Princeton University. She is the author of *City of Women,* from which this selection is taken.

The city has been made the grand lurking-place of vice," a speaker at an evangelical meeting announced in 1835. Since the days of Jefferson, Americans had voiced similar denunciations of urban corruption. This man's point, though, was not a general lament about the inherent baseness of city life but a specifically framed indictment: He was protesting what he saw to be the infestation of one particular city, New York, by the forces of sin. Others echoed his condemnation. A map of the city limned bright and dark according to the moral state of the district, another evangelical subsequently speculated, would present an alarming picture. Tucked away off the avenues, down the side streets and alleys, were lodged appalling concentrations of viciousness, multitudes which "probably outnumbered the whole Christian portion of the city . . . ignorant, careless, deprived, perishing." By the 1830s, New York was daunting in its complexity; religious activists were well aware how easily sin—"inebriation, squalid wretchedness, Sabbath profanation and vices"—could conceal itself in such a city from the vigilance of the devout.

These places of vice were the incarnation of bourgeois perceptions of the working-class neighborhoods. The evangelicals were devout Protestants who, spurred by a series of revivals that began after the War of 1812, invaded the poor neighborhoods in search of souls lost to grace. Their numbers swelled in the years 1829–35, when the great evangelical minister Charles Finney preached his New York revivals; by 1835, the evangelical movement encompassed a score of moral reform organizations. The pious view of the iniquity of working-class life had developed from attitudes toward the "unworthy" poor which had been germinating in the city's elite since 1812. But there were also new elements in the evangelicals' metaphors of danger, sin and secrets, which embodied the class prejudices and perceptions they formed as they saw firsthand the realities of the working poor. The imagery of concentrated vice was one response to the movement of laboring people into recognizably working-class neighborhoods.

Ideals of family life and womanhood also played into the images of depravity. On their errands of mercy into the tenements, evangelical men and women encountered patterns of womanly behavior and child rearing that clashed with their deepest-held beliefs. As genteel writers and ministers after 1820 articulated more clearly their expectations of women in the home, the evangelicals sharpened their own ideas about domesticity in the context of their disapproving encounters with the laboring poor. Antebellum domesticity—at least in its urban form—emerged within a field of class antagonisms and in turn incited and intensified those antagonisms. Through the efforts of the evangelicals to transform working-class neighborhoods, issues of gender and family entered into class conflicts.

In 1829, the New York City Tract Society, the city's leading evangelical organization, reorganized its work with the unregenerate. Volunteers were assigned a group of families on whom they would regularly call with inspirational tracts, Bibles, and the message of salvation. These home visits, the evangelicals hoped, would penetrate the entire city: Christ's legions would leave no resident untouched.

The emphasis on mass conversions came from the evangelicals' view of the role of human will in securing salvation. While orthodox

Calvinists had believed that God saved whom He chose, the evangelicals gave much more credit to human agency. God would help with His divine grace those who helped themselves. By 1829, the evangelicals had taken their faith in human ability one step further: If people could help to save themselves, then they could also expedite the salvation of others. Divine grace, moreover, had a social as well as a spiritual purpose. From its beginnings, the evangelical movement had concerned itself with urban poverty. Fortified by a faith in the limitless powers of the redeemed to transcend earthly circumstance, the evangelicals saw salvation . . . as the solution to the problem of poverty in the city. . . .

The public life of the evangelical revivals was especially valuable to women. Nationwide, they poured into the fold in great numbers, "the workers, the fund raisers, the emotionally committed supporters of tract and Bible societies, of Sunday schools and of charity sewing societies." They took spiritual command of their own families, assigning themselves traditionally patriarchal duties like leading family prayers. In the excitements of the revivals, women put the finishing touches on the new imagery of womanhood they had been promoting since the late eighteenth century. Evangelical women and the ministers who encouraged them turned the republican mother into a moral leader. This figure, the "true" woman, powerfully repudiated misogynist assumptions about the weaker character of the sex and studiously ignored the well-worn tales of Eve's transgressions in favor of more flattering Biblical texts about industrious, faithful and pious females. Banished to the upper and lower reaches of society (to the frivolous rich and the depraved poor) was the image of the vain, foolish, sexually duplicitous woman. The dignified Christian woman demanded respect and esteem for her sex. . . .

Clear boundaries delimited respectable, propertied womanhood: To violate them was to find oneself in the shady realm of the demimonde. Home visiting, however, allowed respectable women to cross with impunity some of the same class boundaries that gentlemen-about-town habitually transgressed. The Society for the Relief of Poor Widows (SRPW) was founded in 1797 as New York's first female charity; after 1820 it was closely allied with the evangelicals. This women's association, one of the city's largest and most powerful, confronted the geographical circumscriptions of gender, beginning in the early 1820s, with a string of resolutions that limited home visits to certain sections of the city. Off-limits were streets "the managers cannot visit with propriety" like those around Five Points, a veritable sink of iniquitous pleasures in the eyes of the genteel. The ladies continually expanded the limits of propriety, however, as the laboring poor moved uptown. Others were bolder. The zealous members of the Female Moral Reform Society, founded in 1834 to abolish prostitution, traveled to the "low" brothels of Corlears Hook and Five Points, the most powerfully tabooed spots for women in the entire city, to stand outside and read Scripture, to pray and to urge repentance on all who entered and exited. Admittedly, the Moral Reform ladies were extreme in their ardor and their actions. Nonetheless, evangelicalism gave women the spiritual armor . . . to defend their reputations from the slurs women incurred when they ventured onto men's sexual terrain.

Through religiously motivated exploration, then, bourgeois women made some progress in making the city their own. What their advances meant for their laboring sisters is a more complicated question. Deeply invested in a particular construction of gender as the basis of respect for their sex, the religious women encountered in the neighborhoods of the working poor an alien mode of womanhood and family life. To some extent they responded sympathetically, in ways that differed from moralistic male charities and reform associations. While empathy for their sex tinged evangelical women's perceptions of the poor, however, those perceptions still drew upon and reinforced bourgeois biases.

For charitable women, a strong commitment to proving the "worthiness" of applicants reconciled stringent exclusionary policies with a genuine solicitude for some who sought aid. Women's charities required verifiable character references and marriage certificates from applicants, a practice which ruled out the great majority of those in the most desperate straits, the immigrants. Although travelers' guides advised emigrating Irish to take along such papers, many did not (or could not, if theirs were common-law marriages), and those who did often found the letters from Ireland useless, since they could not be verified in New York. Practical concerns, of course, also entered into this policy. The ladies needed principles of selection all the more because they were inundated with requests for help. Moral criteria helped the ladies justify to themselves and to their applicants why they could help some and not others, and at times soothed their own distress at their inability to give aid.

The logic of reconciliation between gender-based sympathies and class-based moralism is especially striking among the ladies who ran the Asylum for Lying-In Women, where the appeal to the common afflictions of womanhood was especially strong. The asylum was a refuge for pregnant women bereft of the resources for giving birth. For a small fee the patients obtained room and board, a midwife's services and postpartum care. "It is our own sex appealing to us," the ladies stressed to members and supporters. Poverty, they believed, only increased the burdens that all women endured in pregnancy and childbirth. "Daughters of affliction, how hard is your lot!" the recording secretary exclaimed in 1830, in sympathy with a woman in an especially sad situation.

But is was virtue, not affliction, the ladies were willing to succor. However "interesting" or miserable a woman's circumstances, she could not enter without references. The ladies found Mrs. Donnally's case, for instance, especially touching. Pregnant and with four small children, she had followed her husband to New York; the day she arrived he took sick and died. This unfortunate woman's letters of character were good, but "the testimonials of marriage were wanting" (even if her husband was dead, the ladies needed to be sure the pregnancy was legitimate) and the board regretfully turned her away, noting that "her widow'd heart seem'd ready to burst as she spoke of her helpless children." Mrs. Byrnes, already handicapped by her residence in the disreputable Five Points, was damned by the very urgency of her need: "From her abject appearance she appeared not a fit association for patients." But the most chilling instance of the limits of sisterly charity was that of Maria Burley in 1827. Her case was "pitiable and urgent," the admissions committee noted. Her husband had left her and their child to go tramping for work. She had spent the money he left her on caring for her sick mother, who had then died. Destitute, she went to live with a friend, but she had no bed of her own: Nine months pregnant, "she was shivering with cold without comfortable apparel." Yet Mrs. Burley lacked the requisite letters and the ladies sent her back out into the bitter cold of a New York January until they could ascertain her character from reliable sources. Consequently, the woman almost died.

It is painful to relate that after a walk of two miles in this extreme cold she was obliged to seek refuge for the night in an open garret with only one quilt for covering and before morning and alone she was delivered of a female infant, which when she was found by two men was frozen to her clothing and with great difficulty restored to life.

By the next day the ladies had made their inquiries, and the half-frozen Mrs. Burley could be admitted. But even these terrible travails were not enough to convince the ladies they had given charity to a "proper object." The following summer, the admissions committee noted sorrowfully that they had learned that "Mrs. Burley who was confined here last winter does not appear to sustain as good a character as was hoped." Such were the contradictions embedded in sisterly charity or, as the ladies of the asylum described it, "the difficulties of meeting at the same time the demands of justice and charity." . . .

Generally, the evangelically inspired women's charities did not actively contribute to the evolving discussion of social depravity, but rather embroidered a sentimentalist image of the female victim, a gentle and wounded spirit who partook of the piety and deference of the traditional worthy poor. The virtues of the image were elaborated within the emerging ideal of true womanhood. Such a proper object of women's sympathy was "poor yet industrious, modest quick neat," frail, vulnerable, timid and self-sacrificing:

> Warm'd by labor all day long. . . .
> Ill clad, and fed but sparsely. . . .
> The frugal Housewife trembles when she lights
> Her scanty stock of brush Wood, blazing clear. . . .
> And while her infant race with outspread hands
> And crowded knees, still cow'ring o'er the sparks—
> Retires, content to quake, so they be warm.

Above all, the worthy poor woman was alone (except for her children). She abnegated the "bad associations" which surrounded her; she was, accordingly, a "lonely" and "desolate" woman who tearfully "look'd round in vain for friend or succour," the metaphorical (if hardly actual) inhabitant of a "solitary dwelling." Her moral independence from the milieu in which she lived—or, from another perspective, her social isolation—made her dependent on womanly charity not just for material help but for emotional support. "The thought that there is someone who cares for her . . . is like a balm to her wounded spirit, and causes hope to spring up where before, nothing but withering despondency was felt." In practice, then, sentimentalism did little to promote understanding across class lines; rather, it reinforced the categories of worthy/unworthy and fleshed them out with a specifically female content. . . .

The figure of the solitary woman quaking in her garret allowed the members of female charities to acknowledge the specific injustices to which their sex was subject and at the same time to maintain their contempt for the milieu in which poor women lived. It was an image fashioned from both sex and class loyalties, the progenitor of all the shivering seamstresses and disinherited match girls, weepy but valiant, who frequented the pages of charity reports and urban fiction in the Victorian period. Insofar as the ladies of religious charities could associate the women they helped with this image, they extended to them the emotional bonds of womanhood. In effect, however, such a community of sex could only incorporate a tiny minority of laboring women. By the very unsolitariness of their lives, most of the female laboring poor excluded themselves.

The sentimentalist imagery of female poverty became a convention of nineteenth-century urban social thought. For all its remoteness from the actualities of experience, it nonetheless embodied a new empathy for women; as such, it could only have developed within a reform movement in which women were active. In practice, however, such figures of the imagination did little to help female benevolent associations cope with the realities of poor women's lives in those dense neighborhoods laced through with the intimacies of loyalty, anger and affection. Sentimentalism did, however, serve to reconcile, however unevenly, the competing claims of class and sex.

The urban geography of vice charted by the ministers and tract visitors was neither an accurate rendition of plebeian reality nor a figment of an anxious bourgeois imagination. Rather, it represented the charities' hostile perceptions of certain kinds of working-class assumptions and associations. Prepared to aid the silent and solitary sufferers, charitable visitors were repelled by the gregarious clamor of the tenements. Nathaniel Willis, although not himself a reformer, voiced what must have been the surprise many experienced when he discovered the distance between what he had imagined the poor to be like and what he saw firsthand: "At the Five Points," he observed on a tour of the city's exotica of poverty, "nobody goes in doors except to eat and sleep. The streets swarm with men, women, and children. . . . They are all out in the sun, idling, jesting, quarrelling, everything but weeping, or sighing, or complaining. . . . A viler place than Five Points by any light you could not find," he concluded. "Yet to a superficial eye, it is the merriest quarter of New York." . . .

A developing history of family instability framed the passions and dramas of the tenements. Men's relationships to their families shifted, as old patterns of involvement and authority disintegrated. The same circumstances that loosened men's ties bound their wives in all the more tightly. Situated at the heart of the household economy, mothers almost always stayed on, no matter how dire the situation. Consequently, it was they who often felt most keenly the hardships of wages insufficient to feed their children, and the fatigue of enforced dependency on others who themselves had little to share. The exigencies of working-class life, on the one hand, increasingly assigned women major responsibilities for their children's survival and, on the other, denied them the means to support their families.

It was, in part, the consolidation of these domestic networks that contributed to the evangelicals' perceptions of the "concentration" of wickedness in the city. As they came to identify working-class mores as inherently vice-ridden, the neighborhood took on the appearance of the breeding ground of sin. The ways laboring women helped one another, raised their children and played out their pleasures and grievances on the streets only seemed to the pious to manifest a belligerent iniquity. Home visiting provided all the more opportunity to witness the supposed coalescence of depravity in the tenements and on the streets. Journalists and writers, in translating the experiences of the home visitors into narratives, popularized the geography of vice as a metaphor through which genteel New Yorkers could see themselves as both brave explorers of a dangerous city and elect guardians of civilized culture.

By constituting themselves in evangelical work as *especially* moral, women could also set off to investigate the geography of vice. Through the cult of domesticity, they thus gained some freedom of movement and a wider sphere of influence and activity. These improvements in bourgeois women's lives, however, generated few benefits for the women they sought to help. Their sympathy for the collectivity of women, real indeed in some cases, took the form of an imagined womanhood which had little to do with the actual difficulties of laboring women and their working-class neighborhoods.

David R. Roediger

RACE, ETHNICITY, AND WORKING-CLASS FORMATION

Nineteenth-century American cities were magnets for foreign immigrants seeking to better their lives in an industrializing economy. In the 1850s, roughly one-third of the residents of Baltimore, Boston, and Philadelphia were foreign-born, as were approximately half the inhabitants of Cincinnati and New York. Many native-born workers responded to the massive influx of immigrants with a combination of suspicion, fear, and anger. Irish Catholics, in particular, were the target of nativist wrath and violence. Yet according to David Roediger's provocative account, Irish and native-born white workers found a common bond in their mutual animus toward blacks, who composed a small proportion of the northern urban population but came to symbolize for metropolitan whites all the dangers of otherness. By muting ethnic tensions, Roediger contends, racism contributed to the development of class consciousness and solidarity among white workers while deepening the oppression of black workers. Roediger is professor of American history at the University of Minnesota. This excerpt is from his book *Wages of Whiteness*.

Coming into American society at or near the bottom, the Catholic Irish sorely needed allies, even protectors. They quickly found them in two institutions that did not question their whiteness: the Catholic Church and the Democratic party. Although the former proved more open to promoting Irishmen to positions of power—most bishops in

From David R. Roediger, *The Wages of Whiteness: Race and the Making of the American Working Class* (London: Verso, 1991), is reprinted by kind permission of the publishers, Verso.

the United States were Irish by the 1850s—the Democratic party was far more powerful as a national institution and more consistently proslavery and white supremacist in its outlook. The church did reflect the racial attitudes of its members, with Kentucky Catholic newspapers carrying advertisements for the return of runaway slaves. New York church publications hinted at, and then spelled out, the view that the "negro is what the creator made him—not a rudimentary Caucasian, not a human in the process of development but a negro." The official Catholic paper in New York City meanwhile advised that emancipated slaves moving North be "driven out, imprisoned or exterminated." However, these strong and unpalatable Catholic stances, which existed alongside softer calls for amelioration of the slave's plight, at most reproduced existing white supremacist attitudes without challenging them. The Democratic party did more.

Jean Baker, a leading historian of the Democrats between the Age of Jackson and the Civil War, has acutely observed that the Democratic party reinvented whiteness in a manner that "refurbished their party's traditional links to the People and offered political democracy and an inclusive patriotism to white male Americans." This sense of white unity and white entitlement—of white "blood"—served to bind together the Democratic slaveholders and the masses of non-slaveholding whites in the South. It further connected the Southern and Northern wings of the Democracy. But less noticed by scholars has been the way in which an emphasis on a common whiteness smoothed over divisions in the Democratic ranks within mainly Northern cities by emphasizing that immigrants from Europe, and particularly from Ireland, were white and thus unequivocally entitled to equal rights. In areas with virtually no Black voters, the Democrats created a "white vote."

From the earliest days of the American republic, Irish immigration to the United States had caused political division. The "wild Irish," a term that invoked images of both "semi-savage" Catholics and political rebels who were sometimes Protestants, excited particular concern among conservative Federalist politicians. Defense of immigration by the Jeffersonian Democrats helped to create a lasting preference for the Democracy among newcomers, though party lines blurred considerably. In any case, how immigrants voted was of small importance nationally through 1830, when only one ballot in thirty could come from the foreign-born. By 1845, that figure was to rise to one in seven, with the Great Famine exodus still to produce, between 1845 and 1854, by far the greatest decade of immigration in antebellum American history. Immigration largely meant Irish immigration, with between 43 percent and 47 percent of migrants each year between 1820 and 1855 coming from Ireland.

By the early 1830s, the pattern of a strong Catholic Irish identification with the Democratic party, and with Andrew Jackson specifically, had strongly taken hold in urban centers like New York City. Although the existing urban Democratic political machines took time to inch away from the suspicion of immigrants felt by many of their artisan followers, Irish Catholics were welcomed as voters, party members and political muscle, though not typically as officeholders, by Democrats before the Civil War. The Catholic Irish, the immigrant group most exposed to nativist opposition, accepted protection from Democrats. Lacking a nationalist tradition of agitation for land redistribution in Ireland, too poor to move West and perhaps soured on farm life after the famine, the Catholic Irish were particularly immune to late antebellum Free Soil criticisms of Democratic opposition to homestead laws. Democrats and Irish-American Catholics entered into a lasting marriage that gave birth to new ideologies stressing the importance of whiteness.

From the 1830s, Democrats appreciated the ways in which the idea that all Blacks were unfit for civic participation could be transmuted into the notion that all whites were so fit. Pennsylvania Democrats, for example, solidified white unity by initiating the movement to codify the disfranchisement of the state's Blacks via constitutional amendment. Conflict with Mexico, and to some extent the rise of Chinese immigration, made it possible in the 1840s and 1850s for leading Democrats to develop racial schemes unequivocally gathering all European settlers together as whites against the "colored" races. At a time when most Democratic theorists were coming to accept polygeniticist ideas regarding the separate creations of the "black" and "white" races, they were also defining "white" in such a way as to include more surely the Irish and other immigrants. Thus, James Buchanan contemptuously branded the Mexicans as a "mongrel" race unfit for freedom but was glad that "Americans" were a "mixed" population of English, Scotch-Irish, French, Welsh, German and Irish ancestry. Missouri's Thomas Hart Benton wrote of a "Celtic-Anglo-Saxon race," superior to, in descending order, the yellow, brown and red "races." Caleb Cushing aroused the Massachusetts legislature by announcing late in the 1850s that he admitted "to an equality with me, sir, the white man,—my blood and race, whether he be a Saxon of England or a Celt of Ireland." He added, "but I do not admit as my equals either the red man of America, or the yellow man of Asia, of the black man of Africa." . . .

Democratic paeans to whiteness must have seemed a godsend to Irish Catholics, especially amid hardening anti-Irish attitudes after 1845. By the time of the famine, it could be argued—and was argued by Irish-Americans themselves—that longstanding British oppression had kept the Irish in political "slavery" and brought utter economic dependency. Irish-Americans were deeply offended in the 1856 campaign when a remark by Buchanan implied that England had *not* made "slaves" of the Irish. But to make this argument, and to compare Irish and African oppression, forfeited any claim of Irish-Americans to be qualified for freedom by republican criteria. Past and present, their history seemed to be one of degradation. As John Ashworth has perceptively put it, since Irish-Americans were in many cases as economically dependent as free Blacks, no "empirical" case could be made that the immigrants had shown themselves fit for freedom, and Blacks by comparison had proven themselves unfit to be "true Americans."

Nativists were somewhat constrained by the historic American acceptance of Irish immigrants, by the cultural proximity of Irish Catholics with clearly assimilable Celtic Protestants from Ireland, Scotland and Wales, and by the ease with which Irish Catholics could pass as mainstream "white" Americans. Anti-immigrant politicians therefore generally did not dwell on the popular ethnological theories that identified the Celts as genetically inferior. They instead concentrated on Irish subservience to religious authority and Irish degradation, loosely arguing at times that the famine itself had helped produce an Irish "race" incapable of freedom. Some unfavorably compared the Irish with free Blacks, not so much as racial types as in terms of their alleged records of fitness to function as republican citizens. Black leaders like Frederick Douglass generally avoided anti-Catholicism but charged that the ignorance and intemperance of the Irish and their roles as "flunkeys to our gentry" made it certain that Irish Catholics were not more desirable than Blacks as citizens of a republic.

The Democratic emphasis on natural rights within a government "made by the white men, for the benefit of the white man" appealed to Irish Catholics in large part because it cut off questions about their qualifications for citizenship. Under other circumstances, Irish-American Catholics might not have accepted so keenly the "association of nationality with blood—but not with ethnicity," which racially conflated them with the otherwise hated English. They might not have so readily embraced a view of "American nationality that stressed the relevance of 'race' while putting the Irish safely within an Anglo-Celtic racial majority." But within the constrained choices and high risks of antebellum American politics such a choice was quite logical. The ways in which the Irish competed for work and adjusted to industrial morality in America made it all but certain that they would adopt and extend the politics of white unity offered by the Democratic party.

In 1856, Henry C. Brokmeyer, then a wage-earning immigrant German molder in St. Louis, wrote in his diary a question posed about one of his German-American friends: "Why doesn't he learn . . . a trade; and he wouldn't have to slave like a nigger?" Brokmeyer, who was to become not only independent of wage work but eventually lieutenant governor of Missouri, had picked up a pattern of usage common in American English since the 1830s. Not only was *nigger work* synonymous with hard, drudging labor but to *nigger it* meant "to do hard work," or "to slave." "White niggers" were white workers in arduous unskilled jobs or in subservient positions.

But not all European immigrants had the same prospects to "learn a trade," let alone to acquire independence from "slaving like a nigger," by owning a workshop or a farm. English and Scandinavian immigrants were especially likely to achieve such mobility, while the Irish and Germans faced most directly the question of how and whether their labor was different from "slaving like a nigger." But the Irish confronted the question much more starkly. Both before and after the famine, they were far more likely than the Germans to be without skills. The famine Irish infrequently achieved rural land ownership. Within large cities Irish-American males were skilled workers perhaps half as often as German-Americans, and were unskilled at least twice as often. Although frontier cities, perhaps attracting Irish migrants with more resources and choices, showed less difference between Irish and German occupational patterns, the Irish stayed at the bottom of white society. . . .

Job competition has often been considered the key to Irish-American racism. From Albon Man to Bruce Laurie, historians have emphasized that Irish workers, especially on the docks and shipyards in cities like Cincinnati, Philadelphia, Baltimore, and above all New York City, fought to keep away Blacks as job competitors and as strikebreakers. Many such direct incidents of Irish violence to intimidate Black workers did occur, especially during the Civil War, and there is some justification for Laurie's view that in Philadelphia Irish gangs undertaking racist violence were exercising job control. But to go from the fact that Irish workers really fought with Blacks over jobs on occasion to the proposition that Irish racism was really a cover for job competition is an economic determinist misstep that cuts off important parts of the past. Why, for example, when Irish Catholic immigrants said that they feared the "amalgamation of labor" should historians hearken to their emphasis on labor and not to their emphasis on amalgamation?

Moreover, to say that Irish-Americans acted as militant white supremacists because of job competition only invites the further question: why did they choose to stress competition with Black workers instead of with other whites? In 1844, Philadelphia Irish Catholics who mobbed Blacks to clear them from dockworking jobs had themselves recently been removed from handloom weaving jobs via concerted actions by Protestant weavers. Why did they not mob the Protestants? In most cities, even when we consider only unskilled work, the Irish had far more German-American competitors than Black ones. Why was the animus against working with Blacks so much more intense than that of against working with Germans? Indeed, as Harold Brackman has argued, the main competitors of the Irish for unskilled work were other arriving Irish. Why, given the strength of "countyism" in Ireland and the patterns of intra-Irish factional fighting for canal-building jobs in the 1830s, did race and not time of emigration or county or even kin network become the identity around which Irish dockworkers in New York City could mobilize most effectively in the 1850s and during the Civil War?

By and large, free Blacks were *not* effective competitors for jobs with the Irish. A small part of the urban labor force, negligible in most Midwestern cities, they at best held on to small niches in the economy and small shares of the population, while the immigrant population skyrocketed in the 1840s and 1850s. Discrimination of the "No Irish Need Apply" sort hurt Irish opportunities. Sometimes, as in an 1853 New York *Herald* ad reading "WOMAN WANTED—To do general housework . . . any country or color will answer except Irish. . . .", such job prejudice was scarcely distinguishable from racial discrimination. But what was most noteworthy to free Blacks at the time, and probably should be most noteworthy to historians, was the relative ease with which Irish-Americans "elbowed out" African-Americans from unskilled jobs. By 1850, for example, there were about twenty-five times as many Irish-American serving women in New York City as Black serving women.

One obvious reason that the Irish focused so much more forcefully on their sporadic labor competition with Blacks than on their protracted competition with other whites was that Blacks were so much less able to strike back, through either direct action or political action. As Kerby Miller has argued, Irish Catholic immigrants quickly learned that Blacks in America could be "despised with impunity." They also learned that free Blacks could be victimized with efficacy. Even the wholesale wartime atrocities against Blacks in the 1863 draft riots did not draw any opposition for assembled crowds nor vigorous prosecutions by municipal authorities. The attempt of Irish-American dockworkers in New York to expel *German* longshoremen from jobs under the banner of campaigning for an "all-white waterfront"—perhaps the most interesting and vivid antebellum example of the social construction of race—reflects in part ill-fated Irish attempts to classify Germans as of a different color. But it also suggests how much easier it was for the Irish to defend jobs and rights as "white" entitlements instead of as Irish ones.

Had the Irish tried to assert a right to work because they were Irish, rather than because they were white, they would have provoked a fierce backlash from native-born artisans. As it was, in major cities North and South immigrants comprised a majority or near-majority in artisanal jobs by the 1850s. Despite their concentration in unskilled labor, Irish-Americans were also a large percentage of the artisan population and of the factory-based working class, especially in sweated and declining trades. Native-born artisans often complained that Irish and German immigrants undermined craft traditions and sent wages down by underbidding "American" workers. Historians as diverse in approach as Robert Fogel and W. J. Rorabaugh have held that the native-born workers were at least partly right in connecting the immigrants with a downward spiral of wages and a loss of control over work. Similar arguments have linked Irish immigration with the lowering of wages and the undermining of a promising labor movement of native-born women textile workers. By no means is the case connecting Irish immigration with the degradation of native-born workers the only one that can be made. Edward Everett Hale observed at the time that with the coming of the Irish, "Natives [were] simply pushed up into Foremen . . . , superintendents, . . . machinists," and other skilled occupations. Hale's view has some defenders among modern historians, but the important issue here is that many native-born artisans, rightly or wrongly, paired the arrival of the Irish with unfavorable changes in their crafts and wages and participated in both anti-immigrant riots and anti-immigrant political movements. By casting job competition and neighborhood rivalries as racial, rather than ethnic, the Irish argued against such nativist logic.

Thus, the struggle over jobs best explains Irish-Americans' prizing of whiteness if that struggle is considered broadly, to include not only white-Black competition but white-white competition as well. Similarly, we must widen the focus from a struggle over jobs to include an emphasis on the struggle over how jobs *were to be defined* to understand more fully why the Irish so embraced whiteness. Specifically, the specter of "slaving like a nigger" hung over the Irish. In Ireland, peasants with small holdings had commonly described loss of a parcel as a descent to "slavery." Irish-Americans did not mind referring to Britain's "enslavement" of Ireland. Sometimes, as in the 1856 presidential campaign, they insisted on it. Would-be friends of Irish-Americans as diverse as Edward Everett Hale, Orestes Brownson and the labor reformers of the *Voice of Industry* all alluded to the British imposition of slavery or worse on Eire. Irish-Americans were also receptive to appeals from Democratic politicians who emphasized the threat of "white slavery" in the United States and were cool to Republican attempts to portray talk of "white slavery" as reckless and demeaning to white workers.

But there were few specific attempts by the Irish or their friends to talk about a specifically Irish-American "slavery"—a distended metaphor, as Frederick Douglass pointed out, but considerably less so than the generalized concept of "white slavery," which was used.

Immigrants, so hopeful of escaping slavery in Ireland, were hesitant to acknowledge a specifically ethnic defeat in the Promised Land, and real differences between the suffering in Ireland and that in America discouraged use of "Irish slavery" to describe both situations.

Most important, Irish-American Catholics did not want to reinforce popular connections of the Blacks and the Irish. If they could live with being called "white slaves," it was harder to abide being called "Irish niggers." When Irishmen repeated jokes about slaves complaining that their masters treated them "like Irishmen," the laughter had a decidedly tense edge. But it was difficult to get out from under the burden of doing unskilled work in a society that identified such work and (some craft jobs) as "nigger work." If they were to sever this connection, the Irish could not just achieve a favorable labor market position vis-à-vis Blacks. They had to drive all Blacks, and if possible their memories, from the places where the Irish labored. Frederick Douglass warned the Irish worker of the possibility that "in assuming our avocation he also assumed our degradation." Irish workers responded that they wanted an "all-white waterfront," rid of Blacks altogether, and not to "jostle with" African-Americans. They thought that, to ensure their own survival, they needed as much.

Expansion, Concentration, and Invention in the Age of Capital

William Cronon

RAILROADS AND THE REORGANIZATION OF NATURE AND TIME

Directly tied to the emergence of the metropolis was the expansion of agricultural hinterlands that quite literally fed—and figuratively fed off of—urban growth. The technological basis for this dynamic connection was a series of improvements in transportation that culminated in the triumph of the steam-powered railroad by midcentury. In the following selection from *Nature's Metropolis,* William Cronon describes how railroads transformed not only the way goods were moved from country to city and vice versa, but also the way people related to their environment, including their very conceptualization of nature and time. Cronon takes as his case study the rapid growth of Chicago and the Great West, but he argues more generally that railroads, by transcending longstanding geographical limitations, enabled the development of a truly national market and the rise of corporations with unprecedented economic power. Cronon is Frederick Jackson Turner Professor of American History at the University of Wisconsin at Madison.

As Chicagoans and other Americans groped for language to convey their excitement at the new [railroad] technology, they found themselves drawn to two metaphors that would recur endlessly in booster rhetoric. On the one hand, they assimilated the railroad to the doctrine of natural advantages. . . . The railroad's presence was no less inevitable, no less "natural," than the lakes and rivers with which it competed. Wealth would come to Chicago because its "system of railroads branching in every possible direction throughout the length and breadth of the producing district" made it "the natural outlet and market" for its region. A writer for the *Lakeside Monthly* went so far as to argue that Chicago could expect a speedy recovery from its disastrous 1871 fire because the railroads constituted a natural force compelling it back to economic health. "The routes of traffic passing through this city," he wrote,

> are as truly "natural" routes as though the great lakes were a mountain-chain, and the Mississippi, instead of flowing to the tropics, swept around the southern base of that impassable range, and emptied its volume, swollen by a score of great tributaries into the waters of New York, Delaware, or Chesapeake Bay. The routes thus established, not merely by capital, but by nature and necessity, are as truly fixed facts as are the Mississippi and the Lakes; and they are far more commanding. . . .

People who wrote of the railroad in this way never paused to explain how so "natural" a route could be constructed from rails, ties, and locomotives. Instead, they seemed to see it less as an artificial invention than as a force of nature, a geographical power so irresistible that people must shape their lives according to its dictates.

Wherever the rails went, they brought sudden sweeping change to the landscapes and communities through which they passed, suggesting the second metaphor that occurs repeatedly in nineteenth-century prose about them. Railroads were more than just natural; their power to transform landscapes partook of the supernatural, drawing upon a mysterious creative energy that was beyond human influence or knowledge. The steam engine on the prairie evoked genies and wands and the magic that could make dreams come true merely by wishing them so. "Railroads," wrote one Chicagoan, "are talismanic wands. They have a charming power. They do wonders—they work miracles. They are better than laws; they are essentially, politically and religiously—the pioneer, and vanguard of civilization." Because the flat glaciated landscape was peculiarly suited to railroads, "adapted as it is by nature for their advantageous construction," the arrival of these "powerful iron agencies" meant that the land would "spring at once into teeming life and animation." When the locomotive appeared on the horizon, it soon called forth "the wave of population . . . rolling a mighty tide of subjugation over the prairies," with "hamlets, towns, and cities . . . springing up like magic and realizing in a day the old time history of an age." One editor compared such villages to the quail that "whirls up before the whistle of the engines."

Nobody probably intended such metaphors literally, so we can if we choose read them as mere rhetorical excess. There seems little question, though, that many nineteenth-century Americans did feel genuine awe in the face of the new technology. The locomotive was an inanimate object that had somehow sprung to life, the mechanical herald of a new age. People who described it by appealing to nature and magic—often in the same breath—were seeking some analogue that would help them make sense of a phenomenon unlike any they had encountered before. Our own faith in technology has been so chastened by our knowledge of Faust's bargain—also magical, but finally hollow and self-destructive—that we may find it hard to take seriously the rhetoric of wonder as applied to so profane an object as a railroad locomotive. We recognize such rhetoric as an exercise in mystification. Those who shrouded the railroad in the language of deep mystery, making it seem the expression of a universal life-force beyond human ken, obscured the social and economic processes that lay behind it. Despite the metaphors it evoked, the railroad was neither a direct product of nature nor the creation of a sorcerer's magic. It was a human invention at the heart of an equally human economic system. "Nature," wrote one booster who came closer than most to this perspective, "built Chicago through her artificer, Man."

Still, writers who waxed poetic about the railroad were surely right to regard it as much more than just a machine. It touched all facets of American life in the second half of the nineteenth century, insinuating itself into virtually every aspect of the national landscape. As Caroline Kirkland remarked in 1858 in describing the sunset over an Illinois prairie community, "Fancy the rail gone, and we have neither telegraph, nor school-house, nor anything of all this but the sunset,—and even that we could not be there to see in spring-time," because of the mud that would prevent us from reaching the place. The railroad left almost nothing unchanged: that was its magic. To those whose lives it touched, it seemed at once so ordinary and so extraordinary—so second nature—that the landscape became unimaginable without it. The railroad would replace the waterways of first nature with the myriad complexities of its own geography, thereby becoming the unnatural instrument of a supposedly "natural" destiny. It would rapidly emerge as the chief link connecting Chicago with the towns and rural lands around it, so the city came finally to seem like an artificial spider suspended at the center of a

great steel web. To understand Chicago and its emerging relationship to the Great West, one must first understand the railroad.

Compared with earlier transport systems—lakes, rivers, and canals,
on the one hand and rural roads, on the other—railroads exhibited
several key innovations. For one, they broke much more radically
with geography. Railroad engineers certainly had to consider any environmental factors that might affect a line's operating costs—the relative steepness of topographic gradients, the bearing load of subsoil
structures, the bridgeability of watercourses, and so on. Still, their
chief task was to draw the straightest possible line between market
centers that might contribute traffic to the road. The same principle
applied to nonrail transport systems as well, but the railroads came
closer to realizing it than any of their water-based competitors.

As a result, the boosters' geographical determinism affected railroads only indirectly, as a kind of cost-benefit analysis that engineers
performed in selecting from among a nearly infinite set of possible
routes. Railroads did follow existing rivers and valleys to reach existing harbors and towns—but not because of mysterious environmental forces. Such places usually offered the largest concentration
of prospective customers for freight and passenger traffic. Railroad
engineers sought above all to route their lines through country that
promised high market demand and low operating cost. Nineteenth-
century rhetoric might present the railroad network as "natural,"
but it was actually the most artificial transportation system yet constructed on land.

The railroads' liberation from geography took many subtle forms.
Aside from being able to go virtually anyplace where potential demand was great enough, they could also operate quite independently
of the climatic factors that had bedeviled earlier forms of transportation. Farmers who used a railroad like the Galena and Chicago Union
probably regarded its invulnerability to mud as its single greatest
attraction. No longer did trade and travel have to stop during wet seasons of the year.

The railroads also alleviated many of the worst effects of winter.
The period from November to April had always been the dullest
season of the business year, when trade ground to a virtual halt for
farmers and merchants alike. With the railroad, rural farmers could
travel to urban markets whenever they had the need and funds to do

so, even in the deep cold of February. Chicagoans no longer had to wait for months on end to view the latest fashions from New York. As one railroad promoter wryly remarked, "It is against the policy of Americans to remain locked up by ice one half of the year." The railroads could not break the wheel of the seasons entirely: the fall harvest, for instance, remained a particularly active time for travel, straining all forms of transportation. But they did reduce the seasonal economic cycles that followed the rising and falling curves of temperature and precipitation.

Just as the railroad changed the ways people experienced the seasons of the year, so too did it begin to change their relationship to the hours of the day. No earlier invention had so fundamentally altered people's expectations of how long it took to travel between two distant points on the continent, for no earlier form of transportation had ever moved people so quickly. In prerailroad days, before the Michigan Southern made its triumphal entrance into Chicago on February 20, 1852, the trip from New York took well over two weeks; shortly thereafter, it took less than two days. Even more striking was the accelerated flow of *information* after the arrival of the telegraph in 1848: messages that had once taken weeks to travel between Chicago and the East Coast now took minutes and seconds. Railroad and telegraph systems would expand in tandem, often following the same routes, and together they shrank the whole perceptual universe of North America. Because people experience distance more in hours than in miles, New York, Chicago, and the Great West quite literally grew closer as the lines of wire and rail proliferated among them.

Conversely, time accelerated and became more valuable the greater the distance one could travel in any given period. Once farmers had access to a railroad, most no longer thought it worth their while to spend a week or more driving a team of horses over bad roads to sell their crops in Chicago. More than twice as much wheat came to Chicago in 1852 via the Galena and Chicago Union than came in farmers' wagons, the latter having fallen by half in just the previous year. In 1860, Chicago received almost a hundred times more wheat by rail than by wagon; ten years later, no one even bothered to keep statistics on the latter. Beneath these seemingly straightforward commodity movements lay a much subtler cultural change: farmers now valued their time too much to contemplate making extended wagon journeys of the sort they had taken for granted just ten or twenty years earlier. As one Chicagoan later remembered, the railroad relieved "the farmers at every stopping place from their long and tedious journeys by team, enabling them to utilize their own labor, and the services of their teams, in improving their farms, and adding every season to the amount of grain sown," thereby increasing the pace of agricultural improvement throughout the hinterland landscape.

As railroads decreased the cost of distance and increased the value of time, they also raised people's expectations about the regularity and reliability of transportation services. Earlier forms of western transport had involved single vehicles carrying small loads. The individuals or firms that ran them operated on a limited scale and had little ability to predict local demand or avert potential delays caused by weather, accidents, or other hazards. As a result, canal boats, steamships, and road vehicles had trouble keeping regular schedules. As one frustrated eastern traveler reported of his western journey in 1851, "For a boat to lie at her wharf hours after the time set for starting, and by innumerable stops to prolong her trip a day or two beyond the promised time, is an event of common occurrence." Because people had no choice but to tolerate such delays, they had to plan very loose schedules for when they might be able to conduct business, receive shipments, or complete a trip. With so erratic a transportation system, one could not place a very high value on one's own time. "Indeed," the same traveler reported, *"time* does not yet seem to enter as an element into Western thought. It answers about as well to do a thing next week as this; to wait a day or two for a boat, as to meet it at the hour appointed; and so on through all the details of life."

Because railroads ran more quickly and reliably, and could carry more people and goods over greater distances, they changed this irregular sense of time. Trains too could be delayed. But whereas earlier western stage and steamship operators had measured their service by how many trips they made in the course of a *week,* railroads measured the same service in terms of the scheduled trips they made in a *day.* On this scale, a train delayed by several hours was very late indeed, a fact that suggests how railroads changed people's ability to schedule and predict their use of time. The long-term consequence was to move timekeeping into the realm of the mechanical clock, away from the various natural cycles which had formerly marked the flow of time.

Distinctions that had once been crucial in dividing the days and months of the year—separating night from day, wet times from dry, hot times from cold, good weather from bad—gradually became less important to travel even if they did not disappear altogether. No longer did one have to stop traveling and find lodging for the night when the sun went down; no longer did one have to delay a journey until ice disappeared from rivers or lakes; no longer did one have to fear snowstorms as a life-threatening hazard on the open road. When one boarded a train, one entered a world separated from the outside by its own peculiar environment and sense of time. Train passengers had less and less need to interact physically with the landscapes through which they were passing. They became spectators who could enjoy watching the world go by instead of working their way across it on foot or horseback. Unless an accident occurred—and railroad accidents, like those of steamboats, entailed horrors of a sort never before seen—the train promised what its passengers increasingly came to expect: the safety and clockwork regularity of an artificial universe.

The most dramatic proof that this new universe had extended its influence to the outside world came in 1883, when the major railroad companies imposed on North America new, "standard" times to replace the hundreds of "local" times which had previously been used to set clocks throughout the country. Before the invention of standard time, clocks were set according to the rules of astronomy: noon was the moment when the sun stood highest in the midday sky. By this strict astronomical definition every locale had a different noon, depending on the line of longitude it occupied. When clocks read noon in Chicago, it was 11:50 A.M. in St. Louis, 11:38 A.M. in St. Paul, 11:27 A.M. in Omaha, and 12:18 P.M. in Detroit, with every possible variation in between. For companies trying to operate trains between these various points, the different local times were a scheduling nightmare. Railroads around the country set their clocks by no fewer than fifty-three different standards—and thereby created a deadly risk for everyone who rode them. Two trains running on the same tracks at the same moment but with clocks showing different times could well find themselves unexpectedly occupying the same space, with disastrous consequences.

And so, on November 18, 1883, the railroad companies carved up the continent into four time zones, in each of which all clocks would be set to exactly the same time. At noon, Chicago jewelers moved their clocks back by nine minutes and thirty-three seconds in order to match the local time of the ninetieth meridian. The *Chicago Tribune* likened the event to Joshua's having made the sun stand still, and announced, "The railroads of this country demonstrated yesterday that the hand of time can be moved backward about as easily as Columbus demonstrated that an egg can be made to stand on end." Although the U.S. government would not officially acknowledge the change until 1918, everyone else quickly abandoned local sun time and set clocks by railroad time instead. Railroad schedules thus redefined the hours of the day: sunrise over Chicago would henceforth come ten minutes sooner, and the noonday sun would hang a little lower in the sky.

The railroads broke with the sun in one other respect as well. All previous forms of land transport had relied on biological sources to power their movement, in the form of food calories consumed by people, horses, or oxen to move vehicles and goods through space. All such energy ultimately derived from the sun, and its use was strictly constrained by the physiological ability of animal metabolisms to convert food into work. Speed of movement had well-defined biological limits, as did the total quantity of work that people or animals could perform in a day: a good-sized man might deliver two to three horsepower-hours in the course of a hard ten-hour day, while a horse might deliver eight to ten horsepower-hours during the same period. The railroad broke this age-old restrictive relationship between biological energy and movement, much as the steamboat had done for water transport several decades earlier. Although early locomotives burned wood, they gradually shifted toward coal, and so ended their reliance on biological energy sources by replacing them with fossil fuel. Locomotives were not more efficient than horses, but they could consume vastly greater quantities of fuel much more quickly, and thus had much higher limits for work, speed, and endurance. Typical locomotives of the 1850s could deliver well over three hundred horsepower. By the Civil War, they could pull enormous loads at better than twenty miles per hour for hours on end—far longer than horses or people could move a tiny fraction of that load at less than half that speed. No longer would solar energy and animal physiology set limits to human movement across the landscape.

The greater speed, distance, volume, and power of railroads enabled them to break free from the economic and environmental constraints of earlier transport systems. Compared with its predecessors, railroad geography rested on differences in degree that people experienced as differences in kind, shifting the human sense of scale in a way that itself became second nature in subtle ways. With the possible exception of great armies, no human organization had ever posed such extensive and elaborate management problems before. The railroads moved immense volumes of goods and people at high speeds on closely timed schedules over great distances, creating a far-flung network in which responsibility for the entire system fell to a small group of managers. Operating such a system required concentrations of private capital greater than ever before. By 1860, total American investment in canals, which had been the largest comparable corporate enterprises, was still less than $200 million after forty years of operation, while railroad investment, more than tripling in the preceding single decade, had already passed $1.1 *billion*. Unlike their predecessors, the corporations that ran railroads generally owned the entire operation: lands, rails, locomotives, cars, and stations, not to mention the labor and fuel that kept everything moving. The companies that operated stagecoaches, ships, and canalboats generally paid only their vehicles' operating costs, not the expense of maintaining the right of way, while canal companies and toll roads maintained the right of way without owning or running vehicles themselves. Railroads did both and simultaneously incurred large fuel, labor, and equipment costs. Although such extensive ownership rights conferred great power, with them came truly daunting levels of risk and responsibility as well. Running a railroad meant trying to achieve unprecedented levels of coordination among engineering technologies, management structures, labor practices, freight rates, resource flows, and—not least—natural environments, all spread over thousands of square miles of land.

Control of this sort required techniques for gathering and interpreting information at a level much more detailed than had previously been typical of most business enterprises. The railroads faced as much of a challenge in processing data as in moving people or freight. For every station, managers had to set rates, maintain schedules, and keep records of what the firm was hauling at how much cost during which period of time, so that in the end the corporate account books would all balance. Managing this accounting problem generated vast new quantities of statistics which themselves helped revolutionize the American economy by making possible increasingly intricate analyses of trade and production. Responsibility for using the new statistics fell into the hands of a new class of managers, engineers, and accountants whose emerging professional skills became essential to the system as a whole. Out of their work would come an increasingly hierarchical power structure which gradually proliferated through the entire economy.

At the most abstract level, the railroads' hierarchies of corporate wealth and managerial power represented a vast new concentration of capital. Whether one understands that word to mean the accumulated surplus value extracted from rail workers, the aggregate financial investments represented by company stock, or the real resources and equipment required to operate trains, it carries one basic implication. As perceived by those who ran it, a railroad was a pool of capital designed to make more capital. Railroads spent money moving goods and passengers in order to earn a profit out of the difference between their receipts and their operating expenses. Actual practice did not always turn out so happily, but this at least was the theory of the enterprise: invested capital would grow or at least earn back costs so that the system as a whole could expand. Because investments and costs were enormous, everything that moved by railroad—and every place through which the railroad ran—became linked to the imperatives of corporate capital. The railroad thus became the chief device for introducing a new capitalist logic to the geography of the Great West.

Alfred D. Chandler, Jr.

THE COMING OF MASS PRODUCTION AND MODERN MANAGEMENT

As the nation's transportation and communication networks expanded, technological and organizational efficiency proved increasingly critical to business success. The faster an industrial enterprise could transform raw materials into finished products, the greater its chance of boosting output and achieving a competitive advantage in the marketplace. Speed, size, and market share went hand in hand. Yet as Alfred Chandler has argued in a number of highly influential books and articles, business efficiency also required managerial bureaucracy. Indeed, according to Chandler, the defining characteristics of modern business enterprise are that "it contains many distinct operating units and it is managed by a hierarchy of salaried executives." In the following excerpt from his Pulitzer Prize–winning volume *The Visible Hand,* Chandler traces the development of mass production and the emergence of modern managerial structures in the American steel industry during the second half of the nineteenth century. Chandler is Straus Professor of Business History Emeritus at the Harvard Business School.

Modern factory management was first fully worked out in the metal-making and metal-working industries. In metal-making, it came in response to the need to integrate (that is to internalize) within a single works several major processes of production previously carried on in different locations. In metal-working, it arose from the challenges of coordinating and controlling the flow of materials within a plant where several processes of production had been subdivided and were carried on in specialized departments. In both metal-making and metal-working, the processes of production became increasingly mechanized, capital-intensive, and energy consuming. But because the materials were so hard to process and more difficult to work than in the mechanical or refining industries, mass production came in a slower, more evolutionary manner. In the metal-making and

Reprinted by permission of the publisher from *The Visible Hand: The Managerial Revolution in American Business,* by Alfred D. Chandler, Jr., Cambridge, Mass.: Harvard University Press. Copyright © 1977 by Alfred D. Chandler, Jr.

metal-working industries the drive to mass production required far more intricate and costly machinery, a more intensive use of energy, an even greater attention to the design of works and plants, and for the first time, concentration on the development of systematic practices and procedures of factory management.

In metal-making, the challenge of scheduling, coordination, and controlling the flow of work came only after more than one process had been placed in a single works. On the old "iron plantations" facilities had been too small and the technology too crude to create a need for internal scheduling and control or to permit a greater increase in output through careful plant design and improved management procedures. Then, the iron industry began to "disintegrate" in the 1830s and 1840s, when the availability of coal permitted a greater and steadier output and when many of the plantations had exhausted their ore supplies. Blast furnaces, forges, and rolling and finishing mills were soon operating in different establishments.

The reintegration of the iron-making processes came quickly. It first appeared with the building of the earliest large rail mills in the 1850s. As one rail mill normally consumed the output of two or three blast furnaces, there was an obvious advantage to placing the blast furnaces and final shaping mills within a single works. By 1860 the four biggest integrated rail mills were the largest enterprises in the iron industry. Soon they were producing wire, beams, and merchant bar iron as well as rails. The capitalization of each was over $1 million. Not only was equipment costly but also the labor force in these mills was large. The ratio of capital to worker was still relatively low; the mills remained relatively labor-intensive. In 1860 the Mountour Iron Works at Danville employed close to 3,000 employees; the Cambria Iron Works at Johnstown, 1,948; the Phoenix Iron Company at Phoenixville, 1,230 (all three were in Pennsylvania); and the Trenton (New Jersey) Iron Works, 786. During the Civil War the number of large integrated iron-making works increased, though they remained about the same in size.

In such integrated rail mills the Bessemer steel process—the first to produce that metal on a massive scale—was introduced into the United States in the late 1860s and early 1870s. And it was in these same mills that the open-hearth process made its appearance in the

1880s. Between 1865 and 1876 eleven iron and steel enterprises installed Bessemer converters. In most cases the converters worked alongside or took the place of the existing puddling and rolling mills. However, Andrew Carnegie's Edgar Thomson Works in Pittsburgh and one or two other rail plants were entirely new ones.

One man, Alexander Lyman Holley, was responsible for the design of these eleven new steel works. This brilliant and versatile engineer had found his calling in bringing to fruition the ideas and plans of Henry Bessemer for the mass production of steel. Holley's achievements were less in technological innovation than in the designing of equipment and facilities and their arrangement within the works. He defined as his primary goal "to assure a very large and regular output." He improved machinery by placing removable bottoms in the converters to shorten the time needed to reline them and by reshaping the form of converters themselves. In Holley's mind, however, the design of the works and the quality of its management were as important as machinery in increasing the velocity of throughput. He emphasized this point in an article printed in the *Metallurgical Review* in 1877, in which he compared steel-producing works in Great Britain and the United States:

> In the United States, while the excellent features of Bessemer and Longsbon's plant have been retained, the very first works, and in a better manner each succeeding works, have embodied radical improvements in arrangement and in detail of plant, *the object being to increase the output of a unit of capital and of a unit of working expense.* . . . It will have been observed that the capacity of these works for a very large and regular output, lies chiefly in an arrangement which provides large and unhampered spaces for all the principal operations of manufacture and maintenance, while it at the same time concentrates these operations. The result of concentration which is realized is the saving of rehandling and of the spaces and machinery and cost required for rehandling. A possible result of concentration which has been avoided is the interference of one machine and operation with another. At the same time a degree of elasticity has been introduced into the plant, partly by the duplication and partly by the interchangeableness of important appurtenances, the result being that little or no time is lost if the melting and converting operations are not quite concurrent, or if temporary delays or failures occur in any department of manufacturing or maintenance.

The fact, however, must not be lost sight of that the adaptation of plant, which has thus been analyzed, is not the only important condition of large and cheap production; the technical management of American works has become equally improved. Better organization and more readiness, vigilance and technical knowledge on the part of the management have been required to run works up to their capacity, as their capacity has become increased by better arrangement and appliances.

Holley considered the Edgar Thomson Works his finest creation. He was proud of the installation he had built at his Cambria works at Johnstown, Pennsylvania, but that involved only the placing of the Bessemer units within a large, already existing works. In building the Edgar Thomson Works for Andrew Carnegie he could start from scratch. The comparison of the layout of the two works is illuminating. Cambria was originally built in the 1850s before manufacturers fully appreciated the importance of plant design to productivity. It was constructed with little attention to flow of materials within the works. This had been the case with the layout of other large early works, such as the Du Pont Company's establishment on the Brandywine Creek and the Springfield Armory on the Connecticut River. On the other hand, at Carnegie's new works the site itself, on the Monongahela River at the junction of three railroads—the Pennsylvania, the Baltimore & Ohio, and the Pittsburgh & Lake Erie—was selected to make the fullest use of existing railroad transportation. The plant was designed to assure as continuous a flow as possible from the suppliers of the raw materials through the processes of production to the shipment of the finished goods to the customers. Holley described the works in 1878, three years after operations began, by saying:

> As the cheap transportation of supplies of products in process of manufacture, and of products to market, is a feature of first importance, these works were laid out, not with a view of making the buildings artistically parallel with the existing roads or with each other, but of laying down convenient railroads with easy curves; *the buildings were made to fit the transportation.* Coal is dumped from the mine-cars, standing on the elevator track . . . , directly upon the floors of the producer and boilerhouses. Coke and pigiron are delivered to the stockyard with equal facility. The finishing end of the rail-mill is accommodated on both sides by low-level wide-gauge railways. The

projected open-hearth and merchant plants have equally good facilities. There is also a complete system of 30-inch railways for internal transportation.

The works relied at first on Carnegie's nearby Lucy and Isabella blast furnaces for their pig iron. Then in 1879 large blast furnaces were built at the plant site. The design of the works permitted the E. T. Works, as they were always called, to become the most efficient steel producer in the nation, and indeed the world.

In addition, Carnegie's blast furnaces—Lucy, Isabella, and then those at the E. T. Works—were the largest and most energy-consuming in the world. By "hard driving," through the use of more intense heat and improved and more powerful blast engines, the Lucy furnace increased production from 13,000 tons in 1872 to 100,000 tons in the late 1890s. By 1890, other furnaces besides those of Carnegie were producing over 1,000 tons a week—an enormous increase over the 70 tons a week of the blast furnaces even as late as the early 1870s.

In the same period similar increases occurred in the output of the succeeding stages of the process and in quickening the flow from the blast furnace to the shipment of the final product. As Peter Temin has noted: "The speed at which steel was made was continually rising, and new innovations were constantly being introduced to speed it further." At the Carnegie works, for example, Bessemer converters became larger, the Thomas-Gilchrist process made possible a large output from open-hearth furnaces, and the Jones mixer accelerated the flow of materials from the blast furnace to converter. Here and at other works the cooling of ingots in the soaking pits was done faster and carrying rollers improved. "Steam and later electric power replaced the lifting and carrying action of human muscle, mills were modified to handle the steel quickly and with a minimum of strain to the machinery, and people disappeared from the mills. By the turn of the century, there were not a dozen men on the floor of a mill rolling 3,000 tons a day, or as much as a Pittsburgh rolling mill of 1850 rolled in a year."

Technological innovation and improved plant design, which continued to accelerate velocity of throughput, made the processes more capital-intensive and energy consuming. This was true not only of the largest and most efficient works, including those using the new open-hearth furnaces installed in the 1880s, but also of the industry as a whole. Between 1869 and 1899 the average annual output of the blast furnaces rose from 5,000 to 65,000 tons and that for steel works and rolling mills from 3,000 to 23,000 tons. For the same period, the average capital investment for a blast furnace establishment increased four and a half times, from $145,000 to $643,000, and rolling mills eight times, from $156,000 to $967,000. The working force grew more slowly. That for a blast furnace increased from an average of 71 to 176, or two and a half times, and for rolling mills from 119 to 412, or three and a half times. In the same period the number of blast furnace establishments fell from 386 to 223, while the number of steel works and rolling mills stayed at about 400. This great expansion in the speed and volume of output required an immense amount of fuel. Coke, which was just beginning to be used in the United States as fuel in the 1850s, consumed 8.1 million tons of coal in 1885 and 49.5 million tons in 1905.

The greatly increased velocity of flow through these works, as Holley suggested, placed increased demands on their managers. Overall coordination and control was difficult, for unlike an oil or sugar refinery, each part of the production process involved different activities. Moreover, the subunits within the works—the coke ovens, the blast furnaces, the Bessemer converters or open hearths, the rail, wire, beam, and other finishing mills—were managed, in the words of one of the most able steel-makers, John Fritz, as "small principalities, each of them being governed by a despotic foreman." These autocrats handled the day-to-day activities in their units. They hired, fired, and promoted the men who worked under them. Effective coordination of throughput required the placing of vigorous management controls over these despots.

In no metal-making enterprise were the techniques of coordination and control more effectively developed than in those of Andrew Carnegie. In building the administrative structure for his new steel works, Carnegie and his subordinates drew directly from the railroads. Carnegie himself was an experienced railroad executive before he entered iron- and steel-making. At the age of seventeen he had become an assistant to Thomas Scott, who was then the first superintendent of the Western Division of the Pennsylvania Railroad. When Scott moved up to be vice president, Carnegie succeeded him as division superintendent. He quickly proved himself a most effective manager on one of the busiest divisions of what was then the nation's best-managed railroad.

The Carnegie Company's close relation to the railroads was not unique. The entire output of the first Bessemer plants went into rails. "All of the Bessemer plants had ties of one sort or another with the railroads, usually through the medium of common ownership or directorships." Railroads, in order to assure themselves of such essential supplies, provided much of the capital investment required in the new Bessemer works. The transfer of administrative techniques from the railroads to iron- and steel-producing plants was perfectly natural.

In organizing his steel company, Carnegie put together a structure similar to the one he had worked in on the Pennsylvania Railroad. He appointed the nation's most accomplished steel-maker, Captain William Jones, as general superintendent to oversee the day-to-day work of the superintendents in charge of the blast furnaces, Bessemer converters, railroad mills, bridge-making plants, and other departments. As general managers, Carnegie selected William P. Shinn, a highly competent railroad executive who had been appointed the general agent of the Pennsylvania Company (the subsidiary that operated the Pennsylvania's lines north and west of Pittsburgh) when it was formed in 1871. "It was Shinn," notes Carnegie's biographer, Joseph Frazier Wall, "who had coordinated the various parts and created an effective unit of production."

Shinn's major achievement was the development of statistical data needed for coordination and control. According to James H. Bridge, who worked in the Carnegie enterprises, Shinn did this in part by introducing "the voucher system of accounting" which, though it had "long been used by railroads, . . . was not [yet] in general use in manufacturing concerns." By this method, each department listed the amount and cost of materials and labor used on each order as it passed through the subunit. Such information permitted Shinn to send Carnegie monthly statements and, in time, even daily ones providing data on the costs of ore, limestone, coal, coke, pig iron (when it was not produced at the plant), spiegel, molds, refractories, repairs, fuel, and labor for each ton of rails produced. Bridge called these cost sheets "marvels of ingenuity and careful accounting."

These cost sheets were Carnegie's primary instrument of control. Costs were Carnegie's obsession. One of his favorite dicta was: Watch the costs and the profits will take care of themselves. He was forever asking Shinn and Jones and the department heads the reasons for changes in unit costs. Carnegie concentrated, as he had when he was a division manager on the Pennsylvania, on the cost side of the operating ratio, comparing current costs of each operating unit with those of previous months and, where possible, with those of other enterprises. Indeed, one reason Carnegie joined the Bessemer pool, which was made up of all steel companies producing Bessemer rails, was to have the opportunity to get a look at the cost figures of his competitors. These controls were effective. Bridge reports that: "The minutest details of cost of materials and labor in every department appeared from day to day and week to week in the accounts; and soon every man about the place was made to realize it. The men felt and often remarked that the eyes of the company were always on them through the books."

By 1880 Carnegie's cost sheets were far more detailed and more accurate than cost controls in the leading enterprises in textile, petroleum, tobacco, and other industries. In the metal-working industries comparable statistical data were only just being perfected. In addition to using their cost sheets to evaluate the performance of departmental managers, foremen, and men, Carnegie, Shinn, and Jones relied on them to check the quality and mix of raw materials. They used them to evaluate improvements in process and in product and to make decisions on developing by-products. In pricing, particularly nonstandardized items like bridges, cost sheets were invaluable. The company would not accept a contract until its costs were carefully estimated and until options had been obtained on the basic materials of coke and ore.

Nevertheless, Carnegie's concern was almost wholly with prime costs. He and his associates appear to have paid almost no attention to overhead and depreciation. This too reflected the railroad experience. As on the railroads, administrative overhead and sales expenses were comparatively small and estimated in a rough fashion. Likewise, Carnegie relied on replacement accounting by charging repair, maintenance, and renewals to operating costs. Carnegie had, therefore, no certain way of determining the capital invested in his plant and equipment. As on the railroads, he evaluated performance in terms of the operating ratio (the cost of operations as a percent of sales) and profits in terms of a percentage of book value of stock issued.

Although Carnegie had by the end of the 1870s created a plant organization at the E. T. Works that could be considered modern, the number of managers was still low and the staff was small. The staff executives included only the accountants who provided statistical controls, three engineers in charge of maintenance of plant and equipment, and a chemist, "a learned German, Dr. Fricke," whose laboratories played an important role in maintaining the quality of output and in improving the processes of production. The enterprise was still very much an entrepreneurial one with Carnegie making nearly all the top management decisions.

The history of the American steel industry illustrates effectively how technological innovation, intensified use of energy, plant design, and overall management procedures permitted a great increase in the volume and speed of throughput and with it a comparable expansion in the productivity of operation. Carnegie's preeminence in the industry came from his commitment to technological change and from his imaginative transferral to manufacturing of administrative methods and controls developed on the railroads. Technological and organizational innovation paid off. Carnegie's prices were lower and his profits higher than any producer in the industry. As soon as the E. T. Works was opened in 1875 it recorded profits of $9.50 a ton. In 1878 Carnegie's rail mill recorded a profit of $401,000 or 31 percent on equity. It rose in the next two years to $2.0 million. As the business grew, so did its profits. At the end of the 1890s Carnegie's larger and more diversified enterprise had profits of $20 million. For the year 1900 they stood at $40 million. By becoming a pioneer in the methods of mass production in steel, Carnegie quickly accumulated, as John D. Rockefeller had done in petroleum, one of the largest fortunes the world had ever seen. . . .

Paul Israel

INVENTION AND CORPORATE STRATEGIES

For large corporations, the dynamic character of technology presented both significant risks and major opportunities. Inventions and other technological improvements could either upset or reinforce the status quo in a given industry, depending on which firm or firms could best take advantage of a particular innovation. To ensure continuing market dominance and reduce the potential threat posed by upstart competitors, leading firms in several industries began to invest in research and development on a continuing basis. One of the first major corporations to adopt such a strategy was Western Union, which emerged as the nation's preeminent provider of telegraph service in the late nineteenth century. In the following selection, Paul Israel describes how Western Union strove to maintain its near monopoly over telegraphy by funding the work of inventors and acquiring crucial patent rights. Israel is an editor of the Thomas A. Edison Papers and author of *From Machine Shop to Industrial Laboratory,* from which this selection is taken.

Corporate officials conceived their attempts to establish greater control of technology primarily in market terms, but they were also influenced by their own beliefs regarding the technical and business characteristics of telegraphy. Control of technology could be used for a variety of purposes: an existing company could maintain or expand its market share, or enter new markets, while a new company might use technology to enter an existing market or to create a new one. Firms competing with Western Union in the long-distance market required technology that would reduce their line construction costs and give them technical advantages over Western Union's ability to provide national service. During the 1870s, when telegraph technology seemed to be undergoing rapid development, Western Union officials found it advantageous to pay close attention

From Paul Israel, *From Machine Shop to Industrial Laboratory: Telegraphy and the Changing Context of American Invention, 1830–1920,* pp. 121, 128–131, 135–138, 140–141, 151. Copyright © 1992 by the Johns Hopkins University Press. Excerpted by permission of the publisher.

to new inventions in order to prevent such technology from falling into the hands of competitors. . . .

Because Western Union emerged from the Civil War with a near monopoly over intercity message service, Western Union's managers focused their market strategy on maintaining dominance in the telegraph industry. Western Union's managers initially focused their attention on "minor" technical improvements in the company's existing system, to consolidate the myriad lines acquired from former competitors and improve the quality of service to western cities. Western Union's rivals, on the other hand, needed technological advantages to compete with its national network and service. They sought improvements that could substantially increase productivity or reduce costs while at the same time using far fewer lines. Such improvements also became attractive to Western Union's managers in the face of renewed competition in the 1870s.

Both Western Union and its rivals desired inventions that would increase the speed of message transmission or the capacity of a single telegraph wire to carry messages. Technical development involving line capacity and transmission speeds focused primarily on two types of systems. One system, multiple telegraphy, could be adapted to the existing Morse system and was designed to increase the number of messages that could be transmitted over a single wire. Automatic telegraphy, on the other hand, was intended to replace the Morse system with automatic machinery that transmitted at higher speeds than the Morse and also used less skilled, and hence, less costly operators. In determining which inventions to adopt and which inventors to support, telegraph officials' decisions reflected a set of conceptions and assumptions about the nature of telegraph business and technology. This "business-technology mindset" mirrored cultural values concerning the role of the telegraph and the nature of invention.

The principal architect of Western Union's strategy in regard to invention was William Orton. . . . He came to believe that the best way to improve his company's competitive position would be to increase the volume of business with a minimum of additional expense. He saw that this could best be accomplished by improving the condition of the company's wires, thereby increasing their capacity, and by increasing the number of new lines operated by the company, thus attracting additional business. As president of Western Union,

Orton often returned to these themes. For example, in a letter of 4 December 1868, addressed to T. H. Wilson, a Western Union stockholder, he stated that "our policy concerning [opposition lines] is to put up more wires and otherwise constantly increase our facilities. In short, to grow faster than they and at the same time to do our business better." Orton perceived that quality of service was more important than price to most Western Union customers, especially businessmen.

Early in his career at Western Union, Orton elaborated his definition of quality service, arguing that time was the company's real competitor. By taking all possible steps to provide the most rapid service, he would cause "the customers of our competitors to come to us for the protection of their own interests." Therefore, it was in Western Union's interest "to adopt every improvement whereby the dispatch of business within a given time can be materially increased." . . . Initially, however, Orton's willingness to adopt new machinery did not lead him to develop a strategy for obtaining such needed improvements. Instead, he waited on the initiative of independent inventors. Most firms interested in acquiring technical improvements adhered to this passive approach, because they considered invention to be a product of individual inspiration, which could be guided in only the most general fashion. It was up to the inventors themselves to direct their efforts toward particular markets in the hope they might gain fame and fortune. Only slowly did companies such as Western Union perceive the value of attempting to direct inventors' efforts. . . .

The advantages offered by multiple telegraphs became apparent to Orton when they were demonstrated by inventor Joseph B. Stearns. In 1867, Stearns, then president of the Franklin Telegraph Company, faced the problem of insufficient wires for the increasing volume of the company's business. Lacking the necessary funds to undertake a construction program, Stearns consulted general superintendent James G. Smith and decided to try duplexing the wires—that is, simultaneously sending two messages over a single wire in opposite directions. Stearns, whose knowledge of electrical science and telegraphy developed during his years as an operator and manager of the Farmer-Channing fire-alarm telegraph, combined elements of several existing designs into a device that increased the capacity of the

Franklin wires by almost 50 percent. However, Franklin Telegraph's directors failed to take advantage of the potential competitive advantages afforded by the duplex, refusing either to buy it from Stearns or to pay development costs. As a result, Stearns resigned from the company in 1871 and convinced Orton to allow him to conduct tests on Western Union's lines. . . .

Stearns began his new experiments on Western Union lines in the fall of 1871 with the assistance of company electrician George Prescott. Within six months he had radically improved his system by adding a condenser to overcome the effects of static discharge. This improved duplex had an immediate and dramatic impact on Western Union's lines. Because the duplex nearly doubled the capacity of a wire, company officials found that they needed fewer new wires, saving construction costs. Fewer wires also meant substantial maintenance savings, as lines had to be reconstructed on an average of every twelve years. Even more important, in Orton's opinion, was the ability of the apparatus to increase the capacity of a line temporarily when wires failed or when particularly heavy traffic taxed the capacity of a line being worked in one direction only. Duplexing also allowed the company to better serve tourist resorts, which needed extensive communications facilities only during certain seasons. Orton came to view the Stearns duplex as the most important improvement in telegraphy since Morse's original invention. In a letter to its inventor, Orton stated that he considered it so valuable that he would not sell it for a million dollars. Thus, he moved quickly to acquire all the patent rights to Stearn's duplex system and to place it into service on the company's lines.

The successful outcome of Western Union's support for Stearn's experiments and his growing awareness of the importance of patents in preventing use of a technology by competitors encouraged Orton to pursue a more aggressive strategy in regard to invention. He moved to prevent further use of the Stearns duplex by the Franklin Company and also engaged the services of another inventor to work on duplex telegraphy. Thomas Edison had come to Orton's notice through his work for Gold and Stock on printing telegraphs, which had given him a reputation for devising ingenious variations on the existing technology. After Edison approached Orton in the fall of 1872, claiming he could achieve comparable success with duplex telegraphs, the Western Union president wrote Stearns, saying

> I became apprehensive that processes for working Duplex would be devised which would successfully evade your patents, and also that your [Stearns's] attorneys had not done their work in shutting out competitors, as might have been done. I therefore, sent for Edison, and after several conferences and much discussion with him, I employed him to invent as many processes as possible for doing all or any part of the work covered by your patents. The object was to anticipate other inventors in new modes and also to patent as many combinations as possible.

Edison put it more simply, claiming he was hired to invent duplexes "as an insurance against other parties using them—other lines."

Edison's work on multiplex telegraphy reinforced Orton's interest in new inventions and led to an increase of company funding to inventors for specific projects. While working on duplex telegraphy with assistance from Prescott and the electrician's office, Edison developed an unexpected bonus for Western Union when he invented a practical quadruplex telegraph, by which two messages could be sent simultaneously in each direction. But Western Union failed to secure a formal agreement with Edison for control of any inventions he had developed with Western Union support, and this led to a protracted court battle with Jay Gould's Atlantic and Pacific Telegraph Company for control of the quadruplex. As a result, Orton also gained a new appreciation for the necessity of more formal relationships with inventors working for the company. Subsequently, when Edison had a falling-out with the managers of Atlantic and Pacific, Orton again acquired the inventor's services to make further improvements in multiple telegraphy and to prevent him from working for the opposition. This time, however, Orton drew up a formal contract that called for Edison to develop a telegraph system that could send more than four messages at a time, in return for experimental expenses of two hundred dollars per week, as well as other assistance from the company.

Thomas Edison was not the only beneficiary of Orton's farsighted strategy. Western Union also provided assistance to Elisha Gray, another inventor whose printing telegraph patents were controlled by Gold and Stock. Both Edison and Gray were working on acoustic telegraph systems designed to transmit multiple messages by means of different harmonic frequencies using tuning forks or reeds. Western Union first became interested in acoustic systems in May 1874, when Elisha Gray demonstrated his system of harmonic telegraphy to company officials. By 1874, Gray was well known to company officials for his printing telegraph inventions and for his work as electrician of the Western Electric Manufacturing Company of Chicago, which was partly owned by Western Union. Nothing immediately came of the demonstration and Gray went to Europe to exhibit it, but after his return he and the company renewed their discussions. The company apparently agreed to give him a five-thousand-dollar loan, using his stock (approximately one-third of the total interest) in the Harmonic Telegraph Company as collateral. Western Union also provided Gray with the facilities of [George] Phelps's shop.

Western Union's support for acoustic telegraph experiments paid off when Alexander Graham Bell, who was working independently on acoustic telegraphy, announced in May 1876 that his instrument could be made to transmit speech. Orton initially rejected Bell's offer to sell the new invention to Western Union, believing that it was technically inadequate for long-distance transmission. Edison and Gray therefore continued to focus their work on acoustic telegraphy. When Bell and his backers began using the telephone to compete with intraurban telegraph services, such as those supplied by Gold and Stock, thus threatening Western Union's own interests in this field, Orton responded by acquiring Gray's inventions suited to telephony, as well as encouraging Edison's work on the new technology. Edison's experiments resulted in a new contract with Western Union, which moved the company toward a potentially significant innovation in corporate support for invention.

Prompted by the unexpected development of both the quadruplex and the telephone, Orton decided to support an ongoing research program rather than to pay an independent inventor for specific improvements in the company's apparatus or for work on a new device. Using money from his contract for work on acoustic telegraphy, along with royalties from his earlier telegraph work, Edison had built his Menlo Park, New Jersey, laboratory in early 1876. At the inventor's initiative, Western Union entered into a new agreement with Edison in March 1877, which provided general support for the laboratory's investigations related to telecommunications. During the negotiations over this contract, Edison had pointed out the advantages the laboratory offered for further enhancing his proven abilities to turn out new inventions with startling regularity. Under the new arrangement, Western Union provided one hundred dollars per week for the "payment of laboratory expenses incurred in perfecting inventions applicable to land lines of telegraph or cables within the United States." . . .

Companies in the telegraph industry were among the first to seek the competitive advantages made possible by controlling invention. By the turn of the century, companies in many other industries sought to exercise similar control. Recognizing that patents were "the best and most effective means of controlling competition," a few firms such as Bell Telephone, General Electric, and the United Shoe Machinery Company began to employ corporate inventors to produce inventions that not only improved their products but also created patents to help protect their dominant position in the market. While the patent system remained the principal means by which society sought to encourage invention, that system was increasingly being used to secure the industrial property of large, economically powerful corporations rather than the intellectual property of individual inventors. Changes in the postwar telegraph industry reflected a general transformation taking place in American society, as economic and political power began to shift from individuals to large-scale bureaucratic organizations.

IMAGES OF INDUSTRIALIZATION:
SOCIAL CONFLICT AND CELEBRATION

Beginning in the late 1820s, boosters in Baltimore, Boston, and other major American cities began pressing for the development of railroads to enhance local economic prospects. By 1840, the United States boasted over one and a half times the total miles of rail in all of Europe. Yet not every American was enamored of early locomotives, which made a good deal of noise, polluted the air, caused numerous accidents, and threatened existing social arrangements. Reproduced above is a poster circulated by opponents of railroad expansion in Philadelphia in 1839. Note how the appeal of this broadside is framed explicitly in terms of both gender and class. (Union Pacific Museum)

The Centennial Exhibition held at Philadelphia during the summer and fall of 1876 celebrated not only the one-hundredth anniversary of the Declaration of Independence but also the growing industrial might of the United States. Although the nation was in the midst of an economic depression and still recovering from the horrendous bloodshed of the Civil War, the Exhibition's organizers found cause for optimism in the apparently unceasing progress of American technology. The greatest technological spectacle at the Exhibition was the gigantic Corliss engine in Machinery Hall, pictured above, which produced enough power to drive all the other machines on display throughout the building's fourteen acres of floor space. (Library of Congress)

"The Strike," reproduced above, was painted by the German-American artist Robert Koehler in 1886 and may be the first major painting ever to focus on the theme of industrial confrontation. Although inspired by the Great Railway Strike of 1877, the painting represented not a particular historical event but the general phenomenon of class struggle. The popular magazine *Harper's Weekly* reproduced "The Strike" in its issue of May 1, 1886—the date hundreds of thousands of workers nationwide walked off their jobs to support the call for an eight-hour work day. (Collection of Lee Baxandall)

This 1890 poster advertises the advantages of traveling in the Pullman dining and sleeping cars featured by the Chicago and Alton Railroad. Note how the affluent female passenger reclines in fashionable comfort while the train moves peacefully through a pastoral midwestern landscape. The poster projects a sense of harmony between technology and nature and betrays no hint of class conflict. It may seem ironic, then, that a strike by workers at the Pullman Palace Car Company in 1894 led to a nationwide boycott by the American Railway Union and one of the fiercest social confrontations in late nineteenth-century America. (Library of Congress)

Held in Chicago during the summer of 1893, the World's Columbian Exposition (also known as White City) highlighted the artistic and cultural dimensions of industrial progress. The fair's motto was "Not Matter, But Mind; Not Things, But Men." Yet the Exposition was designed to be fun as well as educational, and it drew crowds of eager visitors from across the country and around the globe. Pictured above is the fair's huge ferris wheel, measuring 250 feet in diameter and towering over the surrounding structures. (Culver Pictures)

Progress and

Its Discontents

T. J. Jackson Lears

CHAMPIONS AND CRITICS OF MODERNITY

Like their forebears of the Revolutionary era, social and intellectual leaders in the late nineteenth century debated the implications of industrial development for the health and welfare of the American republic. On one side were the champions of modernization who argued that material and moral progress went hand in hand, promoting simultaneously physical comfort, civility, and personal autonomy. On the other side were cultural critics who feared that American society was becoming "overcivilized," corrupt, and dangerously unstable. Beneath the complacent surface of respectable appearances these critics perceived an erosion of moral character among the "haves" as well as the "have nots" of industrial America. In the following excerpt from his book *No Place of Grace*, T. J. Jackson Lears locates these conflicting perspectives on modernity within the context of both economic change and ideological continuity. Lears is professor of American studies at Rutgers University.

Late-nineteenth-century enthusiasm for material progress is difficult to chart because it was omnipresent and often implicit in the emergent modern culture. It united businessmen, politicians, ministers, journalists—all the stout thought-leaders of the urban bourgeoisie. Even many labor leaders, socialists, and dissident farmers accepted the progressive faith: they attacked the maldistribution of wealth, not the fundamental beneficence of economic growth; they accepted the conventional link between technological development and national greatness. Americans who despised the steel magnate Andrew Carnegie would have echoed his claim in *Triumphant Democracy* (1886): "The old nations of the earth creep on at a snail's pace; the Republic thunders past with the rush of the express." Carnegie revealed a major foundation of the belief in progress: the idea that nations (like individuals) can never stand still. They must always be growing, changing, improving their material lot; life is a race to be won by the swiftest. Like the progressive faith itself, this notion was often left

165

implicit. Yet its impact has been incalculable. It accounts for the re-
lentless dynamism at the heart of capitalist development, spreading
an obsessive need for change throughout modern culture. And for
most educated and affluent Americans in the late nineteenth century,
"change" meant "progress." . . .

An idea of progress had existed in Western culture for centuries,
but in the nineteenth century it became more sweeping in its implications and more widely held than ever before. Of all Victorian
habits of mind, this tendency to equate material and moral progress
is perhaps most difficult to swallow today. Among later generations,
it has helped earn Victorian moralists a reputation as consummate
hypocrites. One can easily see why by looking (for example) at a
symposium called "The Moral Drift of Our Time," sponsored by
the Congregational Club of New York and held at the Vienna Café,
corner of Tenth Street and Broadway, on May 25, 1883. After a
huge seven-course meal (which included salmon à la hollandaise,
sirloin of beef braisé, breaded breast of lamb, and stewed prunes),
the symposium participants settled down to a chorus of sober self-
congratulation. Judge Noah Davis noted the elevated tone of politics
since the banishment of the "slave power"; the literary critic Hamilton Wright Mabie applauded the application of the scientific spirit to
literature; Professor William Tucker of Andover Theological Semi-
nary was sure that religious sentiment was on the rise because church
membership was up. From the banquet vantage, the "moral drift of
our time" seemed hardly drift but inevitable, calculable ascent.

This sort of optimism is difficult to credit today, when it survives
only among a few vapid futurologists. But it epitomized the pattern
of evasive banality which pervaded modern culture. To try to catch
the significance of this pattern, we need to see the equation of material and moral progress not simply as complacent hypocrisy but as
a natural outgrowth of nineteenth-century bourgeois morality.

The center of that morality was the autonomous individual, whose
only moral master was himself. For centuries, the internal dynamic
of bourgeois individualism had been undermining all the older, external forms of moral authority—the authority of king over subject,
priest over communicant, master over slave. Freed from older constraints, each masterless man needed a moral gyroscope to keep him
on course or else market society might dissolve into a chaos of self-

seeking individuals. The destruction of old oppressive forms created new problems of social control; in order to preserve any semblance of public order, oppression had to yield to repression. Even as they attacked the old, external forms of moral authority, bourgeois moralists labored to create a new, internalized mode of moral authority. As Weber brilliantly suggested, Protestant ministers played a major role in beginning the work; they were joined in the more secular nineteenth century by medical men, public educators, and social reformers of all sorts. Health and morality became intertwined. By the 1880s, whether sanctioned by secular or religious authority, an internalized ethic of self-control had become the unquestioned norm for the middle and upper classes as well as for much of the rest of society. . . .

The official creed held not only that progress was inevitable but that the key to it was the disciplined, autonomous self, created in the bosom of the bourgeois family. From the dominant view, the autonomous self was a Promethean figure, conquering fate through sheer force of will. Faith in autonomous selfhood required a denial of inner conflict and an insensitivity to actual social conditions; it epitomized the evasiveness of modern culture.

This faith emerged most clearly in nineteenth-century success ideology, which held aloft the example of the self-made man. In the popular imagination, that figure possessed neither intellectual brilliance nor unusual physical prowess; what he had in abundance were industrious work habits, extraordinary moral discipline, and above all an indomitable will. "To the man of vigorous will, there are few impossibilities," said a clerical success adviser in 1878. "Obstructions melt before his fiat like spring snowflakes." The career of the self-made man embodied the dynamism inherent in all capitalist development. Autonomous achievement required perpetual motion; the modern self never stood still. Like the heroes of Horatio Alger's novels, the self-made man would forever *Strive and Succeed;* he would always be *Struggling Upward.*

The image of the Promethean self-made man was mythic in a double sense: it was part of a world view which provided many Americans with meaning and purpose; and it was false. Social historians have conclusively demonstrated that gross inequalities of opportunity existed in the United States during the Jacksonian era; by the 1880s the growth of organized corporate capitalism had made genuine economic independence a near impossibility. Yet the ideal of self-made manhood persists. One can find traces of it today at all levels of our culture, from the calls for "self-starters" in the want ads to the fascination of ego psychologists with autonomy to the assertions of sociologists about workers in modern industrial societies. According to Clark Kerr, for example, the modern worker is fully committed, "dedicated to hard work, a high pace of work, and a keen sense of individual responsibility for performance of assigned norms and tasks"; he is moved not by grudging acquiescence but by "an ideology and an ethic." He is, in other words, an embodiment of autonomous achievement. . . .

Historians have long castigated Gilded Age culture for its failure to grapple with the realities of a raw, new industrial society; in actuality that "failure" served an important social purpose. By denying the dilemmas posed by modernization, the official doctrines provided both a source of escape from unprecedented conflict and a means of legitimizing continued capitalist development in a liberal polity. In the official doctrines of our own time, the same bland reassurances serve the same social purpose: they legitimize the hegemony of capitalist proprietors and managers. But the reassurances are cast in a new moral and cultural mold. According to the conventional wisdom, we have thrown aside the cumbersome mental furniture of our Victorian ancestors and liberated ourselves from the burden of our puritan past: a cultural "revolution" has taken place. The problem with this view is that the "revolution" has done little or nothing to alter the structure of social relations. Despite momentous changes in manners and morals, wealth and power remain in the hands of a few. Everything has changed, yet nothing has changed.

The key to this anomalous situation lies in the late nineteenth century, when modern culture began to show signs of strain, cracks in the surface of official optimism. Among educated Americans there was a growing sense of dis-ease, a barely articulated feeling that denial and evasion were inadequate strategies for containing the unprecedented social and psychic conflict in the emerging industrial society. It was not so much that late Victorians reacted consciously against modern culture as that they began half-consciously to perceive its limitations and contradictions, its failure to live up to its claims of perpetual progress and perfect autonomy. Ultimately that critical perception helped to generate a crisis of cultural authority, rooted in the social and psychic turmoil of the late nineteenth century.

The social dimensions of the crisis were the clearest. By the early 1880s, it became apparent that the evasive banality of modern culture might no longer be adequate to maintain social order. The technical rationality of industrial capitalism was *merely* technical; the irrationalities of the business cycle continued to generate mass unemployment and heightening class conflict. As upper-class orators denounced labor unrest and fretted publicly about "impending revolution," their audiences began to rethink official optimism and resurrect an alternative cultural tradition: the darker strain of Puritan and republican moralism. Subterranean but strong even at the apex of mid-Victorian optimism, the republican tradition allowed troubled Americans to make moral sense of the social conflicts bred by industrial capitalism. From the republican vantage, historical development was not linear but cyclical; material progress contained the seeds of moral decline. Every paean to economic growth evoked, in many minds, the old republican fears of overcivilization. . . .

Throughout the last two decades of the nineteenth century, critics warned against the effects of European luxury and fashion on national character. They agreed that Americans, whether artists or ordinary citizens, should not be ashamed of their provincialism but should wear it proudly as an emblem of their freedom from aristocratic foppishness. Despite such exhortations, fears persisted that America would repeat the classical republican pattern. As George Frederic Parsons of the *New York Tribune* mused in 1887: "Poverty, thrift, prosperity, wealth, luxury, corruptness, degradation: in these seven words the fate of many great empires is told. No nation following in that track has escaped the common destiny. Shall we?"

Though Parsons's worries recalled those of John Adams, a century of industrial transformation separated the two men. By the 1880s urban landscapes blotted out pastureland from the Atlantic to the Great Lakes. The folkways of the countryside began to succumb to the standardized "chromo civilization" of the city. And the city was the republicans' *bête noire;* it offered no fertile ground for the growth of righteous leaders. In republican mythology, the virtuous husbandman had long been counter-posed to the corrupt cosmopolitan, but as rural populations declined, urban writers increasingly idealized farm life. A host of "local color" writers imagined republican virtue in a wide variety of preindustrial communities. In 1888 a pathologist writing in the *North American Review* summarized the conventional wisdom: "Once let the human race be cut off from personal contact with the soil, once let the conventionalities and artificial restrictions of so-called civilization interfere with the healthful simplicity of nature, and decay is certain."

Concern about urban luxury was intensified by embryonic but momentous changes in the economy. As the leaders of organized capitalism solved the problems of mass production by adopting technical innovations, they began to face new problems of marketing and distribution. For many the central question became: how could one persuade people to consume the articles now being mass produced? (The example of the tobacco magnate James B. Duke is illustrative. In 1882 he adopted the Bonsack machine for mechanically rolling cigarettes; within two years he had saturated the market and moved from North Carolina to New York, where he concentrated his attention on marketing, distributing, and advertising cigarettes rather than producing them.) Major enterprises began to place heavier emphasis on advertising consumer goods for an expanding urban market. As the economy started slowly to shift from a producer to a consumer orientation, the urban bourgeoisie were encouraged to place an even higher premium on purchasing material comfort and convenience—or "luxury" from the old republican view. Thorstein Veblen's famous satire of "conspicuous consumption" in *The Theory of the Leisure Class* (1899) was rooted in part in republican outrage over sybaritic waste among an overcivilized elite.

Most critics of overcivilization . . . feared urban comfort as a source of both bodily and spiritual enervation, and their fears were reinforced by intersecting racial and class anxieties. Worry about an irresponsible elite's destruction by an unleashed rabble, always a component of republican tradition, intensified in the face of unprecedented labor unrest, waves of strange new immigrants, and glittering industrial fortunes. An overcivilized bourgeoisie was vulnerable to "race suicide" on the one hand, revolutionary overthrow on the other.

The mingling of race and class fears emerged most clearly in the hysterical response to the explosion during an anarchists' assembly at Haymarket Square, Chicago, in 1886, when a policeman was killed and six other persons wounded. "The enemy forces are not American

[but] rag-tag and bob-tail cutthroats of Beelzebub from the Rhine, the Danube, the Vistula and the Elbe," a typical editorial trumpeted. Another advised that "if the master race of this continent is subordinated to or overrun with the communistic and revolutionary races, it will be in grave danger of social disaster." Surveying the class strife of 1886, which included not only Haymarket but also numerous clashes between strikes and police, the Reverend Theodore T. Munger concluded: "This horrible tyranny is wholly of foreign origin." . . .

Yet as labor troubles continued, increasing numbers of affluent citizens grew determined to fight. They armed themselves and their police as never before. President Charles W. Eliot of Harvard pointed the way when he began drilling the Harvard riflemen in 1877, to defend propertied New Englanders against the eastward spread of rioting workers. Concerned community leaders banded into a number of vigilante "Law and Order Leagues" during the 1880s. By the end of that decade, massive armories brooded at the center of every American city—testimony to the official fears of domestic insurrection. Amid such precautions, warnings against the dark designs of labor leaders and anarchist assassins proliferated in the established press, and expectations of apocalyptic class warfare pervaded both fiction and journalism. The publisher Henry Holt employed a dominant image when he wrote in 1895 that "the large majority of intellectual people . . . are peacefully sitting reading physical science and the classics, on a crust covering a mephitic chasm or, as many think, a volcano."

The Volcano under the City embodied the social sources of the crisis of cultural authority. Concern about overcivilization was heightened by ethnic and class antinomies, impossible to ignore, in the emerging industrial society. Earlier republican moralists, though they expressed concern about restive lower orders, had never faced such widespread evidence of lower-class discontent. Even by the 1890s, when urban elites were extraordinarily well organized and prepared to meet any disturbance, working-class discontent still seemed volcanic in its white-hot explosiveness—unpredictable and unmanageable. Despite all ruling-class precautions the forces of social chaos smoldered; modern culture seemed unable to contain them.

Yet many problems involved in this crisis of cultural authority were even less manageable than the threat posed by the Volcano under the City. Threats came from aboveground as well—not merely the familiar urban danger of physical and moral decay but a subtler menace, unknown to earlier moralists. The spread of technical rationality bred more than social chaos; it also produced spiritual and cultural confusion. In an emerging national market dominated by bureaucratic corporations, the bourgeois ideal of the independent self seemed barely tenable. As new theories in sociology and psychology gave scientific sanction to the notion of an overcivilized, diminished human personality, the bourgeois vision of individual autonomy began to seem sharply circumscribed. And if autonomy was circumscribed, personal moral responsibility was undermined as well. Familiar ideas of character and will were shaken by the triumph of organized capitalism.

These difficulties were exacerbated by religious changes. As Calvinism softened into platitudinous humanism, Protestant Christianity lost the gravity provided by older, sterner creeds. Lacking spiritual ballast, bourgeois culture entered what Nietzsche had called a "weightless" period, marked by hazy moral distinctions and vague spiritual commitments. Gradually personal identity itself came to seem problematic. Part of the difficulty was that individual will and action were hemmed in by the emerging iron cage of a bureaucratic market economy. But the trouble ran deeper: the rationalization of urban culture and the decline of religion into sentimental religiosity further undermined a solid sense of self. For many, individual identities began to seem fragmented, diffuse, perhaps even unreal. A weightless culture of material comfort and spiritual blandness was breeding weightless persons who longed for intense experience to give some definition, some distinct outline and substance to their vaporous lives. . . .

David Montgomery

THE STRUGGLE FOR CONTROL OF PRODUCTION

The Great Railway Strike of 1877 ushered in an era of labor protest and industrial violence on an unprecedented scale in the United States. One of the most notorious confrontations of the period took place at Homestead, Pennsylvania, in 1892. The Homestead conflict pitted members of the Amalgamated Association of Iron and Steel Workers against the management of Carnegie Steel, one of the nation's largest companies and a pioneer of modern business administration. In this selection, David Montgomery interprets what happened at Homestead as an instance of class struggle over the fundamental question of who should control the process of production in a capitalist enterprise. Montgomery is Farnum Professor of History at Yale University and the author of several major works on the history of American labor. This selection is excerpted from his book *The Fall of the House of Labor.*

With the revival of the steel industry between 1888 and 1892, the [Amalgamated Association of Iron and Steel Workers] began to grow rapidly. . . . At the 1891 convention, 294 delegates transacted business for 24,068 members (the largest union of ironworkers and steelworkers in the world and the largest number to belong to the Amalgamated Association until 1934), about one-fourth of the eligible tonnage men in the country. Delegates to this and other conventions during this militant half decade responded to the decay of their trades with draconic work rules: ordering promotion by seniority in rolling crews, "blacklegging" inside contractors, reducing the amount of iron that could be pulled per heat by any one member, and banning overtime turns where anyone was out of work. "Corruption" at the local level was thus challenged by the adoption of uniform and rigid rules at the union's national level. Moreover, because the technology, the managerial controls, and the very size of the new steel mills made such self-discipline increasingly

From David Montgomery, *The Fall of the House of Labor: The Workplace, the State, and American Labor Activism.* Copyright © 1987 by Cambridge University Press. Reprinted with the permission of Cambridge University Press.

difficult to enforce, the union members had to resort to ostracism, boycotts, and threats of violence against deviants, and when strikes came, they used mass picketing, sympathetic strikes, and even armed force. As this happened, the employers appealed increasingly to the community at large to support the freedom of property owners and of individual workers from "union tyranny," and to support "law and order." Thus, the battle for control between craft and managerial authorities within the mill spilled over into a social and political confrontation of social classes and of social ideals. At the Homestead works in 1892, that confrontation assumed legendary proportions.

The lockout that gripped Andrew Carnegie's Homestead works from the beginning of July to the end of November 1892 put the amalgamation movement to the acid test. Of the thirty-eight hundred workers in the mill, roughly eight hundred tonnage men belonged to one of eight Amalgamated lodges on the eve of the lockout. Not only had they won a strike in January 1889, forcing the company to deal with the Amalgamated Association and pay according to its sliding scale of tonnage rates for the next three years, but also they formed the keystone in the structure of ninety-four lodges in the district, which constituted one-third of all the lodges in the union. They also dominated the borough's government, Burgess John McLuckie himself being a mill worker and a union leader. When the county sheriff had led a posse into Homestead during the 1889 strike, he and his men had simply been chased away by the strikers, and the sheriff had concluded that the better part of valor was to offer his services as a mediator in effecting a settlement.

In the spring of 1892, however, the situation was quite different. For three years the Carnegie company had made careful preparations for a showdown over the question of who controlled the mills. Henry Clay Frick had assumed direction of the works, bringing with him a reputation for having smashed strikes in the coal and coke end of the industry, and he promptly erected fortifications around the plant. Moreover, the latest boom in railroad construction had clearly ended; rail prices were falling and many mills in the Midwest were laying off or shutting down. The manufacturers' association in the iron-rolling mills rejected the union's proposed scale and demanded major wage cuts. In steel, however, the union did not deal with an association, but simply and directly with Frick. He brooked no compromise with the drastic tonnage reductions he proposed, and when the negotiators for the Amalgamated Association refused to accept his terms, Frick began closing down parts of the mill. On July 2 the company discharged all its workers and served public notice: "Hereafter, the Homestead steel works will operate as a non-union mill."

The union lodges rallied the workers with enthusiastic mass meetings, elected an advisory committee of thirty-three members to direct their struggle, and set up special committees that patrolled the streets, warned tavern keepers to allow no drunkenness, and cut down effigies of company officials, with which inhabitants had liberally decorated the town. As the Pittsburgh journalist Arthur Burgoyne concisely put it:

> The government of Homestead had now passed absolutely into the hands of the advisory committee of the Amalgamated lodges, and the committee was determined to use its arbitrary authority for the preservation of order and decency and the protection of life and property as well as the exclusion from Homestead of non-union men, better known to the unionists as "scabs" or "black sheep."

Four days later, two barges filled with Pinkerton detectives arrived at the waterfront entrance to the mill, and on their refusal to obey the committee's instruction to depart, the great battle of July 6 began. While the Pinkertons fired through gun slits in the armor plating of their barges, the populace of Homestead hastily erected steel barricades of their own and assaulted the invaders with rifle fire, dynamite, flaming oil, cannon fire, and fireworks left over from the Fourth of July. When the detectives surrendered to the advisory committee toward the end of the day, they were forced to run a bloody gauntlet of men, women, and children and were saved from death only by the efforts of the committee members. The "Fight for Hearth and Home," through which the steelworkers cleansed their town of the hated lackeys of capital, was soon celebrated in song and legend in working-class homes throughout the land:

> Now the man that fights for honor, none can blame him,
> May luck attend wherever he may roam,
> And no son of his will ever live to shame him,
> Whilst liberty and honor rule our home.

The "Battle of Fort Frick" had projected the contest for control of Carnegie's mills into the community for all America to observe.

Newspaper reporters who swarmed into Homestead remarked on the prominence of the borough's women in the armed confrontation with the Pinkertons and in the bloody gauntlet the detectives had to run after their surrender. They were equally impressed by the way the mill hands who did not belong to the Amalgamated Association supported the union. A committee of mechanics and laborers had approached management on the eve of the strike with proposals for a scale of wages for their work and had been rebuffed. That committee ardently endorsed the strike of the tonnage men on July 2, and its adherents remained off the job until November 18. In the ominous calm that followed the battle of July 6, the union's advisory committee was absolute master of the community. Its representatives patrolled the streets and the silent mill, organized huge funeral processions in collaboration with local churches and lodges, and even arrested a group of anarchists who came from Pittsburgh to distribute leaflets. No one expressed the craftsmen's image of themselves better than the Reverend J. J. McIlyar of the Fourth Avenue Methodist Episcopal Church, who pronounced John Morris, slain in the battle with the Pinkertons, "a perfect citizen; an intelligent man; a good husband who was never lacking in his duty; a brother who was devoted and loyal and who will surely find his reward."

Three days after Reverend McIlyar's eulogy, eight thousand soldiers of the Pennsylvania National Guard arrived in Homestead to begin ninety-five days of military occupation. It was the army, not the Pinkertons, that allowed Frick gradually to reopen the mill with strikebreakers. But its commander, General George R. Snowden, envisaged his mission as far more important than simply deciding the outcome of an industrial dispute. As he explained in his official report, "Philadelphians can hardly appreciate the actual communism of these people [in Homestead]. They believe the works are their's [*sic*] quite as much as Carnegie's."

That view was seconded by Chief Justice Edward Paxson of the Pennsylvania Supreme Court. Coming to Pittsburgh in September for the court's annual session, after 167 Homestead residents had already been indicted on charges of murder, riot, and conspiracy for the events of July 6, the chief justice handed down a further bill of charges against the union's advisory committee, that they did "unlawfully, falsely, maliciously and traitorously compass, imagine and intend to raise and levy war, insurrection and rebellion against the

Commonwealth of Pennsylvania." Proof of their treasonous intent was found by Justice Paxson in the fact that they had not participated in "a mob driven to desperation by hunger as in the days of the French Revolution," but were rather "men receiving exceptionally high wages . . . resisting the law and resorting to violence and bloodshed in the assertion of imaginary rights." Their act had been "a deliberate attempt by men without authority to control others in the enjoyment of their rights."

This crisp and firm declaration that workers' control was illegal—that the group discipline in the workplace and community by which workers enforced their code of mutualism in opposition to the authority and power of the mill owners was tantamount to insurrection against the republic—clearly illuminated the ideological and political dimensions of workplace struggles. It also made clear to Justice Paxson himself the "diseased state of public opinion" regarding the respective rights of labor and capital that "finds expression in the assurances of demagogues who pander to popular prejudices and in the schemes of artful politicians." . . .

As early as mid-October, the *Homestead News,* . . . which had consistently supported the strikers, had begun to editorialize that the struggle was lost and should be abandoned. Mounting anxiety among the laborers that all their jobs were being taken by newcomers led a mass meeting of mechanics and laborers . . . to vote to ask for their jobs back. Defeat now being certain, a mournful gathering of tonnage men voted to "declare the mill open" by the narrow margin of 101 to 91.

In the eight years after the defeated workers seeking reemployment filed past two hiring clerks under the watchful eye of Superintendent Charles Schwab, steel production in Carnegie's mills tripled—from 878,000 tons to 2,870,000 tons. "Ashamed to tell you profits these days," Andrew Carnegie wrote a friend in 1899. His word for them was "Prodigious!" In place of the $4 million net return of 1892 stood a profit of $21 million that year (and almost $40 million the next). The 2,663,412-ton output of Carnegie's Monogahela Valley plants (Homestead, Duquesne, Braddock, etc.) in 1899 surpassed Great Britain's world-historic record of 1885 by 35 percent. No longer, to use the words of Carnegie's one-time colleague James H. Bridge, was "the method of apportioning the work, of regulating the turns, of altering the machinery, in short, every detail of working the great plant . . . subject to the interference of some busybody representing the Amalgamated Association." Tonnage rates were slashed, twelve-hours turns were extended to at least one-third of the workers, breaks in the working day that had once been prescribed by union rules were eliminated, and workers were reassigned at management's discretion, while new charging machines, heating furnaces, automatic roll tables, and other equipment eliminated an estimated five hundred jobs in Homestead alone by the end of the decade. . . .

Our brief look at work relations and strife in the iron and steel industry of the late nineteenth century has suggested some of the most important characteristics of the workers' movement of the epoch. The line of battle did not run between "industrialism" (or "modernity") and its foes. On the contrary, class conflict was an inherent part of industrial life. The production of iron and steel was a collective undertaking, involving the coordinated teamwork of thousands of workers, whose technical expertise and intense physical exertion were applied to ever more imposing furnaces, rolling mills, molds, and transfer machinery, all of which were legally owned by other men and set in motion in such a way, and only such a way, as to earn a profit for the owners.

The industry's rapid development, therefore, involved simultaneous social accumulation of capital and of knowledge. The former legally belonged to the firms' partners and shareholders, and its perpetual increase was their driving ambition. But to whom did the knowledge belong? From the vantage point of society's real wealth, Karl Marx argued that

> . . . the accumulation of the skill and knowledge (scientific power) of the workers themselves is the chief form of accumulation, and infinitely more important than the accumulation—which goes hand in hand with it and merely represents it—of the *existing objective* conditions of this accumulated activity. These objective conditions are only nominally accumulated and must be constantly produced and consumed anew.

The process of accumulation involved social conflict not only because workers and owners disputed over the division of the product between wages and profits but also because the social character of production clashed with the private nature of ownership. The "skill and knowledge" accumulated by workers assumed decisive importance in determining the outcome on both levels of conflict, and indeed in determining the way in which capital itself was "constantly produced and consumed anew." Such "prodigious" profits as had made Carnegie himself "ashamed" could not have been earned without Carnegie's triumph over workers' power that had its roots in their accumulated "skill and knowledge."

This contest placed the skilled workers of late-nineteenth-century industry in a position of unique importance. They were producers, whose "mass of rule-of-thumb or traditional knowledge," in the words of Frederick Winslow Taylor, was their "principal asset or possession" and made their "initiative" indispensable to the operation of the enterprise. The craft workers' initiative was both indispensable to the employers and a source of controversy for them. Because the firm was an agency for the generation of profits out of money invested in buildings, land, machinery, raw materials, and labor power, its success depended on management's exploitation of all those factors of production in the generation of salable products. But because that process involved the creation of goods needed by society, the "manager's brains," to quote Bill Haywood and Frank Bohn, were "under the workman's cap." By the turn of the century, the steelmasters' quest for greater and more secure profits had led them not only to integrate "backward" for control of every operation from the iron or coal mine to the rolling mill but also to attack the menace of collective workers' control over any part of those operations and ultimately to search for ways in which to cut the taproot of nineteenth-century workers' power by dispossessing the craftsmen of their accumulated skill and knowledge. . . .

Alan Trachtenberg

COMPETING VISIONS FOR THE FUTURE

In 1893 millions of people flocked to Chicago to visit the World's Columbian Exposition, also known as White City, a huge fair celebrating the benefits of material progress and the achievements of modern culture. In 1894, in nearby Pullman, Illinois, thousands of workers went out on strike against the Pullman Palace Car Company and triggered a nationwide labor boycott of railroads that used the company's cars. In the following selection, Alan Trachtenberg takes the close juxtaposition of these two events as a starting point for exploring contemporaries' competing visions for the future of American society after a century of industrialization. The contest between "corporation" and "union" as social ideals, Trachtenberg contends, extended well beyond the economic conflicts of the 1890s and is still with us today. Trachtenberg is Neil Grey Professor of American Studies and English at Yale University. This selection comes from his book *The Incorporation of America*.

October 12.—*The Discovery.*—It was wonderful to find America, but it would have been more wonderful to miss it." Pudd'nhead Wilson's mordant calendar entry in Mark Twain's bleak comedy of race and class, *Pudd'nhead Wilson,* with its wicked pun on "wonderful," may well have seemed apt to at least some of the book's readers when it appeared in 1894. It was the year of the great railway strike which spread like a prairie fire from its origins in Pullman, Illinois. An epic insurgence of sympathy in the form of a national boycott in support of the Pullman strikers, the event pitted the United States Army against the American Railway Union, and the clash resulted in the most destructive civil violence since the Civil War. But the previous summer, when close to 30 million people had trekked by railroad to visit the Fair staged in Chicago on reclaimed swamplands on the shores of Lake Michigan, in commemoration of the four hundredth anniversary of that same discovery, Pudd'nhead's

From *The Incorporation of America: Culture and Society in the Gilded Age* by Alan Trachtenberg. Copyright © 1982 by Alan Trachtenberg. Reprinted by permission of Hill and Wang, a division of Farrar, Straus and Giroux, Inc.

coy remark would not have made a hit. Surely Chauncy M. Depew's view of the occasion carried the day. In his oration at the dedication ceremonies in October 1892 (the Fair itself would not open its gates until May of the following year), the New York senator and industrialist summed up the common belief: "This day belongs not to America, but to the World. The results of the event it commemorates are the heritage of the people of every race and clime. We celebrate the emancipation of man." Of course, what he meant, and what the Fair would proclaim, is that America *represents* the world, is itself the world's heritage, itself the "emancipation of man." Inviting the world to come and see (though not to stay: Depew included a timely warning against unrestricted immigration, against admitting "those who come to undermine our institutions and subvert our laws"), White City would display just how wonderful America had become.

How shall we take this event, which lasted but a summer—an oasis of fantasy and fable at a time of crisis and impending violence? Given its time and place, the Fair invites ironic scrutiny as few other events and objects in the age. Not the gesture alone of planting a new "city upon a hill" for the world to admire, but the accidental setting of that gesture between the financial panic of 1893 and the strike of 1894 makes White City seem a fitting conclusion of an age. The fruition of the alliance between "the word Culture" and corporate powers, it closes out an era. But it also inaugurates another. It lays bare a plan for a future. Like the Gilded Age, White City straddles a divide: a consummation and a new beginning.

We shall take it as a pedagogy, a model and a lesson not only of what the future might look like but, just as important, how it might be brought about. And in our analysis we shall look not only at what it says but at what it fails to say, what it keeps hidden. For example, as a model city it taught a lesson in the coordination of spaces and structures: some 400 buildings covering almost 700 acres of once swampy land dredged and filled and inlaid with canals, lagoons, plazas, and promenades, and a preserve of woods. Based on Olmsted's unifying ground plan, it taught the public utility of beauty, the coordination of art with the latest mechanical wonders: railroads, dynamos, electrical bulbs. It was, of course, a city without residences, though it offered advice in great detail about how families might live in cities of the near future: the model electrical kitchen, for example. How did its manifest harmony of parts (and

in the central Court of Honor, of architectural style, height of buildings, color: a uniform whiteness) come about? The overt message
stressed the structure of authority, a structure which gave to the
Director of Works, Daniel H. Burnham, a free hand in selecting de-
signers, architects, engineers, and approving their plans. Burnham's
task seemed a model "commission," aloof from politics and practical
economics, answerable only to the corporation which employed it: a
private entity created by the laws of the state of Illinois as "World's
Columbian Exposition" and authorized to raise capital by selling
stock certificates. The Official Manual of the Fair consisted of the
bylaws of this body, an account of its structure (board of directors
elected by stockholders, standing committees), many lists of names of
the prominent Chicago citizens among its ranks (businessmen,
bankers, lawyers), and a complete text of the Act of Congress which
authorized a "World's Columbian Commission" of appointed officials to deal with the corporation in matters of selection of site and
specification of buildings and exhibits. The overt message about the
origins of the Fair appeared, then, in the chain of authority devolving
from legislative acts to private enterprise, a structure which gave the
Department of Works its own authority and freedom to coordinate
spaces and buildings according to its own lights.

The manual did not mention "labor." But one covert message
about how a model future might be built lies in Walter Wyckoff's
account of his experiences as a "road builder" on the fairgrounds in
the spring of 1892. A Princeton graduate who had undertaken an
"experiment" of tramping across the country to learn firsthand how
the world looks and feels from the point of view of a working stiff,
Wyckoff published his extraordinary narrative of hard knocks and
wrenched perspectives in *Scribner's* and then in two volumes. In the
second, *The Workers: An Experiment in Reality: The West* (1899), he
described his experiences as a laborer on the fairgrounds. His employment there was a happy reprieve after a bleak winter of unemployment on the streets of Chicago. Now he finds himself with
"wholesome labor in the open air," and has no complaints. He lives
in a temporary "hotel" on the site "of the future 'court of honor'"
with about four hundred other workers. They include "half a score
of nationalities and of as many trades," including the unskilled, "who
work in gangs." "Housed and fed in this one house," they seem

altogether in an ideal situation. Yet the picture contains an ambiguous note: "Guarded by sentries and high barriers from unsought contact with all beyond, great gangs of us, healthy, robust men, live and labor in a marvelous artificial world. No sight of misery disturbs us, nor of despairing poverty out in vain search for employment." Regimentation on one hand, artificial security on the other: the picture suggests that White City's proposal for a future includes a distinct solution to the "labor problem." "Work is everywhere abundant and well paid and directed with the highest skill. And here, amid delicate, web-like frames of steel which are being clothed upon with forms of exquisite beauty, and among broad, dreary wastes of arid dunes and marshy pools which are being transformed by our labor into gardens of flowers and velvet lawns joined by graceful bridges over wide lagoons, we work our eight hours a day in peaceful security and in absolute confidence of our pay." A work force tranquilized by security, by beauty of environment, and by barriers and sentries which protect it from "unsought contact with all beyond": such is the utopia of labor implied.

Of such weavings of the overt and covert is White City made. By design, the Fair set itself against what lay beyond its gates. It enforced its lessons by contrast. The irony of opening its gates almost at the exact moment in May 1893 when banks and factories closed theirs in the worst financial panic of the nation's history only highlights the contrast, the dialogue of opposites between the Fair and the surrounding city, between White City and the great city of Chicago. As Julian Ralph pointed out in *Chicago and the World's Fair* (1893), a book written for Harper's and "approved by the Department of Publicity," Chicago displayed an energy and an exuberance in need of discipline: its politics, for example, showing the worst features of the spoils system, while its parks governed by a commission above politics (responsible business leaders appointed by the county or state, not the city itself), represented a hopeful direction. With its own corporate structure, its chain of command, and its contented labor force (in fact, a number of strikes delayed construction), White City would show how a place like Chicago might be governed as well as how it might look. Just as the ground plan of the Fair implicitly rebuked the monotonous grid of Chicago's streets, so the Department of Works and its master plan rebuked the rule of mere competition, of commercial domination over beauty and order. By model and example, White City might thus inaugurate a new Chicago, a new urban world. . . .

In the Rand McNally *Handbook* (Andrew McNally was one of the chief backers of the Fair and member of the board of directors), Daniel Burnham explained to the public how the Fair's unfamiliar organization of space should be understood. After describing the work of transforming the "desolate wilderness" and "dreary landscape" of the original site, he wrote:

> Three distinct motives are apparent in the grouping of the buildings. Those about the Grand Basin—the Administration, Manufactures, Agriculture, Machinery, Electricity, Mines, and also the Art Building—are essentially dignified in style; those lying farther to the north—the Horticultural, Transportation [Sullivan's contribution], and Fisheries—being less formal, blend readily with the more or less homelike headquarters buildings of the States and foreign governments, which are grouped among the trees of the extreme northern portion of the grounds. Upon the Midway Plaisance no distinct order is followed, it being instead a most unusual collection of almost every type of architecture known to man—oriental villages, Chinese bazaars, tropical settlements, ice railways, the ponderous Ferris wheel, and reproductions of ancient cities. All these are combined to form the lighter and more fantastic side of the Fair.

It might seem peculiar that Burnham should describe the Midway, with its mixture of modern machinery and vernacular buildings, as fantastic "reproductions," implying that the real and the original were to be found in the academic classicism of the Court of Honor. But the spatial divisions proclaimed just what Burnham implied, that reality must be sought in the ideality of high art. The Court of Honor provided the center around which the rest of White City was organized in hierarchical degree; indeed, the carnival atmosphere of the Midway Plaisance confirmed by contrast the dignity of the center. And, of course, the center represented America through its exhibitions, the outlying exotic Midway stood for the rest of the world in subordinate relation.

The design, then, encompassed a schematic set of contrasts, and by this it further promulgated its message of unity through subordination. But the heart of the message did not lie in the geometric form alone; it lay in the fact that the formal center of the Fair was derived from "art," from "culture." The Fair insinuated this primacy at every turn. Its organized spaces and classified exhibitions were an intellectual edifice indispensable to the message, as were the religious, educational, and scholarly events of the World's Congress Auxiliary. The motto of these events and meetings scheduled throughout Chicago during the months of the Fair articulated the message of White City: "Not Matter, But Mind; Not Things, But Men." . . .

For a summer's moment, White City had seemed the fruition of a nation, a culture, a whole society: the celestial city of man set upon a hill for all the world to behold. It seemed the triumph of America itself, the old republican ideal. But . . . that ideal had taken on another look and signified another meaning: the alliance and incorporation of business, politics, industry, and culture. The spectacle proclaimed order, unity, coherence—and mutuality now in the form of hierarchy. White City manifested the conversion of the old ideal, its transvaluation into not a communal but a corporate enterprise. Business and politics provided the structure, the legitimacy of power, the chain of command. Industrial technology provided the physical power, forces of nature mastered and chained to human will, typified by tens of thousands of electric bulbs controlled by a single switch. And culture served as the presiding genius, orchestrating design and style, coordinating effort. Illumination, clarity of design, a perfectly comprehensible ground plan dividing the Fair into distinct regions—all such signs of lucidity seemed to proclaim mystery overcome by an artfully composed reality: a reality composed, that is, in the mode of theatrical display, of *spectacle*. White City seemed to make everything clear, everything available. This indeed had been the prime function of industrial expositions in the nineteenth century, to display the fruits of production as universal culture, to construct of the performances of economy a modern spectacle. Moreover, in choosing neoclassicism as its dominant style, White City made obvious allusion to European Baroque, to the monumental neoclassicism of capital cities in which radial avenues, open plazas, and façades of columns signified royal power, the authority of the state on display.

   White City implied not only a new form of urban experience but a new way of experiencing the urban world: spectacle. Visitors to the Fair found themselves as *spectators*, witnesses to an unanswerable performance which they had no hand in producing or maintaining. The

Fair was delivered to them, made available to them. And delivered, moreover, not as an actual place, a real city, but as a frank illusion, a picture of what a city, a real society, might look like. White City represented itself *as* a representation, an admitted sham. Yet that sham, it insisted, held a truer vision of the real than did the troubled world sprawling beyond its gates.

In sum, White City seemed to have settled the question of the true and real meaning of America. It seemed the victory of elites in business, politics, and culture over dissident but divided voices of labor, farmers, immigrants, blacks and women. Elite culture installed itself as official doctrine of the Court, claiming dominion over the "low" confined to the outskirts of the Midway. In retrospect, the Fair has seemed not only a culmination of the efforts of ruling groups since the Civil War to win hegemony over the emerging national culture but a prophetic symbol of the coming defeat of Populism and its alternative culture, the alternative "America" it proposed. White City expressed the very outlook later manifested by McKinley and the Republican banner of "peace, prosperity, progress and patriotism," as well as the overseas crusades to spread the blessings of "our deeply incorporated civilization." The power to say what was real, what was America, seemed now safely in the hands of property, wealth, and "the word Culture."

But the ragged edges of 1894 implied that even in defeat advocates of "union" over "corporation" retained their vision, their voice, and enough power to unsettle the image of a peaceful corporate order. At stake in the sympathy boycott of the American Railway Union was more than a legal right, but a way of life and a world view. Arguing before the Supreme Court in October 1894, in defense of Eugene Debs, who had been speedily convicted of violating a federal injunction against the boycott, Clarence Darrow presented the legal issue in the light of a broader defense of the right of workingmen to associate in the first place. It makes no difference whether the members of the American Railway Union were themselves personally at odds with the Pullman Company, he argued. "They doubtless believed that their fellow laborers were unjustly treated, and did not desire to handle the cars of a corporation that was unjustly treating their brothers who were engaged in a struggle with this company." It was the very right to consider each other "brothers" that Darrow insisted upon. "The right to cease labor for the benefit of their fellows" lay at the heart of labor unions. "If no man could strike except he were personally aggrieved, there could be no strike of a combination of workingmen," he explained. For "the theory on which all labor organizations are based is that workingmen have a common interest, and that 'an injury to one is the concern of all.'" "Mutual aid" is "the very object of combination and association." To deny this principle, which indeed the court would do in denying Darrow's plea, "would leave each individual worker completely isolated and unaided to fight his battle alone against the combined capital everywhere vigilant and aggressive, to add to its own profit by reducing the wages and conditions of those who work."

The crux of Darrow's losing argument lay in his joining this familiar notion of mutuality with a developing concept of collective rights which lay "beyond equality." He put the issue pointedly. "Politically and theoretically the laborer is now a freeman, the equal of the employer, the equal of the lawyer or the judge. But freedom does not consist alone in political rights, or in theories of government, or in theories as to man's relations with the state." Effective freedom lay in the right of workers to combine and act in union, in solidarity. "The present system of industry" makes this larger freedom essential, for "so long as steam and electricity are applied to machines in any such manner as at present," and "hundreds and thousands of men must work for single employers," "great masses of men working together to a common end, and subject to regulations from a common head" must enjoy the right of collective action for mutual aid. Political economy itself raised the old mutuality to a new, more radical condition: the need for solidarity among an entire class of people. It was this need which welled up out of Pullman and spread along the railroad network across the land, as it had more spontaneously in 1877. The need arose from conditions, Darrow argued, which lay at the base of industrial life. It also arose from motives, principles, beliefs—from an entire culture—at sharp odds with the implied obedience and deference, the ethos of incorporation celebrated at Pullman and at White City. "No doubt it is difficult for some people to understand a motive sufficiently high," he concluded, "to cause men to lay down their employment not to serve themselves but to help some one else. But until this is understood, the teachings of religionists and moralists will have been in vain."

Darrow spoke out of the accumulated experience of labor, of workers and farmers in the age of incorporation, evoking the spirit of the Knights of Labor as well as the Farmers' Alliance. He spoke in a losing cause before the highest court in 1894, describing a vision of a new political concept arising from a culture of common need. In more figurative language, Eugene Debs invoked that same vision in images sharply at odds with the culture of Pullman and White City. Pausing for a moment to reflect on the events of 1894 while still in their midst, Debs wrote, in "Labor Strikes and Their Lessons" (published by John Swinton in his 1894 volume on the Pullman strike): "on one hand, a great corporation, rich to plethora, rioting in luxuries, plutocratic, proud, and powerful." And on the other, "not a picture of houses and lands, lawns and landscape, 'sacred grass,' violets and rose-trees, sparkling fountains and singing birds, and an atmosphere burdened with the aroma of flowers, but of human beings living amidst such surroundings and toiling for a pittance doled out to them by their employers—as a Heber might say: 'Where every prospect pleases,' and only man is wretched." "Every honest patriotic American" should understand the need to resist such "brazen heartlessness." Indeed, the "great lesson" of the strike at Pullman is "that it arouses wide-spread sympathy." Debs continued:

> This fellowship for the woes of others—this desire to help the unfortunate; this exhibition of a divine principle, which makes the declaration plausible that "man was made a little lower than God," and without which man would rank lower than the devil by several degrees—should be accepted as at once the hope of civilization and the supreme glory of manhood. And yet this exhibition of sympathy aroused by the Pullman strike is harped upon by press and pulpit as the one atrocious feature of the strike. Epithets, calumny, denunciation in every form that malice or mendacity could invent have been poured forth in a vitriol tide to scathe those who advocated and practised the Christ-like virtue of sympathy. The crime of the American Railway Union was the practical exhibition of sympathy for the Pullman employees.

Thus did the events of 1894 reveal to Debs and Darrow not only corporations (and the state) pitted against striking workers, but a clash of cultures: the pleasing prospect against the bonds of sympathy, of solidarity.

That tension would persist in America, submerged in periods of prosperity and wartime nationalism, only to reappear at moments of stress and crisis: the Depression of the 1930's, the agitations of the 1960's and 1970's. To be sure, since World War II a larger number of workers have shared in the abundance of an incorporated America and have seemed to accept its cultural premises. A wider diffusion of comfort and the goods of culture (as well as education) seems to have overshadowed the vista of a solidarity grounded not in consumption but in equality, the dignity of labor, and the sympathy of common need. Yet it seems evident, almost a hundred years since White City and its aftermath at Pullman, that the question remains unresolved. In the conflict of perspectives disclosed in Chicago in 1893–94 lay one of the deepest and most abiding issues accompanying the incorporation of America.

SUGGESTED READINGS

General Interpretations

The best interpretive overview of American industrialization is Walter Licht, *Industrializing America: The Nineteenth Century* (Baltimore, 1995), a concise synthesis of business, labor, and economic history. Also excellent but more tightly focused on workers' experience is Bruce Laurie, *Artisans into Workers: Labor in Nineteenth Century America* (New York, 1989). Books that address the early phases of American industrialization from multiple perspectives include Thomas C. Cochran, *Frontiers of Change: Early Industrialism in America* (New York, 1981) and Brooke Hindle and Steven Lubar, *Engines of Change: The American Industrial Revolution 1790–1860* (Washington, D.C., 1986). Alan Trachtenberg offers a sophisticated interpretation of the later phases in *The Incorporation of America: Culture and Society in the Gilded Age* (New York, 1982). George Rogers Taylor, *The Transportation Revolution 1815–1860* (New York, 1951) and Edward C. Kirkland, *Industry Comes of Age: Business, Labor and Public Policy, 1860–1897* (New York, 1961) are older yet still valuable syntheses.

Intellectual, Legal, and Cultural Histories

The economic thought of the so-called Founding Fathers has attracted considerable scholarly attention in recent years. Important studies include Drew R. McCoy, *The Elusive Republic: Political Economy in Jeffersonian America* (Chapel Hill, N.C., 1980); Joyce Appleby, *Capitalism and a New Social Order: The Republican Vision of the 1790s* (New York, 1984); John R. Nelson, Jr., *Liberty and Property: Political Economy and Policymaking in the New Nation, 1789–1812* (Baltimore, 1987); and Cathy D. Matson and Peter S. Onuf, *A Union of Interests: Political and Economic Thought in Revolutionary America* (Lawrence, Kans., 1990).

For an interpretation of American economic thought during the first half of the nineteenth century, see Paul K. Conkin, *Prophets of Prosperity: America's First Political Economists* (Bloomington, Ind., 1980). Carl Siracusa, *A Mechanical People: Perceptions of the Industrial Order in Massachusetts, 1815–1880* (Middletown, Conn., 1979) is a useful case study of the popular debate over political economy in one state.

James Willard Hurst pioneered the serious study of the relationship between economic development and the evolution of American legal thought. For a summary of his largely optimistic assessment, see *Law and the Conditions of Freedom in the Nineteenth-Century United States* (Madison, Wis., 1956). Morton Horwitz offers a more critical interpretation in *The Transformation of American Law, 1780–1860* (Cambridge, Mass., 1977).

On the evolving legal conceptualization of free (wage) labor, see Robert J. Steinfeld, *The Invention of Free Labor: The Employment Relation in English and American Law and Culture, 1350–1870* (Chapel Hill, N.C., 1991); Christopher L. Tomlins, *Law, Labor and Ideology in the Early American Republic* (Cambridge, England, 1993); and Karen Orren, *Belated Feudalism: Labor, the Law, and Liberal Development in the United States* (Cambridge, England, 1991). On the changing legal understanding of the corporation, see Ronald Seavoy, *The Origins of the American Business Corporation, 1784–1855: Broadening the Concept of Public Service During Industrialization* (Westport, Conn., 1982) and Herbert Hovenkamp, *Enterprise and American Law, 1836–1937* (Cambridge, Mass., 1991).

The classic work on the perception of industrial technology in the American literary imagination is Leo Marx, *The Machine in the Garden: Technology and the Pastoral Ideal in America* (New York, 1964). John F. Kasson extends and modifies Marx's analysis in *Civilizing the Machine: Technology and Republican Values in America 1776–1900* (New York, 1976).

Nicholas K. Bromell, *By the Sweat of the Brow: Literature and Labor in Antebellum America* (Chicago, 1993); Jonathan A. Glickstein, *Concepts of Free Labor in Antebellum America* (New Haven, 1991); and Daniel T. Rodgers, *The Work Ethic in Industrial America, 1850–1920* (Chicago, 1978) explore how American intellectuals and others reevaluated the meaning of work in the wake of industrial transformation. On shifting cultural attitudes toward cities and urban living, see Thomas Bender, *Toward an Urban Vision: Ideas and Institutions in Nineteenth-Century America* (Lexington, Ky., 1975) and Paul Boyer, *Urban Masses and Moral Order in America, 1820–1920* (Cambridge, Mass., 1978). On changing notions of success, see Irvin G. Wyllie, *The Self-Made Man in America: The Myth of Rags to Riches* (New York, 1954); Edward Chase Kirkland, *Dream and Thought in the Business Community, 1860–1900* (Ithaca, N.Y., 1956); and Rex Burns, *Success in America: The Yeoman Dream and the Industrial Revolution* (Amherst, Mass., 1976).

T. J. Jackson Lears focuses on intellectual critics of progress and modernity in *No Place of Grace: Antimodernism and the Transformation of American Culture 1880–1920* (New York, 1981), as does John L. Thomas in *Alternative America: Henry George, Edward Bellamy, Henry Demarest Lloyd and the Adversary Tradition* (Cambridge, Mass., 1983). Howard P. Segal concentrates on the intellectual proponents of technology in *Technological Utopianism in American Culture* (Chicago, 1985).

Economic Histories

The study of American economic history has been transformed over the past forty years by the application to historical data of theoretical models and quantitative analytical strategies developed by modern economists. For an outstanding, "reader-friendly" survey of the findings of this often abstruse scholarship, see Jeremy Atack and Peter Passell, *A New Economic View of American History: From Colonial Times to 1940,* 2nd ed. (New York, 1994). Peter Temin, ed., *Industrialization in North America* (Oxford, 1994) is a fine collection of previously published articles by "new" economic historians.

Important general interpretations of the origins of American economic growth include Douglass C. North, *The Economic Growth of the United States, 1790–1860* (Englewood Cliffs, N.J., 1961); Stuart Bruchey, *The Roots of American Economic Growth, 1607–1861: An Essay in Social Causation* (New York, 1965); and Peter Temin, *Causal Factors in American Economic Growth in the Nineteenth Century* (London, 1975).

In his bold comparative study *The Stages of Economic Growth: A Non-Communist Manifesto* (Cambridge, England, 1960), W. W. Rostow argues that railroads were the key to American economic "takeoff" beginning in the 1840s. The most famous refutation of Rostow's thesis is Robert W. Fogel, *Railroads and American Economic Growth: Essays in Econometric History* (Baltimore, 1964). Also relevant to this controversy is Albert Fishlow, *American Railroads and the Transformation of the Antebellum Economy* (Cambridge, Mass., 1965).

Regional studies that highlight the role of hinterland markets in northern economic development include Diane Lindstrom, *Economic Development in the Philadelphia Region, 1810–1850* (New York, 1978) and Winifred Barr Rothenberg, *From Market-Places to a Market Economy: The Transformation of Rural Massachusetts, 1750–1850* (Chicago, 1992). For a social historical alternative to Rothenberg's interpretation, see Christopher Clark, *The Roots of Rural Capitalism: Western Massachusetts, 1780–1860* (Ithaca, N.Y. 1990).

The most thorough analysis of why the South lagged behind other parts of the nation in industrial development is Fred Bateman and Thomas J. Weiss, *A Deplorable Scarcity: The Failure of Industrialization in the Slave Economy* (Chapel Hill, N.C., 1981).

Economic historians have paid a good deal of attention to how and why the United States overtook Great Britain as the world leader in the use of labor-saving machinery and other innovative technologies during the nineteenth century. H. J. Habakkuk argues that the scarcity of American labor was the decisive factor in *American and British Technology in the Nineteenth Century: The Search for Labour-Saving Inventions* (Cambridge, England, 1962). For challenges to Habbakuk's interpretation, see Nathan Rosenberg, *Technology and American Economic Growth* (New York, 1972) and Paul A. David, *Technical Choice, Innovation, and American Economic Growth: Essays on American and British Experience in the Nineteenth Century* (London, 1975).

On the once hotly debated question of whether the Civil War sped or slowed American industrialization, see Ralph L. Andreano, ed., *Economic Impact of the American Civil War,* 2nd ed. (Cambridge, Mass., 1967) and David Gilchrist and W. David Lewis, eds., *Economic Change in the Civil War Era* (Greenville, Del., 1965). On the similarly large question of whether industrialization mitigated or promoted economic inequality in the United States, see Clarence Long, *Wages and Earnings in the United States, 1860–1890* (Princeton, N.J., 1960); Lee Soltow, *Men and Wealth in the United States, 1850–1870* (New Haven, 1975); Jeffrey G. Williamson and Peter H. Lindert, *American Inequality: A Macroeconomic History* (New York, 1980); and Carole Shammas, "A New Look at Long-Term Trends in Wealth Inequality in the United States," *American Historical Review* 98 (April 1993), 412–431.

Histories of Technology

David Freeman Hawke, *Nuts and Bolts of the Past: A History of American Technology, 1776–1860* (New York, 1988) and Thomas P. Hughes, *American Genesis: A Century of Invention and Technological Enthusiasm 1870–1970* (New York, 1989) offer highly readable and optimistic overviews of technological transformation in American history. More difficult yet also more innovative is Robert B. Gordon and Patrick M. Malone, *The Texture of Industry: An Archaeological View of the Industrialization of North America* (New York, 1994).

Recent scholarship has challenged the once popular notion that American technology was crude and unchanging until the advent of large-scale mechanization. On early American production methods, see Brooke Hindle, ed., *America's Wooden Age: Aspects of Its Early Technology* (Tarrytown, N.Y., 1975); Brooke Hindle, ed., *Material Culture of the Wooden Age* (Tarrytown, N.Y., 1981); and Judith A. McGaw, ed., *Early American Technology: Making and Doing Things from the Colonial Era to 1850* (Chapel Hill, N.C., 1994). Also relevant is Neil Longley York, *Mechanical Metamorphosis: Technological Change in Revolutionary America* (Westport, Conn., 1985).

David J. Jeremy, *Transatlantic Industrial Revolution: The Diffusion of Textile Technologies Between Britain and America, 1790–1830s* (Cambridge, Mass., 1981) explores how and why Americans adopted, modified, and occasionally rejected British innovations in the mechanization of textile production. On the transatlantic migration of other important technologies, see Darwin H. Stapleton, *The Transfer of Early Industrial Technologies to America* (Philadelphia, 1987).

One of the most celebrated American technological achievements of the Industrial Revolution was the manufacture of firearms with truly interchangeable parts. Scholarly contributions to a full understanding of this accomplishment include Robert S. Woodbury, *Studies in the History of Machine Tools* (Cambridge, Mass., 1972); Merritt Roe Smith, *Harpers Ferry Armory and the New Technology: The Challenge of Change* (Ithaca, N.Y., 1977); and Robert B. Gordon, "Who Turned the Mechanical Ideal into Mechanical Reality?" *Technology and Culture* 29 (Oct. 1988), 744–788.

Scholars disagree over what defined "the American system of manufacture" as it developed in industries beyond firearms. A good introduction to the issues is Otto Mayr and Robert C. Post, eds. *Yankee Enterprise: The Rise of the American System of Manufactures: A Symposium* (Washington, D.C., 1981). For a more elaborate discussion of the evolving technologies of standardization in manufacturing, see David Hounshell, *From the American System to Mass Production 1800–1932: The Development of Manufacturing Technology in the United States* (Baltimore, 1984). Also useful is Donald R. Hoke, *Ingenious Yankees: The Rise of the American System of Manufactures in the Private Sector* (New York, 1990).

Industrialization requires the conversion of natural energy into productive power on a large scale. For a comprehensive analysis of the technological challenges involved and how they were overcome, see Louis C. Hunter, *A History of Industrial Power in the United States, 1780–1930,* 3 vols. (Charlottesville, Va., and Cambridge, Mass., 1979–1991). For a case study of the environmental consequences, see Theodore Steinberg, *Nature Incorporated: Industrialization and the Waters of New England* (Cambridge, England, 1991).

Inventors and their inventions may forever fascinate readers. In recent years, however, historians of technology have shifted focus away from the lives of great individuals to the social process of innovation. Examples of this approach include Brooke Hindle, *Emulation and Invention* (New York, 1981), which focuses on the development of the steamboat and the telegraph, and Robert Friedel, Paul Israel, and Bernard S. Finn, *Edison's Electric Light: Biography of an Invention* (New Brunswick, N.J., 1986). Judith A. McGaw, *Most Wonderful Machine: Mechanization and Social Change in Berkshire Paper Making, 1801–1885* (Princeton, N.J., 1987) is a brilliant case study of technological change as part of a broader cultural transformation. Paul Israel, *From Machine Shop to Industrial Laboratory: Telegraphy and the Changing Context of American Invention, 1830–1920* (Baltimore, 1992) examines how businesses sought to turn the creativity of inventors to their own advantage.

Crucial to the diffusion of new technologies in the United States were the emergence of mechanical engineering as a profession and the expansion of technical education. Monte A. Calvert, *The Mechanical Engineer in America, 1830–1910: Professional Cultures in Conflict* (Baltimore, 1967) provides a general interpretation of these related phenomena. See also Bruce Sinclair, *Philadelphia's Philosopher Mechanics: A History of the Franklin Institute, 1824–1865* (Baltimore, 1974).

Business Histories

Although there is general agreement that industrialization involved a major transformation in the organization of private enterprise in the United States, the foremost business historians of the last generation differ over the timing and character of this transformation. In "The Business Revolution," *American Historical Review* 79 (December 1974) 1449–1466, and in *Frontiers of Change* (cited earlier under General Interpretations), Thomas C. Cochran argues that both an acceleration in entrepreneurial activity and a decisive shift to corporate forms of enterprise occurred before 1840. By contrast, in *The Railroads: America's First Big Business* (New York, 1965), and in *The Visible Hand: The Managerial Revolution in American Business* (Cambridge, Mass., 1977), Alfred D. Chandler, Jr., contends that traditional modes of enterprise prevailed through the mid-nineteenth century. According to Chandler, the key breakthrough was the emergence of the multiunit firm, headed by a class of professional managers, which appeared first in the railroad industry during the 1850s.

Chandler's emphasis on railroads downplays the importance of early textile firms in the United States. Yet the individuals who financed and managed New England's early cotton mills have long commanded the attention of business historians. On the founders of the Rhode Island system, see James B. Hedges, *The Browns of Providence Plantations: The Nineteenth Century* (Providence, R.I., 1968), and Barbara M. Tucker, *Samuel Slater and the Origins of the American Textile Industry, 1790–1860* (Ithaca, N.Y., 1984). The most comprehensive study of the founders of the Waltham or Lowell system is Robert F. Dalzell, Jr., *Enterprising Elite: The Boston Associates and the World They Made* (Cambridge, Mass., 1987). See also Naomi R. Lamoreaux, *Insider Lending: Banks, Personal Connections, and Economic Development in Industrial New England* (Cambridge, England, 1994).

The diversity of early textile enterprises in the mid-Atlantic region is well conveyed by Anthony F. C. Wallace, *Rockdale: The Growth of an American Village in the Early Industrial Revolution* (New York, 1978) and Philip Scranton, *Proprietary Capitalism: The Textile*

Manufacture at Philadelphia, 1800–1885 (Cambridge, England, 1983). On the early iron industry in the mid-Atlantic region, see Paul F. Paskoff, *Industrial Evolution: Organization, Structure, and Growth of the Pennsylvania Iron Industry, 1750–1860* (Baltimore, 1983).

Business histories of nineteenth-century railroads and their promoters abound. In addition to Alfred Chandler's works cited above, see, for example, Thomas C. Cochran, *Railroad Leaders, 1845–1890: The Business Mind in Action* (Cambridge, Mass., 1953); Stephen Salsbury, *The State, the Investor, and the Railroad: The Boston & Albany, 1825–1867* (Cambridge, Mass., 1967); Arthur M. Johnson and Barry E. Supple, *Boston Capitalists and Western Railroads: A Study in the Nineteenth-Century Railroad Investment Process* (Cambridge, Mass., 1967); and Maury Klein, *Union Pacific: Birth of a Railroad, 1862–1893* (Garden City, N.Y., 1987). Colleen A. Donlavy, *Politics and Industrialization: Early Railroads in the United States and Prussia* (Princeton, N.J., 1994) is a comparative analysis.

Glenn Porter, *The Rise of Big Business, 1860–1920*, 2nd ed. (Arlington Heights, Ill., 1992) is an excellent introduction to its subject, which is explored at much greater length in Chandler's *Visible Hand*. Important case studies of the rise of big business include Harold P. Williamson, *The American Petroleum Industry: The Age of Illumination, 1859–1899* (Evanston, Ill., 1959), and Harold C. Livesay, *Andrew Carnegie and the Rise of Big Business* (Boston, 1975). On the transformation in marketing that accompanied the rise of big business, see Glenn Porter and Harold C. Livesay, *Merchants and Manufacturers: Studies in the Changing Structure of Nineteenth-Century Marketing* (Baltimore, 1971).

The ethics of the businessmen who built the great enterprises of the late nineteenth century have been hotly debated from the start. The classic hostile assessment is Matthew Josephson, *The Robber Barons: The Great American Capitalists, 1861–1891* (New York, 1934). More favorable treatments include Joseph Frazier Wall, *Andrew Carnegie* (New York, 1970); Maury Klein, *The Life and Legend of Jay Gould* (Baltimore, 1986); and David Freeman Hawke, *John D.: The Founding Father of the Rockefellers* (New York, 1980).

The emergence of big business did not mean the elimination of small enterprises. On the continuing role of small business in the industrial era, see Stuart W. Bruchey, ed., *Small Business in American*

Life (New York, 1980) and Mansel G. Blackford, *A History of Small Business in America* (New York, 1991). John N. Ingrahm, *Making Iron and Steel: Independent Mills in Pittsburgh, 1820–1920* (Columbus, Ohio, 1991) is a good case study.

Labor Histories

Beginning in the early 1960s, labor historians shifted their attention from the history of labor unions and other formal organizations to the cultural experience of workers in a variety of contexts. A leading pioneer of this new approach was Herbert G. Gutman, whose pathbreaking essays have been collected in two volumes: *Work, Culture & Society in Industrializing America: Essays in American Working-Class and Social History* (New York, 1976) and *Power and Culture: Essays on the American Working Class* (New York, 1987). Other valuable collections of the "new" labor history include Michael H. Frisch and Daniel J. Walkowitz, eds., *Working-Class America: Essays on Labor, Community, and American Society* (Urbana, Ill., 1983) and Charles Stephenson and Robert Asher, eds., *Life and Labor: Dimensions of American Working-Class History* (Albany, N.Y., 1986). Bruce Laurie, *Artisans into Workers* (cited earlier under General Interpretations), and Melvin Dubofsky, *Industrialism and the American Worker, 1865–1920,* 3rd ed. (Arlington Heights, Ill., 1996) are important syntheses of old and new labor history.

Several case studies have focused on the role of artisans in early industrialization and working-class formation. Among the best are Alan Dawley, *Class and Community: The Industrial Revolution in Lynn* (Cambridge, Mass., 1976); Paul G. Faler, *Mechanics and Manufacturers in the Early Industrial Revolution: Lynn, Massachusetts, 1760–1860* (Albany, N.Y., 1981); Susan E. Hirsch, *Roots of the American Working Class: The Industrialization of Crafts in Newark, 1800–1860* (Philadelphia, 1978); Bruce Laurie, *Working People of Philadelphia, 1800–1850* (Philadelphia, 1980); Howard B. Rock, *Artisans of the New Republic: The Tradesmen of New York City in the Age of Jefferson* (New York, 1979); and Sean Wilentz, *Chants Democratic: New York City and the Rise of the American Working Class 1788–1860* (New York, 1984). W. J. Rorabaugh, *The Craft Apprentice: From Franklin to the Machine Age in America* (New York, 1986) offers an engaging interpretation of the decline of apprenticeship as industrialization took hold.

The experiences of first- and second-generation factory workers have also received considerable scholarly attention. Important case studies include Thomas Dublin, *Women at Work: The Transformation of Work and Community in Lowell, Massachusetts, 1826–1860* (New York, 1979); Jonathan Prude, *The Coming of Industrial Order: Town and Factory Life in Rural Massachusetts, 1810–1860* (Cambridge, England, 1983); and Cynthia Shelton, *The Mills of Manayunk: Industrialization and Social Conflict in the Philadelphia Region, 1787–1837* (Baltimore, 1986). David A. Zonderman offers a balanced overview in *Aspirations and Anxieties: New England Workers and the Mechanized Factory System, 1815–1850* (New York, 1992). Steven J. Ross, *Workers on the Edge: Work, Leisure, and Politics in Industrializing Cincinnati, 1788–1890* (New York, 1985) examines the experiences of both artisanal and factory workers in the Queen City.

The distinctive dilemmas of slaves engaged in industrial activity are explored in Charles B. Dew, *Bond of Iron: Master and Slave at Buffalo Forge* (New York, 1994) and Robert S. Starobin, *Industrial Slavery in the Old South* (New York, 1970). Peter Way, *Common Labour: Workers and the Digging of North American Canals, 1780–1860* (Cambridge, England, 1993) examines the experience of unskilled canal construction workers. On coal miners, see Grace Palladino, *Another Civil War: Labor, Capital, and the State in the Anthracite Region of Pennsylvania, 1840–68* (Urbana, Ill., 1990) and Anthony F. C. Wallace, *St. Clair: A Nineteenth-Century Coal Town's Experience with a Disaster-Prone Industry* (New York, 1987). Walter Licht, *Working for the Railroad: The Organization of Work in the Nineteenth Century* (Princeton, N.J., 1983) and Shelton Stromquist, *A Generation of Boomers: The Pattern of Railroad Labor Conflict in Nineteenth-Century America* (Urbana, Ill., 1987) analyze the world of railway workers. Alex Keyssar, *Out of Work: The First Century of Unemployment in Massachusetts* (Cambridge, Mass., 1986) examines the plight of the unemployed in an industrial economy.

A continuing concern of labor historians has been how to assess the outlook of working-class activists and agitators. For an argument that early labor protest fell within a broader liberal consensus, see Walter Hugins, *Jacksonian Democracy and the Working Class: A Study of the New York Workingmen's Movement, 1829–1837* (Stanford, Calif., 1960). For a counterargument, see Edward Pessen, *Most*

Uncommon Jacksonians: The Radical Leaders of the Early Labor Movement (Albany, N.Y., 1967). On the religious dimension of early labor radicalism, see Teresa Anne Murphy, *Ten Hours' Labor: Religion, Reform, and Gender in Early New England* (Ithaca, N.Y., 1992) and Jama Lazerow, *Religion and the Working Class in Antebellum America* (Washington, D.C., 1995). David Roediger, *The Wages of Whiteness: Race and the Making of the American Working Class* (London, 1991) analyzes how racism distorted early labor radicalism and influenced working-class formation in the United States.

Much of the debate over the character of labor radicalism in the late nineteenth century concerns the Knights of Labor and what they stood for. Gerald N. Grob, *Workers and Utopia: A Study of Ideological Conflict in the American Labor Movement, 1865–1900* (Evanston, Ill., 1961), portrays the Knights as naïve utopians. More sympathetic accounts include Leon Fink, *Workingmen's Democracy: The Knights of Labor and American Politics* (Urbana, Ill., 1983); Kim Voss, *The Making of American Exceptionalism: The Knights of Labor and Class Formation in the Nineteenth Century* (Ithaca, N.Y., 1993); and Robert E. Weir, *Beyond Labor's Veil: The Culture of the Knights of Labor* (University Park, Pa., 1996). Richard Jules Ostreicher, *Solidarity and Fragmentation: Working People and Class Consciousness in Detroit, 1875–1900* (Urbana, Ill., 1986) and Peter J. Rachleff, *Black Labor in the South: Richmond, Virginia, 1865–1890* (Philadelphia, 1984) are important case studies. Alexander Saxton, *The Indispensable Enemy: Labor and the Anti-Chinese Movement in California* (Berkeley, Calif., 1971) examines the xenophobic dimension of late-nineteenth-century labor radicalism.

David Montgomery has written several major books that trace episodically the struggles of industrial wage earners for democratic principles and workers' control: *Beyond Equality: Labor and the Radical Republicans, 1862–1872* (New York, 1967); *Workers' Control in America: Studies in the History of Work, Technology, and Labor Struggles* (Cambridge, England, 1979); *The Fall of the House of Labor: The Workplace, the State, and American Labor Radicalism, 1865–1925* (Cambridge, England, 1987); and *Citizen Worker: The Experience of Workers in the United States with Democracy and the Free Market in the Nineteenth Century* (Cambridge, England, 1993).

Several fine studies cover the great confrontations between capital and labor in the late nineteenth century. See, for example, Robert

V. Bruce, *1877: Year of Violence* (Indianapolis, 1959); Philip S. Foner, *The Great Labor Uprising of 1877* (New York, 1977); Paul Avrich, *The Haymarket Tragedy* (Princeton, N.J., 1984); Paul Krause, *The Battle for Homestead, 1880–1892: Politics, Culture, and Steel* (Pittsburgh, 1992); and Almont Lindsay, *The Pullman Strike: The Story of a Unique Experiment and of a Great Labor Upheaval* (Chicago, 1942).

Urban and Ethnic Histories

Although now nearly three decades old, Stephan Thernstrom and Richard Sennett, eds., *Nineteenth-Century Cities: Essays in the New Urban History* (New Haven, 1969), remains an excellent introduction to the quantitative and qualitative methodologies employed by urban historians over the past generation. For a more theoretical overview, see Thomas Bender, *Community and Social Change in America* (New Brunswick, N.J., 1978). Raymond A. Mohl, *The New City: Urban America in the Industrial Age, 1860–1920* (Arlington Heights, Ill., 1985) is a useful synthesis.

Of particular interest to the "new" urban historians in the 1960s and 1970s was the extent of social mobility in nineteenth century cities. Stephan Thernstrom, *Poverty and Progress: Social Mobility in a Nineteenth Century City* (Cambridge, Mass., 1964), pioneered this type of community study. Other examples of the genre include Peter R. Knights, *The Plain People of Boston, 1830–1860: A Study in City Growth* (New York, 1971); Clyde and Sally Griffen, *Natives and Newcomers: The Ordering of Opportunity in Mid-Nineteenth-Century Poughkeepsie* (Cambridge, Mass., 1978); and Michael B. Katz, *The People of Hamilton, Canada West: Family and Class in a Mid-Nineteenth-Century City* (Cambridge, Mass., 1975). Two noteworthy books that originated as mobility studies but extend their purview to other aspects of urban social organization are Theodore Hershberg, ed., *Philadelphia: Work, Space, Family, and Group Experience in the Nineteenth Century: Essays Toward an Interdisciplinary History of the City* (New York, 1981), and Michael B. Katz, Michael J. Doucet, and Mark J. Stern, *The Social Organization of Early Industrial Capitalism* (Cambridge, Mass., 1982).

An underlying assumption of the early mobility studies was the supposed desire of poor people and immigrants to attain the "American Dream"—understood as material prosperity and cultural assimilation to middle-class norms. Yet over the last twenty-five years, many urban and ethnic historians have questioned the universal applicability of this assumption. The more closely scholars have examined the immigrant experience, in particular, the more they have found evidence of concerted efforts to preserve "Old World" traditions in "New World" contexts. Works that explore this theme include Kathleen Neils Conzen, *Immigrant Milwaukee, 1836–1860: Accommodation and Community in a Frontier City* (Cambridge, Mass., 1976); Kerby A. Miller, *Emigrants and Exiles: Ireland and the Irish Exodus to North America* (New York, 1985); and Brian C. Mitchell, *The Paddy Camps: the Irish of Lowell, 1821–61* (Urbana, Ill., 1988). The relationship between working-class and ethnic identities is examined in Richard B. Stott, *Workers in the Metropolis: Class, Ethnicity, and Youth in Antebellum New York City* (Ithaca, N.Y., 1990); Eric L. Hirsch, *Urban Revolt: Ethnic Politics in the Nineteenth-Century Chicago Labor Movement* (Berkeley, Calif., 1990); and Dorothee Schneider, *Trade Union and Community: The German Working Class in New York City, 1870–1900* (Urbana, Ill., 1994). John Bodnar, *The Transplanted: A History of Immigrants in Urban America* (Bloomington, Ind., 1985) is a provocative synthesis that encompasses the twentieth as well as the nineteenth century.

Even if immigrants did not universally embrace American middle-class norms, the emergence of those norms was critical to the social texture of nineteenth-century urban life. On the dynamics of middle-class cultural development, see Paul E. Johnson, *A Shopkeeper's Millennium: Society and Revivals in Rochester, New York, 1817–1837* (New York, 1978); Karen Halttunen, *Confidence Men and Painted Women: A Study of Middle-Class Culture in America, 1830–1870* (New Haven, Conn., 1982); John S. Gilkeson, Jr., *Middle-Class Providence, 1820–1940* (Princeton, N.J., 1986); and Stuart M. Blumin, *The Emergence of the Middle Class: Social Experience in the American City, 1760–1900* (Cambridge, England, 1989). David A. Gerber, *The Making of an American Pluralism: Buffalo, New York, 1825–60* (Urbana, Ill., 1989), examines in depth the relationship between middle-class formation and ethnic consciousness. Gunther Barth recasts the assimilationist model in *City People: The Rise of Modern City Culture in Nineteenth-Century America* (New York, 1980).

On the changing distribution, use, and mediation of urban space, see the classic works of Sam Bass Warner, Jr., *Streetcar Suburbs: The*

Process of Growth in Boston, 1870–1900 (Cambridge, Mass., 1964), and *The Private City; Philadelphia in Three Periods of Its Growth* (Philadelphia, 1968); David A. Ward, *Cities and Immigrants: A Geography of Change in Nineteenth-Century America* (New York, 1971); and Allan Pred, *The Spatial Dynamics of U.S. Urban-Industrial Growth, 1800–1914: Interpretive and Theoretical Essays* (Cambridge, Mass., 1966). Roy Rosenzweig and Elizabeth Blackmar, *The Park and the People: A History of Central Park* (Ithaca, N.Y., 1992), and Daniel Bluestone, *Constructing Chicago* (New Haven, Conn., 1991), are important case studies of how civic values were reflected—and contested—in urban landscapes. Elizabeth Blackmar, *Manhattan for Rent, 1785–1850* (Ithaca, N.Y., 1989), and Gwendolyn Wright, *Moralism and the Model Home: Domestic Architecture and Cultural Conflict in Chicago, 1873–1913* (Chicago, 1980), focus on urban housing.

Two grand "biographies" of major nineteenth-century metropolises deserve special notice. Edward K. Spann, *The New Metropolis: New York City, 1840–1857* (New York, 1981), is a panoramic "old-fashioned" history of the nation's largest urban center, while William Cronon, *Nature's Metropolis: Chicago and the Great West* (New York, 1991), is a wonderfully innovative environmental interpretation of Chicago's rise to economic prominence.

Women's and Family Histories

In her pioneering essay "The Lady and the Mill Girl: Changes in the Status of Women in the Age of Jackson," *American Studies Journal* 10 (Spring 1969), 5–15, Gerda Lerner argued that industrialization produced a polarization in the social roles of American women along class lines. By endeavoring to integrate gender and class analysis, she charted a course that other scholars have pursued with brilliant fervor over the last three decades. The result has been a rich body of scholarship on both the emergence of domesticity as a middle-class ideal and the struggle of working-class women to achieve economic security and social respect as wage-earners.

Prominent works that link the rise of a middle-class ideology of "separate spheres" to economic development (either market expansion or the mechanization of production) include Nancy F. Cott, *The Bonds of Womanhood: "Woman's Sphere" in New England, 1780–1835* (New Haven, 1977) and Mary P. Ryan, *The Cradle of the Middle*

Class: The Family in Oneida County, New York, 1790–1865 (Cambridge, England, 1981). Jeanne Boydston, *Home and Work: Housework, Wages, and the Ideology of Labor in the Early Republic* (New York, 1990) argues that the rise of "woman's sphere" represented not a gain for middle-class women but the marginalization of their economic contributions to both the family and society at large. Likewise, Ruth Schwartz Cowan, *More Work for Mother: The Ironies of Household Technology from the Open Hearth to the Microwave* (New York, 1983), argues that the decline in household textile manufacture led to more, not less, housework as expectations for domestic comfort increased. Faye E. Dudden, *Serving Women: Household Service in Nineteenth-Century America* (Middletown, Conn., 1983) concludes that relations between matrons and their servants became more exploitative as the cash nexus superseded older models of domestic service.

The impact of industrialization on women who went to work in nineteenth-century factories has been much debated. In his aforementioned *Women at Work* and in *Farm to Factory: Women's Letters, 1830–1860*, 2nd ed., (New York, 1993), Thomas Dublin suggests that the first generation of New England mill women enjoyed unprecedented opportunities for individual fulfillment. Yet in *Transforming Women's Work: New England Lives in the Industrial Revolution* (Ithaca, N.Y., 1994), Dublin finds that later generations of New England working women—both native and foreign-born—had fewer choices and greater family burdens to bear. Mary H. Blewett portrays industrial work as a mixed blessing for female shoemakers in her detailed study *Men, Women, and Work: Class, Gender, and Protest in the New England Shoe Industry, 1780–1910* (Urbana, Ill., 1988). Christine Stansell offers a more uniformly pessimistic assessment of the impact of industrialization on New York City's working women in *City of Women: Sex and Class in New York 1789–1860* (New York, 1986).

Dublin, Blewett, and Stansell agree that women played a distinctive role in nineteenth-century labor protests. For other explorations of this topic, see Susan Levine, *Labor's True Woman: Carpet Weavers, Industrialization, and Labor Reform in the Gilded Age* (Philadelphia, 1984), and Carole Turbin, *Working Women of Collar City: Gender, Class, and Community in Troy, New York, 1864–86* (Urbana, Ill., 1992).

The relationship between class and gender was complicated by the rise of "white collar" women's work in the late nineteenth century. On clerical employment in the public and private sectors, respectively, see Cindy Sondik Aron, *Ladies and Gentlemen of the Civil Service: Middle-Class Workers in Victorian America* (New York, 1987) and Margery W. Davies, *Woman's Place Is at the Typewriter: Office Work and Office Workers, 1870–1930* (Philadelphia, 1982).

The best general interpretation of working-class women's experiences throughout American history is Alice Kessler-Harris, *Out to Work: A History of Wage-Earning Women in the United States* (New York, 1982). See also Rosalyn Baxandall and Linda Gordon, eds., *America's Working Women: A Documentary History, 1600 to the Present*, rev. ed. (New York, 1995) and Ava Baron, ed., *Work Engendered: Toward a New History of American Labor* (Ithaca, N.Y., 1991).

Family historians have tended to be more quantitative in their approach than women's historians, often incorporating the sophisticated statistical models and methodologies of demographers. Works examining the relationship between industrialization and family patterns include Tamara K. Hareven and Maris A. Vinovskis, eds., *Family and Population in Nineteenth-Century America* (Princeton, N.J., 1978), and Maris A. Vinovskis, *Fertility in Massachusetts from the Revolution to the Civil War* (New York, 1981). Steven Ruggles, *Prolonged Connections: The Rise of the Extended Family in Nineteenth-Century England and America* (Madison, Wis., 1987), questions the significance of industrialization as a causal factor. Michael Haines, *Fertility and Occupation: Population Patterns in Industrialization* (New York, 1979) is an important comparative analysis. For an accessible case study, see S. J. Kleinberg, *The Shadow of the Mills: Working-Class Families in Pittsburgh, 1870–1907* (Pittsburgh, 1989).